How Dictatorships Work

This accessible volume shines a light on how autocracy really works by providing basic facts about how post–World War II dictatorships achieve, retain, and lose power. The authors present an evidence-based portrait of key features of the authoritarian landscape with newly collected data on about 200 dictatorial regimes. They examine the central political processes that shape the policy choices of dictatorships and how they compel reaction from policy makers in the rest of the world. Importantly, this book explains how some dictators concentrate great power in their own hands at the expense of other members of the dictatorial elite. Dictators who can monopolize decision-making in their countries cause much of the erratic, warlike behavior that disturbs the rest of the world. By providing a picture of the central processes common to dictatorships, this book puts the experience of specific countries in perspective, leading to an informed understanding of events and the likely outcome of foreign responses to autocracies.

BARBARA GEDDES teaches at University of California, Los Angeles (UCLA). Her 1999 article in the *Annual Review of Political Science* is credited with changing the way social scientists think about dictatorships. She has written extensively on regime transition, dictatorial politics, and research design. She has won awards for data creation and graduate student mentoring.

JOSEPH WRIGHT's research examines how international factors – such as foreign aid, sanctions, human rights regimes, and migration – influence politics in dictatorships. He is the author of multiple articles published in top-ranked political science journals, as well as the award-winning book (with Abel Escribà-Folch) *Foreign Pressure and the Politics of Autocratic Survival*.

ERICA FRANTZ is an assistant professor of political science at Michigan State University. She specializes in authoritarian politics, democratization, conflict, and development. She has published five books on dictatorships and development, the most recent of which is *Authoritarianism: What Everyone Needs to Know*.

How Dictatorships Work

Power, Personalization, and Collapse

BARBARA GEDDES
University of California

JOSEPH WRIGHT
Pennsylvania State University

ERICA FRANTZ
Michigan State University

CAMBRIDGE
UNIVERSITY PRESS

CAMBRIDGE
UNIVERSITY PRESS

University Printing House, Cambridge CB2 8BS, United Kingdom

One Liberty Plaza, 20th Floor, New York, NY 10006, USA

477 Williamstown Road, Port Melbourne, VIC 3207, Australia

314-321, 3rd Floor, Plot 3, Splendor Forum, Jasola District Centre, New Delhi - 110025, India

79 Anson Road, #06-04/06, Singapore 079906

Cambridge University Press is part of the University of Cambridge.

It furthers the University's mission by disseminating knowledge in the pursuit of education, learning and research at the highest international levels of excellence.

www.cambridge.org
Information on this title: www.cambridge.org/9781107535954
DOI: 10.1017/9781316336182

First published 2018

A catalogue record for this publication is available from the British Library

Library of Congress Cataloging in Publication data
NAMES: Geddes, Barbara, author. | Wright, Joseph (Joseph George),
    1976- author. | Frantz, Erica, author.
TITLE: How dictatorships work : power, personalization, and collapse /
    Barbara Geddes, University of California, Los Angeles, Joseph Wright,
    Pennsylvania State University, Erica Frantz, Michigan State University.
DESCRIPTION: New York : Cambridge University Press is part of the University
    of Cambridge, [2018] | Includes bibliographical references and index.
IDENTIFIERS: LCCN 2018017449 | ISBN 9781107115828 (hardback) |
    ISBN 9781107535954 (paperback)
SUBJECTS: LCSH: Dictatorship. | Dictators.
CLASSIFICATION: LCC JC495 .G43 2018 | DDC 321.9–dc23
    LC record available at https://lccn.loc.gov/2018017449

ISBN 978-1-107-11582-8 Hardback
ISBN 978-1-107-53595-4 Paperback

To our (ten) children:

Dylan

Danielle

Darcy

Demetria

Lee

Luca

Enzo

Rania

Luciana

Felix

who help us keep it all in perspective

Contents

List of Figures   *page* xi

List of Tables   xiii

Acknowledgments   xv

1   Introduction   1
     Implementing Our Definition of Regime   5
     The Groups That Initiate Dictatorships   7
     Conflict and Bargaining within the Seizure Group   10
     Plan of the Book   13
     Appendix: Coding Rules for Authoritarian Regimes   18

PART I INITIATION

2   Autocratic Seizures of Power   25
     Who Do Dictatorial Seizure Groups Oust?   26
     How Dictatorships Begin   26
     Before the Seizure of Power   33
     The Morning after a Seizure of Power   36
     Post-Seizure Organization   38
     Conclusion   42

3   What Do We Know about Coups?   44
     Coups for Various Purposes   46
     Preconditions Associated with Regime-Change Coups   47
     Inequality and Coups   54
     Conclusion   56

PART II ELITE CONSOLIDATION

4   Power Concentration: The Effect of Elite Factionalism on
    Personalization   61
    Elite Bargaining in Dictatorships   65
    Handing Power to a Leader   68
    Bargaining over the Distribution of Resources and Power   74
    *Characteristics That Influence the Credibility of Threats to
    Oust the Dictator*   76
    Measuring Personalism   79
    Patterns of Personalism   85
    The Effect of Factionalism on the Personalization of Power   89
    Conclusion   92

5   Dictatorial Survival Strategies in Challenging Conditions:
    Factionalized Armed Supporters and Party Creation   95
    The Strategic Context   97
    The Interaction of Dispersed Arms and Factionalism   99
    The Strategic Creation of New Political Actors   101
    *Evidence That Post-Seizure Party Creation Aims to Counterbalance
    Factionalized Armed Supporters*   105
    Post-Seizure Party Creation and Dictatorial Survival   115
    The Effect of Post-Seizure Party Creation on the Likelihood of Coups 118
    Conclusion   123

PART III RULING SOCIETY: IMPLEMENTATION AND
INFORMATION GATHERING

6   Why Parties and Elections in Dictatorships?   129
    Implementation, Monitoring, and Information Gathering   129
    Elite Competition and Institutions That Engage Citizens   131
    Parties   131
    Dictatorial Legislatures   136
    Elections   137
    Conclusion   150

7   Double-Edged Swords: Specialized Institutions for
    Monitoring and Coercion   154
    Internal Security Agencies   156
    The Army: Bulwark of the Regime or Incubator of Plots?   162
    The Relationship between Counterbalancing and Interference   167
    Conclusion   173

PART IV DICTATORIAL SURVIVAL AND BREAKDOWN

8   Why Dictatorships Fall   177
    How Dictatorships End   178
    Individual Support and Opposition   181

The Effect of Crisis on Decisions to Oppose the Dictatorship   186
Economic Crisis and Breakdown   187
Power Concentration and Regime Survival   190
Leadership Changes and Regime Breakdown   201
The Dictator's Future and the Likelihood of Democratization   206
The Effect of Personalization on Prospects for Democracy   211
Conclusion   214

9   Conclusion and Policy Implications   218

References   237
Index   253

Figures

3.1 Regime-initiating coups against incumbent dictatorships   *page* 49
3.2 Coups against incumbent democracies   53
3.3 Causes of coups in dictatorships, by coup type   55
4.1 Frequency of events that end dictatorships   72
4.2 Illustration of personalism scores   83
4.3 The first dictator's advantage in personalizing power   87
4.4 Personalizing power after the first three years   88
4.5 United versus factionalized seizure groups   91
5.1 Post-seizure party creation and the rotation of dictatorial leadership   109
5.2 Post-seizure party creation and military marginalization   110
5.3 Post-seizure party creation before the leader's election   111
5.4 Post-seizure party creation, age, and rank of first dictator   112
5.5 Effect of age, rank, and previous regime on post-seizure party creation   113
5.6 Post-seizure party creation over time   114
5.7 Parties and regime survival   118
5.8 Coups in dictatorships with post-seizure parties or no parties   119
5.9 Post-seizure party creation and coup risk   121
5.10 Post-seizure party creation and reshuffling versus regime-change coups   123
6.1 Foreign aid and the election of dictators   139
6.2 The electoral spending cycle in dictatorships   146
6.3 Dictatorial elections and health outcomes   148
7.1 Paramilitary forces and interference in the army   171
7.2 Loyalist paramilitary forces and interference   172
8.1 How autocratic regimes end   179
8.2 Semi-competitive elections and coup attempts in dictatorships   180

8.3   Economic crisis, party networks, and authoritarian breakdown   189
8.4   The effect of personalism on authoritarian breakdown   196
8.5   The effects of personalism in dictatorships with different
       leadership configurations   200
8.6   Probability that dictator exit coincides with regime collapse   203
8.7   Effect of personalism on capacity to handle succession   204
8.8   Personalism and post-death regime survival   205
8.9   Personalism and democratization   212
8.10 Personalism, military rule, and democratization   214

Tables

2.1 Proportion of dictatorships begun by different kinds of
seizures of power   *page* 28
2.2 Proportion of dictatorships begun by different kinds of
seizure groups   31
3.1 Area under the ROC for models of regime-change coups
in dictatorships   52

Acknowledgments

This project has lasted longer than many dictatorships. We are grateful to each other for the remarkably enduring and painless power-sharing agreement. We have suffered no purges; all the original plotters remain in the inner circle.

We have incurred many debts while working on this book and the data collection that preceded it. We have presented elements of it at many conferences and universities, and a number of colleagues have read all or part of the manuscript. We are especially grateful to Alex Debs, Alberto Díaz-Cayeros, Abel Escribà-Folch, David Laitin, Ellen Lust, Beatriz Magaloni, Michael Miller, Milan Svolik, Wonjun Song, Clint vanSonnenberg, Mauricio Velásquez, Valerie Wirtschafter, Jessica Weeks, and Matthew Wilson for the gift of their time and for their penetrating and helpful comments.

Generations of our students have suffered through early drafts of the manuscript in classes on authoritarian politics. We thank them for their questions, comments, and enthusiasm. We have learned a great deal from students in our classes and from discussions with students who grew up in dictatorships.

Searching for arcane details about political bargaining and personnel appointments in dictatorships might sound very dull, but coders' meetings became weekly highlights as the coders competed to report the best dictator stories. An old aphorism says power corrupts, but it also nurtures eccentricity, caprice, paranoia, and delusions. Our searches for information yielded many tales to marvel at or be appalled by that found no place in the coding. We have talked about a coffee-table book that would feature photos of charismatic Burkinabe dictator Thomas Sankara with his motorcycle-mounted female bodyguard and the Turkmen dictator who had most of his teeth replaced with gold (and then appointed his dentist as successor). For help with the coding, good-natured tenaciousness, and retaining their senses of humor during immersion in the demoralizing world of dictatorial politics, we thank Joonbum Bae, Shahin Berenji, Ruth Carlitz, Marika Csapo, Sebastián Garrido, Ron Gurantz,

Eric Kramon, Sarah Leary, Zsuzsanna Magyar, Eoghan McGreevy-Stafford, and Amanda Rizkallah.

We also thank Nicholas Bichay, Rosemary Pang, Wonjun Song, and Valerie Wirtschafter for research assistance that helped us to stagger across the finish line.

Even imagining the fine-grained data needed for this book would not have been possible without the Department of Defense's research initiative to fund scholarship on autocracies, Minerva. We gratefully acknowledge funding from the National Science Foundation/Minerva (NSF-BCS #0904478), National Science Foundation (BCS-0904463), and the Minerva Research Initiative (ONR N000141211004).

Finally, and most importantly, we thank our partners, Cliff Williams, Jaimie Wright, and John Zaller. Without their daily support and encouragement, there might have been no book about dictators.

I

Introduction

Since humans began to live in settled communities, most have lived under autocracy.[1] Dictatorships still rule roughly 40 percent of the world's nations. All international wars since the end of World War I have involved dictator-ships. Two-thirds of civil wars and ethnic conflicts since World War II have erupted in countries under authoritarian rule.[2] Since the fall of the Berlin Wall, dictatorships have perpetrated nearly 85 percent of mass killings by govern-ments.[3] In other words, dictatorships affect millions of people's lives (and deaths) and initiate most of the urgent international challenges that policy makers face. We cannot avoid dealing with them. And yet a limited understand-ing of how dictatorships work undermines our ability to influence and negotiate with them.

Most academic analyses of how governments work have focused on democra-cies. We therefore know much less about dictatorial decision-making than about democratic. As a further complication, dictatorships differ not only from democracies but also from each other, and these differences have consequences for citizen welfare and international conflict. Although some dictatorships initiate more than their share of wars and political violence, many other

---

[1] The absence of fair, reasonably competitive elections through which citizens choose those who make policies on their behalf defines autocracy or dictatorship. The coding rules that operational-ize this definition of dictatorship can be found at http://sites.psu.edu/dictators.

[2] These figures were calculated using data on regime type from Geddes, Wright, and Frantz (2014), data on civil wars from Themner and Wallensteen (2014), data on ethnic conflict from Wimmer, Cederman, and Min (2009), and data on mass killings from Ulfelder and Valentino (2008). Civil war statistics are calculated from all civil war years, including internationalized civil conflicts. Ethnic war and mass-killing statistics are calculated from the onset years of conflicts. The years included are 1946–2010.

[3] Calculated from data on one-sided mass killings from 1989 to 2010 from Eck and Hultman (2007). The figure excludes the genocide in 1994 Rwanda, which is hard to classify.

dictatorships live in peace with their neighbors and refrain from oppressing citizens. The fastest-growing countries in the world are dictatorships, but the most economically mismanaged are dictatorships as well. Some dictatorships have followed policies to equalize incomes, but others have raised inequality to astonishing levels. Abstract theories that treat all dictatorships as the same cannot make sense of these differences. We need more realistic theories.

A great deal has been written about specific autocracies by individuals with impressive local expertise, but only a few comparative studies grounded in evidence exist. We also have some interesting theories of dictatorship, but fewer theories firmly anchored in the real world. We know little about why some dictatorships establish stable government while others suffer continuous upheaval, why some create democratic-looking political institutions to engage citizens and others do not, why some distribute benefits broadly while others concentrate wealth within a small group of regime supporters, or why some last many decades but many collapse within a year or two. In short, we understand little about how dictatorships work and why they sometimes fail to work.

Some of the reasons why analysts have made less progress in the study of dictatorship than democracy are obvious. Dictatorial decision-making often occurs in secret, while policy-making and leadership choice in democracies are relatively transparent (Lewis 1978, 622). Decision-making opacity interferes with understanding why dictatorships do things. Small dictatorial elite groups usually make decisions in informal settings: "formal institutions are not necessarily the place to look when you want to understand everyday operating procedures" in dictatorships (Fitzpatrick 2015, 278). Legislative debates and votes often ratify policy choices made elsewhere, and cabinet ministers may be the implementers of decisions, not the decision makers. Democracies publish great quantities of data about themselves, making it easier for scholars to investigate them. Not only do dictatorships publish less, but what they do publish may be purposely inaccurate (Magee and Doces 2014). Election results may reflect the resource advantage enjoyed by the ruling party rather than voters' preferences about who should rule, and published results may not match votes cast.

For all these reasons, in order to make progress in understanding dictatorships, we need much more systematic information about them than has been available. More challenging, the information needs to reflect informal aspects of real dictatorial decision-making, not just the formal characteristics of rule included in many existing data sets. More detailed information has begun to be collected in recent years, facilitating the development of new theories about dictatorship (Goemans, Gleditsch, and Chiozza 2009; Cheibub, Gandhi, and Vreeland 2010; Svolik 2012). In this book we use additional newly collected data to build on these efforts, which enables us to take another step toward explaining political choices in dictatorships.

A second, perhaps less obvious, reason for the difficulty in developing a systematic understanding of authoritarian politics is the great heterogeneity across autocracies in the way decisions are made and leaders chosen, which groups influence these decisions and who is excluded, who supports the dictatorial elite, and who benefits from their decisions. The policy-making process in Saudi Arabia is quite different from that in China, and both differ from decision-making procedures during military rule in Argentina between 1976 and 1983. Thus, while many theories about how democratic governments function fit all democracies, useful theories about authoritarian politics have to explain and take into account the differences among dictatorships.

This means that in order to develop theories about authoritarian politics, we may first need to explain their differences. Our approach to doing that begins with identifying characteristics of the different groups that seize dictatorial power, which we can observe before the dictatorship begins. Groups potentially able to initiate dictatorship have varying capacities, resources, organizational structures, ways of making decisions, and distributions of within-group power. After the seizure of power, these characteristics shape the way decisions are made in the ensuing dictatorship and who can influence them. Preexisting traits of the seizure group, as we show below, affect which citizens outside the group can influence decisions, which part of the citizenry is likely to support the regime, how the dictatorship responds to citizens who oppose it, which domestic and international policies the dictatorship chooses, and what kinds of formal political institutions it establishes to solve its cooperation problems, monitor potential opponents, and incorporate citizens into unchallenging forms of participation.

We use the term "seizure group" to refer to the small group that literally ousts the incumbent and takes over in order to initiate dictatorship, as well as their organized support base. For example, when military officers seize power in a coup, the seizure group includes both the individual coup plotters and the part of the military (possibly all of it) that provides less active support for them. Seizure groups are thus similar to Haber's (2006) "launching groups" except that we make no assumptions about their ability to solve collective action problems or oust the dictator they install. Nor do we assume that the group that helps the dictator seize power takes over the bureaucracy, courts, police, and military because, in the real world, they often do not. Frequently, in fact, these institutions remain staffed or partly staffed by individuals hired by those who ruled before the seizure of power.

As an example, consider a coup such as the one in Argentina in 1976: the commanding officer of the armed forces, supported by a consensus among other high-ranking officers, seizes control of government. In this kind of situation, before the coup most members of the seizure group have direct control of weapons and expertise in using them but less expertise in bargaining. They have a hierarchical organization structure that can usually ensure disciplined implementation of orders by soldiers (though not civilians), as well as a technocratic decision-making style, with decisions concentrated at the top of the military hierarchy. These characteristics can be expected to influence the way decisions are made after the seizure of power. Because of strong norms about the chain of command within the military, for example, military seizure groups usually choose their highest-ranked officer as dictator.

Contrast this portrait of military rule with rule by a party that won an earlier free and fair election, but then used its control of the legislature to pass laws that severely disadvantaged the opposition, thus "authoritarianizing" the government.[4] For example, between 2002 and 2005, the elected Chávez government in Venezuela used harassment and intimidation of the opposition, arrests of opposition leaders, and interference with the media to authoritarianize the political system. Other ways that democratically elected governments have authoritarianized include banning opposition parties and closing legislatures.

A party leadership that initially grew out of competitive election campaigns has developed very different capacities, organization, and resources than a military seizure group. Such party-based seizure groups typically lack weapons and expertise in using them, but have a great deal of experience in bargaining, cooptation, and electoral mobilization. The party may have a hierarchical organization in the sense that decision-making is concentrated in the party leader, but its activists and employees tend to be undisciplined because of the use of jobs and other benefits to coopt opponents and buy support from people with diverse interests. As a consequence, decisions made at the top may be distorted during implementation to benefit local officials or simply not implemented. Like the central traits of military seizure groups, these characteristics also tend to carry over into post-seizure dictatorships established by parties that were once fairly elected.

Several intuitions lie behind the claim that preexisting characteristics of the group that establishes the dictatorship persist and shape political processes that follow. First, we expect the inner circle of the dictatorship to be chosen from the seizure group. Second, we expect groups represented in the inner circles of dictatorships to dominate early decision-making and to have more influence on decisions than excluded groups throughout the life of the dictatorship. We also expect *organized* included groups to wield more power than unorganized ones. Parties and militaries are large, often well-organized groups frequently represented in seizure groups and thus initially in the dictator's inner circle. The dictator's inner circle may also represent the interests of particular class, ethnic, religious, or regional groups, but since such groups tend to be loosely organized, we expect them to have less capacity to influence decisions and implementation than more effectively organized groups. Third, we expect groups that have developed skills and routinized ways of interacting and making decisions to gravitate toward these same ways of doing things immediately after seizures of power. Our theories build on these intuitions.

---

[4] This is a frequent means of establishing dictatorship, as shown in Chapter 2.

We expect preexisting characteristics of the seizure group to influence the kind of autocratic *regime* that emerges after a seizure of power. By "regime" we mean the set of very basic formal and informal rules for choosing leaders and policies. We "measure" regimes as the continuous country-years in which the same group – though not necessarily the same individuals – controls the government and uses the same basic rules. Regimes can and often do include the tenures of more than one dictator, as in China under Communist Party rule or Saudi Arabia under the Al Saud family dynasty. "Very basic" rules include such unspoken requirements as the necessity for paramount leaders to come from particular ethnic groups or from highest-ranking officers, not necessarily electoral rules or constitutional provisions, which the dictatorial inner circle can change and/or abrogate. Because dictatorships lack third-party enforcement of formal political rules (Svolik 2012), the kinds of formal political institutions that shape politics in democracies have less influence on the behavior of elites in dictatorships. The basic rules that define dictatorial regimes are those, whether formal or informal, that really shape the choice of top leaders and important policies.

IMPLEMENTING OUR DEFINITION OF REGIME

For gathering the data on which this study depends, we relied on a set of detailed rules to identify the beginnings and ends of autocratic regimes. In keeping with much of the literature, countries are coded as democratic if government leaders achieve power through direct, reasonably fair competitive election; indirect election by democratically elected assemblies; or constitutional succession to democratically elected executives.

Events that define the beginning of dictatorship include the following:

- Government leaders achieve power through some means *other than* a direct, reasonably fair competitive election; or indirect election by a body at least 60 percent of which was elected in direct, reasonably fair, competitive elections; or constitutional succession to a democratically elected executive.
- The government achieved power through competitive elections, as described above, but later changed the formal or informal rules such that competition in subsequent elections was limited.
- If competitive elections are held to choose the government, but the military either prevents one or more parties for which substantial numbers of citizens would be expected to vote from competing, or dictates policy choice in important policy areas (e.g., foreign policy in the Middle East). We label such regimes "indirect military rule."

These rules are mostly uncontroversial, but they lead to a few coding decisions with which others may disagree. For example, we code the government of Indonesia's popular first leader, Suharto, as authoritarian because he was not elected before taking power. Some other independence leaders whose governments were coded as democratic at independence (because of fair competitive pre-independence elections) were later classified as authoritarian after they banned an opposition party, arrested opposition leaders, or used violence and intimidation against opposition voters.

Once a country-year is coded as authoritarian, successive years in the same country are coded as part of the same regime until one of the following events occurs:

- A competitive election (as defined above) for the executive, or for the body that chooses the executive, occurs and is won by a person other than the incumbent or someone closely allied with the incumbent; and the individual or party elected is allowed to take office. The end date for the regime is the election, but the regime is coded as ending only if the candidate or party elected is allowed to take power.
- Or the ruling group markedly changes the rules for choosing leaders and policies such that the identity of the group from which leaders can be chosen or the group that can choose major policies changes.
- Or the government is ousted by a coup, popular uprising, rebellion, civil war, invasion, or other violent means, *and* replaced by a different regime (defined as above: a government that follows different rules for choosing leaders and policies).

We code competitive elections as ending dictatorships only if the incumbent is defeated because so many dictatorships hold competitive elections. Many of the ways that dictatorships manipulate electoral outcomes do not occur on election day or during vote counting, so foreign observers may not see rigging. This makes it difficult to judge whether elections are free and fair. We use incumbent turnover because it is a clear indicator that the dictatorship did not control the election outcome. This is a conservative rule in the sense that we code dictatorships as continuing unless we are sure they have ended. This rule leads to a few controversial classifications; for example, we code Ghana's last democratization as of the 2000 election, which led to the first incumbent turnover since Flight Lieutenant Jerry Rawlings's seizure of power, but many analysts code it as of 1992, the first multiparty election.

The most difficult coding decisions involve coups (defined as the overthrow of the incumbent leader by members of the *military* of the regime being ousted),[5] which sometimes replace the whole ruling group and sometimes replace only the dictator in an ongoing regime. We classify coups as regime changes if they replace the incumbent government with one supported by regions, religions, ethnicities, or tribes different from those that supported the ousted incumbent or if they eliminate civilian collaborators from the inner

---

[5] Our definition is thus consistent with everyday usage, but differs from that of Svolik (2012) and Roessler (2016), who label any replacement of the dictator by regime insiders as a coup.

circle. Such coups are coded as regime changes because they change the composition of the group that can influence policy and leadership choice. For example, we treat the coup that replaced the military dictatorship led by Colonel Saye Zerbo in Burkina Faso with one led by Captain Thomas Sankara as a regime change because Sankara's military faction was rooted in different ethnic groups than Zerbo's (Englebert 1998, 51–65). If a coup simply replaces a ruling general with another general from the military command council, without changing the underlying group from which leaders are selected, we code it as a leader change, but not a regime change.

In a very small number of instances, we also classified leader changes in party-led dictatorships as regime changes because of dramatic changes in the ethnic, religious, regional, or tribal base of the ruling group initiated by the new dictator. In nearly all situations, a peaceful transition from one leader to another in a dominant-party regime would be considered a leader change in an ongoing dictatorship. However, Paul Biya's succession in Cameroon is one of the handful that we coded as a new regime. The coalition that had supported Ahmadou Ahidjo, Cameroon's first leader, was multiregional and multiethnic though northern Muslims were favored; Ahidjo was a northern Muslim and Biya, his prime minister, a southern Christian. Soon after becoming president, Biya began narrowing the group with political influence and concentrating power in his own small (southern) ethnic group at the expense of the coalition he had inherited. The post-1983 government is treated as a different regime because the regional and ethnic bases of policy influence changed along with the group from which officials were selected (Harkness 2014, 598–99).[6]

THE GROUPS THAT INITIATE DICTATORSHIPS

Two kinds of groups establish most contemporary dictatorships: groups of officers and soldiers, and groups of civilians organized into parties. Historically, tribal or clan leaders supported by armed followers began most monarchies, but this means of establishing dictatorship may have disappeared. Outgoing colonial rulers (re)established a number of post–World War II monarchies.

Seizures Led by a Group of Military Officers

Military officers usually achieve power via coups, though they are sometimes handed political control during popular uprisings. After the seizure, officers initially decide who will rule the country and make basic policy decisions. Policy choice in some areas may be delegated to civilians, especially for decisions that require technical expertise, but officers choose which civilians and

---

[6] For the full coding rules for identifying regime beginnings and ends, see the Appendix to this chapter. The data on regimes and all coding rules for defining them are available at http://sites .psu.edu/dictators.

can dismiss them. Other officers may have the capacity to constrain the military dictator and force him to consult about major decisions, because the wide dispersion among officers of arms and men under orders ensures that they can make credible threats to oust the dictator if he fails to consult or to heed their advice.[7] Such credible threats to depose give the dictator incentives to consult with other officers, but only if they can in turn make credible promises to support him *if* he consults. The dictator has less reason to consult with officers from a recently created, undisciplined, or factionalized officer corps, which cannot make credible promises of support because those bargaining with the dictator cannot count on being obeyed by junior officers and thus cannot prevent rogue coups.

An example of a seizure of power by a unified military is the 1980 coup in Turkey led by General Kenan Evren and the rest of the military high command. The Turkish army has a long history of disciplined professionalism. The coup was planned by the high command and voted on by the generals at the War Academy.[8] They ruled through the National Security Council, a consultative body composed of the service chiefs and the commander of the gendarmerie. During the dictatorship, officers made many key policy decisions and chose civilian technocrats to handle the economy. Officers also planned and oversaw the orderly return to civilian rule that ended the dictatorship.

Seizures Led by Parties

Parties achieve dictatorial power in three main ways: via "authoritarianization" after winning competitive elections, by armed insurgency, and through imposition by a foreign occupier. The different means of establishing dictatorship are associated with different internal party-governing structures and different ways of interacting with ordinary people. But in all, party leaders and procedures control personnel appointments and hence the political careers of those who wish to share power and influence or work for the government after the seizure of power. High party officials, who can include officers as well as civilians, can constrain the dictator if his hold on office depends ultimately on their support. Dictatorial ruling parties range from highly organized, disciplined networks with tentacles reaching into every neighborhood and village to cliques of the dictator's friends who can mobilize public employees to turn out votes for the dictator in sham elections but perform few other functions. Parties that led a

---

[7] Historically, the vast majority of dictators and members of their inner circles have been male. The data set used as the basis for most empirical statements in this book includes one female dictator, who served as regent for a year during the minority of the prince designated as successor to the deceased king of Swaziland.

[8] This experience contrasts of course with the failed Turkish coup of 2016, which was organized by one faction of the military but defeated by a combination of courageous civilian mobilization and loyal troops from opposing factions.

long struggle to mobilize popular support prior to the seizure of power tend to be more organized and disciplined than those that were cobbled together during the last competitive election before authoritarianization or those created after the seizure of power in order to reward the dictator's supporters with public employment and other benefits.

As an example of party seizure of power, the United National Independence Party (UNIP) of Zambia used a typical authoritarianization strategy. UNIP and its leader Kenneth Kaunda had led the independence movement and won a fair pre-independence election in 1964. The party enjoyed widespread popularity at independence and developed an effective grassroots political network by fighting the competitive elections held before authoritarianization. UNIP transformed itself into a dominant-party dictatorship by using intimidation and violence against opponents to ensure its victory in the 1967 by-elections. It then ruled Zambia until 1991, maintaining its grip on power by banning rival political parties and repressing opponents. During UNIP rule, civilian party members dominated policy-making and governance. The party elite had little ability to constrain its leader, however. Until 1967, Kaunda unilaterally chose the party's executive committee members. Then, after the first internal party elections, the executive committee factionalized along ethnic/regional lines, leading Kaunda to reassert personal control over it to reduce ethnic conflict (Molteno 1974, 67–68; Tordoff and Molteno 1974, 9–11, 29, 35). If the dictator chooses the members of the leadership group, they cannot limit his decision-making autonomy.

Seizures Led by What Becomes a Ruling Family

Seizures of power that result in family-controlled dictatorships have occurred via the conquest of territories by a family-led group and their armed supporters, usurpation of the throne of an established monarchy by the armed followers of a different family or clan, and imposition by an outgoing colonial power. After such seizures, a ruling family chooses future leaders and plays an important role in the decision-making inner circle, though economic and some other aspects of policy are often delegated to commoners with expertise. The monarch's brothers, uncles, and/or sons often control the most important ministries and lead the military and security services (Herb 1999). In this way, power is dispersed within the ruling lineage, which both limits the discretion of the monarch and protects the ruling family from external challenges. Powerful members of the family can influence policy decisions because, in extreme circumstances, they can dismiss the monarch.

What became the ruling family of Oman established the Al Said dynasty via traditional military prowess. In 1741 Ahmed bin Said al Busaidi, governor of Sohar on the coast of what is now Oman, led the city's defense against a Persian invasion during a very chaotic time. As a result, he was formally chosen as imam in about 1744. The Al Said have remained in power as traditional sultans ever since. In the current era, Said bin Taimur inherited the throne when his father abdicated in 1932. His son, Qabus bin Said Al Said, ousted him in 1970 at the behest of the rest of the family (and with support from the British) for obstructing investment and development. Qabus continues to rule today (Mohamedi 1994; Smyth 1994; Plekhanov 2004, 94–99).

In contrast to Oman, Jordan's Hashemite dynasty is a British creation. The first Jordanian monarch, King Abdullah I, was the son of the Ottoman emir of Mecca, who claimed a hereditary right to rule in the Hijaz (now part of Saudi Arabia). He was a leader of the Arab nationalist movement against Ottoman rule and sided with the British during World War I. In 1921, the British appointed him emir of Jordan, a state constructed by the British, and he remained in power when Jordan gained independence in 1946. When Abdullah was assassinated in 1951, his oldest son succeeded to the throne but abdicated in favor of his underage son the following year due to mental illness. A Regency Council controlled the country until Crown Prince Hussein came of age. Hussein died in 1999 and was succeeded by his oldest son, who continues to rule (Haddad 1971, 484–91; Lewis 1989; Wilson 1990; "Background Note: Jordan" 2011).

CONFLICT AND BARGAINING WITHIN THE SEIZURE GROUP

The different groups that initiate dictatorship have different arrangements for organizing themselves, making decisions, and taking action. The procedures and norms established in the seizure group before the dictatorship exists then influence who rules after the seizure of power, the kind of institutions they create to organize their rule, and their first policy choices. The group's preexisting rules and procedures for making decisions provide a focal point in the chaos that characterizes the early weeks of many dictatorships. Many seizure groups apparently give little thought to the practical details of what they will do after ousting the old regime. Following the Iraqi coup in 1968, for example, "Like all other post-coup governments in Iraq, al-Bakr and his colleagues had no very clear idea about politics or administration on a day to day basis" (Farouk-Sluglett and Sluglett 1987, 116). After the Sudanese coup in 1958, Woodward says, "it was clear that few plans for the post-coup situation had been made" (1990, 102). Some plotters have not even chosen who will rule the nation. Describing the 2008 coup in Mauritania, Pazzanita notes, "Although the 6 August coup was swiftly and efficiently executed … the composition of the HCE (Haute Conseil d'Etat, the new ruling council) evidently was not well thought-out beforehand" (2008, 160). Sometimes more than one member of the seizure group assumes he will become regime leader.

Under pressure to make many decisions quickly, the new rulers tend to rely on their existing leadership and familiar decision-making structures. After the seizure of power, members of the group must quickly decide who will lead, who will fill other top offices, and how much power the new leader will have relative to other members of the inner circle. These are difficult, hugely consequential, and potentially dangerous decisions that can provoke conflict within the group.

Preexisting traits of seizure groups shape dictatorial choices immediately after they gain power, but power struggles, policy failures, and other events sometimes change the power of the dictator relative to other members of the dictatorial elite in later months and years. Disagreements within the ruling group can trigger splits among previously close allies. Power struggles are common during the early years of dictatorships. Winners may jail or kill losers, torture losers' supporters, and impoverish their families. Power struggles are frequently entangled with institutional innovations and reversals. These conflicts and institutional experiments can change the distribution of power within the ruling group, either strengthening procedures for consultation or increasing the concentration of power and resources in the new dictator's hands. Post-seizure power struggles can result in much greater concentration of power in the dictator's hands than his comrades intended or foresaw.

We label dictators who have concentrated powers in their own hands personalist. Personalism tends to develop after the seizure of power, as we show below, when seizure groups are factionalized and lack discipline. A disunited group cannot prevent the new dictator from playing off first one faction and then another against the others, in the process ridding himself of the supporters most capable of challenging his decisions and power grabs. If dictators can choose the members of the regime's top decision-making inner circle, they can change its composition without taking into account party procedures, the military chain of command, or, in monarchies, the opinions of ruling-family members. The dictator's control over appointments to the inner circle means that he can threaten his lieutenants with exclusion from power and benefits, but the lieutenants cannot credibly threaten him with ouster.

A unified seizure group, in contrast, can enforce its standard procedures for promoting officers or choosing members of the party executive committee because it can overthrow a dictator who violates group norms. It can thus limit the dictator's discretion over the composition of the dictatorial elite. It can also block the dictator's efforts to take personal control of internal security services. A dictator who can spy on, intimidate, or kill other members of the dictatorial elite cannot be constrained by them. Other members of the dictatorial elite who understand this will try to retain control of the security forces within the party or regular military chain of command rather than permitting the dictator to take personal control of them.

The leader of a new dictatorship rarely controls recruitment to the inner circle or the internal security services the morning after the seizure of power. These are weapons he may acquire, however, through the jockeying over power among members of the seizure group during the first months and years after the group has gained control. Personalist rule can arise in any kind of seizure group. Like Idi Amin of Uganda, personalist dictators often originate in the military, leading many observers to refer to the dictatorships they lead as military regimes despite the marginalization of most officers from decision-making. And like Hugo Chávez of Venezuela, personalist dictators often rely on parties to organize supporters. Nevertheless, they achieve so much control over the lives and prospects of party officials and military officers that they are largely unconstrained by these institutions. Though personalization develops after the seizure of power, the internal characteristics of the seizure group that give the dictator advantages in bargaining with other members of the inner circle predate the seizure. Discipline and unity take time to develop in organizations and cannot be produced overnight when the challenge of controlling a new dictator arises.

Bargaining and conflict between the dictator and members of the inner circle are central features of authoritarian politics and among the things we would most like to understand, since they affect international behavior and many other policy choices. Previous research has shown, for example, that dictators who have concentrated great power in their own hands start more wars than more constrained dictators and pursue more erratic economic strategies (Frantz and Ezrow 2011; Weeks 2012). The bargaining and conflict within the dictatorial inner circle can also motivate the initiation or change of formal political institutions, which can help routinize decision-making, end destructive power struggles, or consolidate the power of one man. Institutional choice is another aspect of authoritarian politics we would like to understand since some institutions seem to stabilize authoritarian rule, while others contribute to political chaos.

This book addresses these subjects. It is about authoritarian politics. That is, the book explains why some dictators make certain policy choices while others make different ones, and then how these decisions affect the dictatorship's vulnerability to threats to its survival. It thus takes a step toward answering some of the questions policy makers and other observers would like to answer.

The first stage of our explanation begins with preexisting characteristics of seizure groups, not only because they help explain dictatorial decision processes, but also because these characteristics are exogenous to the dictatorship; that is, they predate it. Other observable features of dictatorships, such as how many parties they allow, whether they have a legislature, and the extent to which they rig their elections, are strategic choices made by the dictatorial elite after the seizure of power and thus are part of what needs to be explained.

Our starting point for thinking about autocratic differences is not the only one possible. Other analysts, such as Hadenius and Teorell (2007), Gandhi (2008), and Boix and Svolik (2013), have proposed alternatives based on whether the dictatorship has a legislature and the number of parties allowed in it. In a related vein, Levitsky and Way (2010) classify dictatorships based on how much competition they allow in elections. These classifications are useful for some purposes, but the characteristics they use as starting points reflect attempts by ruling groups to retain power. These features should not therefore be used to explain authoritarian durability, for example, because we cannot rule out the possibility that something that contributed to the dictatorial decision to establish the institution being investigated also caused the outcome (Pepinsky 2014). We therefore opt for a theoretical approach based on exogenous characteristics of the seizure group, measured before the existence of the dictatorship.

For theory testing purposes, the resources and capacities of the seizure group before it takes control (or the observable traits that reflect unobservable resources and capacities) are exogenous. Capturing these characteristics, however, requires detailed and subtle data. The data need to allow the assessment of characteristics of pre-seizure party organizations and of how factionalized the military that seizes power was before the seizure. Military factionalization and weak party organization, as we show in what follows, predispose seizure groups toward the personalization of dictatorial control.

To test other arguments, we also need to assess post-seizure features of dictatorial rule, and the real world of dictatorships is complicated. Officers sometimes lead regimes in which a ruling party makes central decisions and most officers simply obey orders. In other military-led dictatorships, one officer may manage to concentrate a great deal of power in his own hands, in the process excluding most other officers from decision-making. Since we want to distinguish these kinds of dictatorship from those in which a group of high-ranking officers rule in a somewhat collegial fashion, we need information beyond knowing whether the dictator wears a uniform. Ruling parties exist in most dictatorships, including many regimes controlled by military officers and a couple of monarchies, as well as regimes actually led and controlled by parties. Thus, we cannot use the simple existence of a regime-support party to infer that party institutions really control dictatorial decision-making. Ideally, we would like to be able to distinguish dictatorships led by groups of officers representing the military institution from other dictatorships led by individual officers, and we would like to distinguish dictatorships in which party officials have some ability to constrain the dictator from those with toothless parties. For these reasons, we collected and make use of the Authoritarian Regimes Data Set, which was designed to capture the distinctions we consider theoretically important, including, among other things, specific features of the seizure group both before and after the seizure of power.[9]

PLAN OF THE BOOK

The order of the book follows the common sequence of challenges faced by dictatorial elites: (1) initiation, the seizure of power; (2) elite consolidation; (3) the extension of rule to society – policy implementation and information

---

[9] The dataset, along with a codebook that explains the rules for coding, is available at our data website: http://sites.psu.edu/dictators/how-dictatorships-work/.

gathering; and (4) breakdown.[10] To correct common misperceptions about dictatorships, Chapter 2 provides some concrete facts about how they come into existence and what happens immediately after seizures of power. It shows the frequency of different methods of seizing control, the kinds of regimes that dictatorial seizures of power replace, and which kinds of groups use which methods to gain political power. Most dictatorships replace an earlier autocratic regime rather than a democracy – as, for example, the replacement of monarchies by military officers in Afghanistan, Burundi, Cambodia, Egypt, Iraq, Libya, and Yemen. Knowing something about how dictatorships begin helps us to understand their later political choices.

Coups are the most common means of initiating new dictatorships, simply because they are easier to organize than insurgencies or popular uprisings. Scholars have disagreed about the reasons for military seizures of power. In Chapter 3, we investigate the reasons for coups that initiate dictatorships. We find no relationship between mass popular mobilization, rebellion, or income inequality and coups that replace either democracies or incumbent dictatorships. Thus, we find no evidence that officers represent the interests of economic elites. Instead, we find support for Nordlinger's (1977) claim that coups reflect the interests of officers.

Whether they secure power through a coup or in some other way, once in control of the capital, members of the seizure group immediately confront all the problems that helped make the overthrow of the old regime possible. They also have to establish or reorganize internal security police to prevent the mobilization of opposition. While juggling these problems and tasks, they must also assign spheres of authority to different members of the new ruling group and devise methods for settling disputes among themselves. The starting point for assigning tasks and making decisions is the preexisting organization of the seizure group and its norms and procedures for choosing leaders, making choices, and maintaining internal unity.

Chapters 4 and 5 focus on the elite consolidation stage, which is dominated by sometimes violent struggles over power and distribution within the inner circle of the dictatorship, beginning soon after the seizure of power (Jowitt 1975). Chapter 4 develops our central theory of politics in dictatorships. The choice of one member of the seizure group as regime leader (dictator) creates a serious control problem for the rest of the dictatorial inner circle. Much of the conflict during the first years of dictatorships arises from the inner-circle members' efforts to control the dictator, and the dictator's attempts to escape

---

[10] We revise and extend Kenneth Jowitt's (1975) implicitly evolutionary argument that successful Leninist regimes exhibit different traits during different stages of their existence. Building on Crane Brinton (1938), Morris Janowitz (1977, 8) also describes a "natural history of revolution," in which a chaotic revolutionary period is followed by the consolidation of power by one man, itself followed by some relaxation. We suggest a general explanation for these patterns, which we think apply to nonrevolutionary dictatorships as well as post-revolutionary ones.

control. This struggle leads either to the concentration of power and resources in the dictator's hands or to the reinforcement of somewhat more collegial rule. In order to limit the dictator's personal discretion, his closest allies must be able to credibly threaten him with ouster. Threats of ouster are more credible when the ruling group is unified. This chapter shows how factionalism within the seizure group enables the dictator to consolidate personal power. Using detailed historical data on observable features of dictatorial rule, we offer the first empirical evidence linking pre-seizure characteristics of the seizure group to the consolidation of personal power in the hands of dictators.

Chapter 5 introduces the complication of wide dispersal of control over arms across members of the dictatorial elite. In armed seizure groups, typically most members of the inner circle have direct access to weapons and command over men trained to use them. This makes it possible for many different individuals to threaten the dictator with ouster, thus increasing the bargaining power of members of the inner circle relative to the dictator. All else equal, the increased bargaining power of members of the inner circle should lead to more constraint on the dictator, as the ease of ouster makes the dictator's promises to share more credible. In factionalized armed seizure groups, however, *other members* of the inner circle cannot make the credible commitments to support the dictator that are needed to solidify *their* side of the exchange. Their promises to support the dictator if he shares power are not credible because factionalism or indiscipline undermines their control of their subordinates, who also have guns. Consequently, they cannot sustain power-sharing bargains.

A dictator facing this situation has little reason to share power with other officers. Instead, he has strong incentives both to invest in new security forces loyal to himself to counterbalance his unruly and potentially disloyal military supporters (discussed in Chapter 7) and to create civilian support organizations to diversify his support, thus reducing his dependence on armed members of the ruling group. Military dictators who cannot count on the rest of the military for support because of factionalism or indiscipline in the army try to marginalize most of the military from decision-making, and to shift the support base of the regime to civilians, who are less threatening because unarmed. Dictators often do this by having themselves popularly elected, creating a civilian support party, appointing a civilian cabinet, and dissolving the military ruling council. Observers label this series of events civilianization, and sometimes even interpret it as democratization, but it is a dictatorial strategy to survive and consolidate personal power in the face of a factionalized and unreliable military support group.

Once decision-making within the elite has become somewhat routinized, the next challenge facing dictatorships is extending their rule over society. They must either create new agencies for pursuing the radical changes in policy that motivated the seizure of power or trust implementation to public employees likely to have been the patronage appointments of the ousted government. In order to rule, they have to have information about what is happening in different parts of the country and how their policies are working. They also have to be able to monitor the behavior of lower-level officials to make sure their policies are not being sabotaged. These are difficult problems for dictators and their allies. Officials tasked with reporting on local conditions often have incentives to misreport conditions on the ground.

Dictators use a number of strategies to try to ensure the loyalty of officials and routinize the collection of accurate information about the grassroots. In Chapter 6 we focus on their use of mass organizations that engage citizens, especially ruling parties, elections, and legislatures, to incentivize information gathering and good behavior in officials. Dictatorial elites often make ruling-party membership a condition for public employment to try to ensure the loyalty of officials. Ruling parties link central elites to vast numbers of officials and state employees. Elites hope to exchange jobs and other benefits for loyalty, effort, and honesty from officials. Without monitoring, however, they cannot ensure that officials live up to their side of the bargain.

Elections for legislative and local offices can partially substitute for regular monitoring. Although the ruling party is unlikely to lose elections, individual officials can lose if citizens are fed up with them. Bad local election outcomes notify central authorities about especially corrupt, incompetent, or abusive officials and unworkable policies. Local and legislative offices are highly valuable because of the benefits that accompany office, so the possibility of losing elections incentivizes officials to extend their distributive networks down to the grassroots, limit theft, and lobby central officials for benefits for their areas. Future elections also motivate officials to report local problems and policy failures to the center and to compete for access to local public goods. In these ways, elections and the knowledge that they will face future elections incentivize the transmission of information about local conditions to the center. Even choice-free elections can serve this purpose because competition for ruling-party nominations is intense regardless of whether there is partisan competition.

In Chapter 7 we consider the other side of monitoring and information gathering: spying. We describe the coercive institutions that protect dictatorships. We stress the differences between the interests of army officers and those of internal security police. We describe the sources of military autonomy from the dictatorships they are supposed to protect and how dictators try to overcome their autonomy. In contrast to the army, internal security services are usually created anew to serve dictatorships and thus have less autonomy. Their main tasks are to spy on and intimidate anyone who might oppose the dictator or dictatorship, which includes members of the dictatorial elite, the ruling party, and military officers. Internal security agencies can be controlled by, and thus serve as agents for, the ruling party, the military high command, or the dictator himself. In this chapter, we analyze how control of internal security changes the distribution of power within the dictatorial inner circle.

Chapter 8 analyzes authoritarian breakdown. Events beyond the dictatorship's control can reduce the costs of various behaviors – such as participating in demonstrations, campaigning for the opposition, and plotting – that in turn reduce regime survival chances. In this chapter, we show how characteristics of the dictatorship shape its ability to withstand such challenges. We describe how the relationship between the dictator and his inner circle interacts with institutions originally created for other purposes – such as parties formed to win democratic elections – to reduce vulnerability to different kinds of challenge. This interaction explains why economic crisis dooms some dictatorships but not others and why some have more difficulty surviving succession struggles after a dictator dies. The chapter highlights the relationship between past institutional choices and regime survival. We also show how different expected post-exit fates affect the responses of both dictators and their closest allies to popular opposition. We bring these various strands together to explain, first, why some kinds of dictatorship are more resilient than others in the face of challenges and, second, why some kinds of dictatorship tend to permit fair, contested elections when faced with widespread opposition and thus to exit peacefully, while others clutch desperately at power until bloodily removed.

In Chapter 9, the concluding chapter, we summarize the facts established and arguments made in other chapters. Several of our findings lead directly to policy recommendations. For example, the evidence we offer implies that policy makers should hesitate to intervene in personalist dictatorships (such as Moammar Qaddafi's in Libya or Saddam Hussein's in Iraq). Such dictators may be hated and incompetent, and they may have committed horrific human rights abuses, but deposing them may nevertheless make the average citizen of the countries they have ruled worse off. The ouster of personalist dictatorships is less likely to result in democratization than the overthrow of other kinds of dictatorship (Geddes, Wright, and Frantz 2014). A violent ouster will probably result in a new autocracy, but could end in civil war or a failed state.

These outcomes occur because the destruction of both political and civil society institutions under personalist rule leaves nations that have endured it with very little human infrastructure with which subsequent political leaders can build stable government. The decimation of institutions under personalist rule often includes the military and police, leaving these forces subsequently incapable of maintaining order or defending the new government from violent attacks by supporters of the ousted dictator. In addition, the personalist dictator's systematic elimination of politically talented potential rivals reduces the quality of the pool from which new leaders can come. These several kinds of damage mean that post-intervention governments struggle to carry out ordinary functions such as keeping streets safe and delivering water.

The foreign intervener is then likely to be blamed for the violence and decline in living standards that follow intervention. For these reasons, intervention to overthrow a personalist dictator is unlikely to result in a friendly country with a stable government willing to protect the intervener's economic and security interests.

We conclude with a series of policy recommendations that, like this one, are implied by our findings.

Appendix

Coding Rules for Authoritarian Regimes

Dictatorship begins when any one of the following has occurred:

- The government leader achieved power through some means *other than* a direct, reasonably fair competitive election; or indirect election by an assembly at least 60 percent of which was elected in direct, reasonably fair, competitive elections; or constitutional succession to a democratically elected executive.
  - Elections are not considered reasonably competitive if one or more large party is not allowed to participate; and/or if there are widespread reports of violence, jailing, and/or intimidation of opposition leaders or supporters; and/or if there are credible reports of vote fraud widespread enough to change election outcomes (especially if reported by international observers); and/or if the incumbent so dominates political resources and the media that observers do not consider elections fair.
  - Elections are not considered reasonably fair if less than 10 percent of the population (equivalent to about 40 percent of the adult male population) was eligible to vote.
  - Regimes are not coded authoritarian if an elected executive is ousted by the military, nonconstitutional legislative action, or popular pressure, but is succeeded by a constitutionally mandated successor and the successor behaves in accordance with the constitution. (Such governments may be unconstitutional, but they are not authoritarian *regimes* because they continue to follow democratic rules concerning succession, length of term, means of choosing the next executive, and legislative-executive relationship.)
- Or the government achieved power through competitive elections, as described above, but subsequently changed the formal or informal rules such that competition in subsequent elections was limited.

- o Events and rule changes that should be coded as causing a transition *from* democracy to autocracy in electoral regimes:

  Opposition parties representing more than 20 percent of voters are banned or not allowed to run candidates in elections.

  Most opposition parties are forced to merge with the ruling party.

  Legislature is closed unconstitutionally.

  There are widespread reports of violence and/or intimidation of opposition leaders or supporters; exclusion of opposition deputies from the legislature; the jailing of one or more opposition leaders.

  There are credible reports of vote fraud widespread enough to change election outcomes (especially if reported by international observers).

  Election results are annulled.

- o Start of autocracy dates from change in rules if formal rules are changed, from date the legislature closed, from date of campaign in which violence was first reported, from election in which fraud is reported; from date when annulment occurred; or from date when deputies were excluded or when opposition leaders were jailed.

- o The following irregularities are not coded as authoritarian:

  Reports of vote buying (because it is very common in democracies)

  Scattered reports of fraud

  Fraud complaints by the opposition without supporting evidence or corroboration by neutral observers

  Opposition boycott of election in the absence of other evidence of unfairness

- Or if competitive elections are held to choose the government, but the military either prevents one or more parties that substantial numbers of citizens would be expected to vote for from competing, or dictates policy choice in important policy areas (e.g., foreign policy in the Middle East). We label such regimes "indirect military rule."

- The start date for monarchical regimes is the first year of the dynasty if the country was independent in 1946; or the first year of independence.

Once a country-year is coded as authoritarian, successive years in the same country are coded as part of the same regime until one of the events identified below as ending a regime occurs.

Authoritarian regimes end when any of the following occurs:

- A competitive election (as defined above) for the executive, or for the body that chooses the executive, occurs and is won by a person other than the incumbent or someone closely allied with the incumbent; and the individual or party elected is allowed to take office. The end date is the election, but the regime is coded as ending only if the candidate or party elected is allowed to take power.

  - o Remember that in cases of indirect military rule, the incumbent leader is the top military officer. If leaders of an indirect military regime change the rules such that all major parties and population groups are permitted to compete in fair elections, and the civilian winner is allowed to take office and to make policy in areas previously reserved for the military, this change is coded as democratization. The authoritarian end date is the date of the election, but cases are not included unless the person elected is allowed to take office.

- o If a country has both a popularly elected president and a prime minister chosen by the elected legislature, and it is not clear which has the most political power, loss of either office by the incumbent party indicates the end of the authoritarian regime.

- Or the government is ousted by a coup, popular uprising, rebellion, civil war, invasion, or other violent means, *and* replaced by a different regime (defined as above, as a government that follows different rules for choosing leaders and policies). Regimes should be coded as ending if:

    - o Civil war, invasion, popular uprising, or rebellion brings to power individuals from regions, religions, ethnicities, or tribes different from those who ruled before (i.e., the group from which leaders can be chosen has changed).

    - o A coup (defined as the overthrow of the incumbent leader by members of the military of the regime being ousted) replaces the government with one supported by different regions, religions, ethnicities, or tribes. If a coup simply replaces an incumbent general from one military faction with a general from another without changing the group from which leaders are selected, this is coded as a leader change, not a regime change.

    - o Assassinations are treated like coups; i.e., if the assassinated incumbent is replaced by someone else from within the same ruling group, it is not coded as a regime end. If the assassinated incumbent is replaced by someone from a different group, as described above, the assassination is counted as a regime end.

- Or the ruling group markedly changes the rules for choosing leaders and policies such that the identity of the group from which leaders can be chosen or the group that can choose major policies changes. Examples of regime changes implemented by leaders of the incumbent regime include:

    - o The new regime leader after a regular authoritarian succession (e.g., the dictator dies and is succeeded by his constitutional successor) replaces the most important members of the ruling group with individuals drawn from a different region, religion, tribe, or ethnicity and changes the basic rules of how the regime functions.

    - o Transitions from military rule to indirect military rule, which occur when military regime leaders allow the election of a civilian government that has many of the powers of a democratic government, but military leaders maintain substantial control over leader and policy choice, either by preventing parties for which large numbers of citizens would be expected to vote from competing or by directly controlling the selection of important cabinet posts and policies. Indirect military regimes are coded as distinct from the prior military-led regime because many in the leadership are chosen through fair elections, and these elected officials control important aspects of policy; they are not simply puppets. Transitions from indirect military rule to democracy are coded from the date of the fair, competitive election.

Transitions from indirect military rule to other forms of autocracy occur when the elected civilian partner of an indirect military regime is removed from office by the military partner or some other group. These changes usually occur via coup.

Country-years are excluded from the authoritarian regimes data set if:

- Country is democratic (defined as above)
- Country has a provisional government charged with conducting elections as part of a transition to democracy, *if* the elections actually take place and the candidate and party elected are allowed to take office; or if a provisional government that is following the rules set up as part of a transition to democracy exists on January 1, but is ousted before the transition is complete by a group different from the one that held power before the provisional government was established; or if the provisional government remained in power on January 1, 2010, the last date coded
  - o To be considered transitional, the majority of top leaders cannot have been top members of the prior authoritarian regime during the months preceding the change in leadership.
  - o If instead of holding elections, the provisional government converts itself into the "permanent" government, it is coded as authoritarian.
  - o If elections are held but elected leaders are not permitted to take office, it is coded depending on who prevents them from taking office and who governs instead.

    If actors from the old regime (from before the provisional government) prevent those who won elections from taking office and return to power themselves, the provisional government and the one that succeeded it are coded as a continuation of the authoritarian regime that preceded the provisional government.

    If actors from the old regime prevent those who won the elections from taking office but replace them with a government drawn from a different group than the one that ruled before (e.g., the military that used to rule replaces elected civilians with a civilian whose base of support lies partly outside the military), the new government is coded as a new authoritarian regime.

    If actors from the old regime prevent those who won the elections from taking office, but they are then ousted by a group that forms a government based on a different support group, using different rules for choosing leaders and policies, the new government is coded as a new authoritarian regime.

- Country is not independent
- Cases are excluded if foreign troops occupy the country and the occupier governs it, or if occupation is the only thing that prevents the country from being coded as democratic. Cases are not excluded if a foreign power influences the (authoritarian) government but allows it to make many decisions.
- Country has no government or has multiple governments, no one of which controls most of the resources of the state.
  - Cases are not excluded because of civil war if one government still controls significant territory and the capital.

PART I

INITIATION

2

Autocratic Seizures of Power

Most thinking about dictatorship pictures the starting point as the violent overthrow of democracy – something like the bloody Chilean coup of September 11, 1973, in which military forces led by General Augusto Pinochet overthrew elected President Salvador Allende. But in reality, less than a third (30 percent) of post–World War II autocratic regimes began by replacing democracies. Among these democratic breakdowns, more than a quarter (28 percent) were "self-coups," meaning that a democratically elected government "authoritarianized" itself, usually by banning the opposition, arresting its leaders, or closing the legislature. The Chilean scenario, the *violent* overthrow of a democratic government, initiated only 20 percent of post-1946 dictatorships.[1]

In this chapter, we provide this kind of basic information about how dictatorships form, and we describe the conditions facing seizure groups the day after the seizure of power. The first sections show how dictatorships begin and who begins them. We start with some facts about the initiation of dictatorship because differences among seizure groups have long-term consequences, as we show in later chapters. Next, we analyze the distribution of power between the leader and other plotters before they have seized power. We then describe the situation that faces seizure groups the morning after they oust the old regime and the kinds of ruling groups that different kinds of seizure group typically create. Our aim is to provide some background for the analysis in the chapters to come.

[1] "Violent" is defined here as overthrow by a coup or armed rebellion.

WHO DO DICTATORIAL SEIZURE GROUPS OUST?

The largest proportion of post-war dictatorships began by ousting an earlier dictator and his supporters as, for example, when a popular uprising ousted the Shah of Iran in 1979 and ushered in the theocracy led by Ayatollah Khomeini, or when the insurgency led by Laurent Kabila toppled Mobutu Sese Seku in what is now the Democratic Republic of Congo. The regimes introduced by these interventions differed from the dictatorships they replaced in that the identity of the group controlling government changed. The new rulers altered the pool from which leaders and elites could be drawn, as well as other basic rules for making leadership and policy choices. In short, following the definition of regime used in this book, long authoritarian spells in these and many other countries include two or more different authoritarian regimes.[2] Forty-two percent of autocratic regimes begin with the ouster of a different dictatorship.

Many of the remaining dictatorships, 26 percent of the total from 1946 to 2010, began with the ouster of foreign rulers or a handover from foreigners to an undemocratic government. Most of these foreign initiations involved transitions from colonial control at independence.[3] In the remaining few cases, autocratic rule has succeeded a period of warlordism.

This variation in the status quo ante may explain some of the difficulty scholars have had in discovering systematic reasons for the initiation of dictatorship. The conditions that motivate the creation of an insurgency to end colonial rule may be quite different from the conditions that motivate the ouster of a populist democracy or the overthrow of an arbitrary traditional monarchy. These figures also suggest that studying only those dictatorships that follow democracies, as occurs inadvertently when analysts rely on data sets that code only transitions between democracy and autocracy, could lead to a biased understanding of both the causes of dictatorship and how they operate in practice.

HOW DICTATORSHIPS BEGIN

We sometimes speak of dictators as though they rule alone, but individuals lack the resources to overthrow or transform existing governments (Haber 2006).

---

[2] Of course, not all leadership changes are regime changes, only those that accompany basic changes in the identity of the group in power and the formal and informal rules for choosing leaders and policies. See Chapter 1 for our definition of regime and Geddes, Wright, and Frantz (2014) for an elaboration of how regime changes differ from leadership changes and undifferentiated spells of consecutive years under authoritarian rule.

[3] As colonialism has become uncommon and democracy has spread, these figures may change just because there are fewer foreign occupiers and autocrats to oust. Since democracy is less susceptible to overthrow than autocracy, however, the number of dictatorships may simply fall rather than the proportions changing.

Only groups can do it. Groups plotting to attain dictatorial power choose methods of achieving their goal that make the most of their own resources and capacities relative to those of the group to be ousted or defeated. For example, military officers, who have an advantage in deploying force and the threat of force, tend to take power through coups, which rely on credible threats of armed violence. Democratically elected incumbent groups usually assume dictatorial control through "authoritarianization," a strategy unavailable to nonincumbent seizure groups. They choose this strategy because they already control their countries' legal and judicial systems and can thus most easily initiate dictatorship via legal changes like banning opposition.

The empirical record indicates that modern dictatorships begin in six main ways.

- Coups (defined as ousters carried out by members of the military of the government being overthrown) replace the incumbent government with one preferred by military officers. Coups can replace either democratic or autocratic regimes.
- Insurgents defeat the incumbent militarily and replace it with their own leaders. Insurgency is usually used to replace foreigners or incumbent autocrats with a new dictatorship supported by different groups. This strategy is rarely successful against democracy.
- Popular uprisings persuade incumbents to hand power to opposition or seemingly neutral leaders such as military officers. Popular uprisings can result in dictatorship when the interim leader reneges on promises to democratize. Popular uprisings have occurred against both democratic and autocratic incumbents.
- Foreign conquest or imposition leads to the eventual control of the state by a group preferred by the invaders. Foreign impositions have ended both democratic and autocratic regimes, as well as nonstate forms of rule.
- Autocratic elites initiate rule changes that alter the kinds of groups permitted in the regime's inner circle.
- Competitively elected elites initiate rule changes that prohibit opposition groups from competing effectively, a process we refer to as "authoritarianization." Such rule changes replace democracy with autocracy under the same ruling group.

The last two kinds of seizure differ from the others in that incumbents remain in the ruling group; such "seizures" are motivated not by the desire to redistribute away from incumbents, as most other dictatorial seizures are, but to prevent redistribution away from the group currently in power, which might follow fully competitive elections.

Table 2.1 shows the distribution of these methods of seizure for post–World War II dictatorships.

TABLE 2.1 *Proportion of dictatorships begun by different kinds of seizures of power*

Kind of Seizure	Percentage of All Seizures
Coup	45
Foreign imposition*	16
Authoritarianization	15
Insurgency	14
Popular uprising	5
Elite rule change	5

* Includes colonial handovers to ruling groups not chosen in democratic elections.

As Table 2.1 shows, coups initiate the largest proportion of dictatorships.[4] By definition, military officers carry out coups. Sometimes the officers have civilian supporters, but coups nevertheless usually lead to government controlled by an officer or group of officers. Examples include the 1973 Chilean coup mentioned above and the 1963 ouster by a coalition of officers with Ba'thist sympathies of an earlier Syrian dictatorship led by the military high command in collaboration with an elected civilian president. The 1963 coup was coded as a regime initiation because it replaced a government led by a military high command consciously selected to unify the military despite its partisan factions with one led by a single faction, the pro-Ba'thists (Be'eri 1970, 150–53; Haddad 1971, 294). The 1963 coup eventuated in the Assad dictatorship that still rules much of Syria as this is written.

Foreigners imposed about 16 percent of post-1946 dictatorships, either as outgoing colonial powers or as occupying forces. Outgoing colonial powers created quite a few post–World War II dictatorships by handing power either to a civilian party-led regime with formally democratic institutions or to a monarchy that was constitutional on paper but not in practice. Soviet occupying forces created many of the rest. The first wave was the party-led regimes with communist institutions imposed by Soviet occupation forces during and after World War II. The second occurred when a number of ex-Soviet nations achieved independence under governments chosen before independence by the Soviets. Where we have labeled the initiation of a dictatorship foreign-imposed, occupiers usually influenced the choice of individual leaders as well as the rules and institutions for making future leadership and policy choices. Some foreign impositions involved a finger on the scale rather than all-out coercion, as when foreigners outlawed popular leftist parties during the period leading to pre-independence elections in order to help a favored party or when they chose to

---

[4] Coups have declined in frequency since the end of the Cold War (Kendall-Taylor and Frantz 2014; Marinov and Goemans 2014), but still accounted for more than one-third of all authoritarian initiations between 1990 and 2010.

negotiate independence with monarchists rather than republicans. Military occupation and all-out repression occurred in other cases, as in Eastern Europe. Since few colonies remain, foreign impositions have become less common.

Democratically elected incumbents initiate a surprising number of dictatorships by changing political institutions or practices to authoritarianize the political system. Examples include the incremental transformation of Venezuelan politics from democratic to authoritarian during the presidency of Hugo Chávez and President Alberto Fujimori's unconstitutional closure of Congress and dismissal of judges (*autogolpe*) in Peru. Elected presidents supported by ruling parties carry out most authoritarianizations.

Fourteen percent of autocracies begin when armed rebels defeat incumbents. Parties lead most insurgencies. Until the end of colonization, many insurgencies ousted foreigners. Examples include the Algerian, Vietnamese, and Mozambican wars of independence. Insurgencies that have replaced domestic incumbents include the Sandinistas' defeat of the Somoza family dictatorship in Nicaragua in 1979 and the defeat of the Habré dictatorship in Chad by Idriss Déby's forces in 1990.

Popular uprisings and elite rule changes are the least common ways new autocracies start.[5] Popular uprisings generally demand democracy, and the individuals to whom power is entrusted usually announce transitions to democracy, but they sometimes consolidate authoritarian rule instead. Examples include the uprisings that ousted Robert Guéï in Cote d'Ivoire in 2000 and the Duvalier family dictatorship in Haiti in 1986. Guéï's overthrow brought to power Laurent Gbagbo, who had probably won the election that protesters accused Guéï of stealing, but Gbagbo then governed as an autocrat (Englebert 2003, 332). A military-civilian transitional ruling council tasked with holding elections replaced the Duvaliers, but officers in the council prevented democratization (Payne and Sutton 1993, 80–89).

Elite rule changes initiate new regimes in the sense that they change the identity of groups that control leadership and policy choice, even though the current incumbent remains a part of the inner circle of the new dictatorship. An example is the transition from direct to indirect military rule in Guatemala in 1985, when military rulers agreed to allow competitive elections for the presidency and legislature, but prevented popular leftist parties from participating (which is the reason the case is coded as authoritarian, despite competitive elections). The military also retained control over important aspects of policy as a condition for allowing real civilian control in other policy areas. Elected civilian President Cerezo said he "held no more than 30 percent of power with no control over the armed forces" (Schirmer 1998, 176). Under our definition of regime, Cerezo's election began a new regime because the pre-1985 political system limited leaders to high-ranking military

---

[5] Since 1990, popular uprisings have become more common.

officers, but the post-1985 regime involved a power-sharing arrangement between officers and competitively elected civilians.

The initiation of the rump Yugoslavian (Serbian and Montenegrin) government under the same leadership as before the breakup of pre-1990 Yugoslavia is another example of an elite-initiated rule change. Slobodan Milošević, who had led Serbia before the breakup but ruled pre-1990 *Yugoslavia* in coalition with the leaders of five other nationalities, remained Serbia's leader but within a ruling group that included only Serbians and Montenegrins after the breakup. Elite rule changes, like authoritarianizations, do not fit the standard image of autocratic seizures of power, but, as Table 2.1 shows, they initiate a number of dictatorships.

Current (or former) military officers and groups organized as parties carry out a large majority of transitions to autocracy. Organized groups have a big advantage over the unorganized when it comes to difficult and dangerous endeavors like overthrowing governments. Soldiers carry out coups, but they also sometimes lead other kinds of seizures. Ex-officers lead 8 percent of the insurgencies that initiate dictatorships; officers implement more than half of the elite rule changes that result in new regimes; and they are handed power during almost one-third of the popular uprisings that end up failing to democratize. Parties lead three-quarters of authoritarianizations, most insurgencies, and some popular uprisings. Half of autocracies imposed by foreign powers are led by dominant parties, as in Eastern Europe after World War II and a number of postcolonial regimes in Africa and Asia.

Military and party leadership are not mutually exclusive. Some seizures involve both officers or ex-officers and parties. The exceptions to leadership by a party or the military include a few instances in which popular uprisings have catapulted party-less opposition leaders to power; some insurgencies that were not organized as parties before the seizure, though insurgent organizations always perform some of the functions usually taken care of by parties; and some cases in which foreign rulers left power in the hands of individuals not supported by parties (usually monarchs, but Hamid Karzai in Afghanistan is another). Table 2.2 shows the frequency of seizures led by current (or former) military officers and/or parties.

Ousters of incumbent governments, whether democratic or autocratic, usually occur when things are going badly, that is, when the economy is in trouble, when disorder and violence make people feel unsafe, and/or when scandal or arbitrary brutality has discredited incumbents. These are the reasons coups are often "welcomed throughout society because, initially, the military coup means all things to all men. The army is popular not because of what it stands for (which nobody knows, at first), but because of what, quite patently, it has fought against" (Finer 1976, 104). After the overthrow of the Iraqi monarchy, the first army broadcast invited citizens to "go out and watch the edifices of tyranny crumble. Within the hour a mob of hundreds of thousands was milling through the streets screaming its joy and its thirst for vengeance" (Dann 1969, 33).

TABLE 2.2 *Proportion of dictatorships begun by different kinds of seizure groups*

Seizure Leadership	Percentage of All Seizures
Military	50
Party-based	40
Neither	18
Both	8

Note: Leadership of the seizure group is coded as military if the regime seized power via coup or the military put the first regime leader into office. It is coded as party if what became the regime support party existed prior to the seizure. The sample consists of 280 regimes that appear in the post-1946 data, including those that seized power before 1946.

Citizens welcomed the 1980 coup in Burkina Faso and also the 1982 coup that ousted those who had been welcomed in 1980 (Otayek 1986). Surveys carried out after the 1966 coup in Argentina and the 1992 *autogolpe* in Peru show popular support for the takeover in each instance at above 60 percent (O'Donnell 1973, 39; Stokes 2001, 142).

When things are going badly for the incumbent and ordinary people are thoroughly fed up, it is not uncommon for more than one group to plot during the months before the successful ouster and for rumors of coups to circulate. Sometimes newspaper editorials publicly urge the military to end an unsuccessful government.[6] Multiple different actors often reach the conclusion that drastic action is needed to "save" the country or that bold action to advance their own interests has become feasible. Several separate groups of officers may be plotting coups at the same time, and sometimes senior officers stage coups to forestall junior officers whom they know to be plotting. In Libya during the months before Moammar Qaddafi's coup, for example, "at least three and possibly four groups were jostling to unseat the king" (Blundy and Lycett 1987, 53). Because multiple groups were known to be plotting, "Several officers took part in [Qaddafi's] coup without knowing who was leading it" (First 1974, 108–9). In such circumstances, there is quite a bit of luck involved in which plotters complete their preparations first to become the actual seizure group. One of the reasons no one opposed the Qaddafi coup is that the seizure group did not announce their identity, and many other officers assumed that a more senior group known to be plotting was in charge.

The choice of the method by which to replace an incumbent regime and install a new dictatorship is largely opportunistic. Coups are the most frequent method for ousting fellow citizens (as opposed to foreigners) simply because officers' access to weapons and command of soldiers make them much easier to

[6] Stepan (1971), for example, reports the frequency of editorials calling on the military to oust the elected government before the 1964 coup in Brazil.

organize than other overthrows. Minority military factions carry out many coups. Qaddafi was a twenty-seven-year-old captain supported by a small number of other low-ranking officers carrying small arms and forty-eight rounds of ammunition (Singh 2014, 29). Small numbers of conspirators can succeed in part because of military discipline; lower-ranked officers and soldiers usually follow orders so few have to know about the plot. Describing the first Nigerian coup, Robin Luckham writes, "the other officers and men thought they were going out only on a night exercise" (1971, 31). After a coup attempt in Guatemala, Jennifer Schirmer reports that "few lower-ranking officers and none of the soldiers were told that the purpose of the mobilization was to overthrow the government" (1998, 218). Rebellions and popular uprisings, in contrast, require substantial voluntary sacrifices by participants. Coups oust 64 percent of autocracies that are replaced by new autocracies and 60 percent of democracies that suffer breakdowns.[7]

A foreign occupier or colonial power, however, has never been ousted by coup. The reason is obvious, but we mention the point because foreign occupation, whether after invasion or colonial incursion, is almost the only situation in which the armed forces do not have an advantage when it comes to toppling incumbents. Otherwise, the armed forces have a clear edge, which begins soon after a military is created, as the many coups carried out by small, newly created armies shortly after independence demonstrate.

This advantage means that military officers dissatisfied with an incumbent government face fewer impediments to acting than do similarly dissatisfied civilians. As a consequence, civilian groups that rate their chances of getting into power through legal means as low, whether because they cannot attract wide popular support or because they face an incumbent who prevents fair elections, often ally with military factions. They hope to achieve power by outmaneuvering officers after a coup ends the old regime. For example, the communists in Afghanistan and the Ba'th Party in Syria and Iraq used this strategy. It worked, in the sense that the party achieved power rather than being marginalized by its erstwhile military ally, on the first try in Syria, on the second in Afghanistan, and on the third in Iraq. After the first effort in Afghanistan and the first two in Iraq, the military ally who assumed leadership right after the coup quickly eliminated the civilian party ally from the government.

While force is the obvious choice for military officers contemplating a seizure of power, the comparative advantage of party-based groups lies elsewhere, so they choose nonviolent means of seizure when possible. They most often initiate dictatorship via authoritarianization because it is relatively easy once a party controls a democratic government. Authoritarianization also has a high

---

[7] These figures for coups are larger than those in Table 2.1 because the universe of autocratic initiations used for the table includes 26 percent that arose in territory that was either foreign-occupied or not independent prior to the seizure of power that started an autocratic regime. The figures on this page are for coups that end regimes in independent countries.

success rate, though we know of a few cases in which a democratically elected president's proposal to merge all parties into one (and thus authoritarianize) was successfully resisted and a couple in which such a proposal led to the elected government's overthrow. The authoritarianization strategy is obviously available only to groups that already control the government, however. Some of the authoritarianizations included in the data we use happened during the run-up to independence or during foreign occupation. The foreign occupier may have promoted it because it ensured control by a group friendly to the occupier's interests, or foreigners may have cared more about extricating themselves than about who ruled after their departure.

Insurgency, in contrast, has very high costs for participants compared with either coups or authoritarianization. Insurgent leaders must sustain armed forces for long periods compared with those engaged in coups. Insurgencies last about a decade on average (Fearon 2007), whereas coups are typically over within a day or two. Insurgent leaders must find some way to fund their forces since the government does not pay their salaries or buy their weapons – as it does for soldiers involved in coups. The chances of death, disability, privation, and loss of livelihood are much higher for participants in insurgencies than for participants in coups or popular uprisings. Furthermore, insurgency is unlikely to succeed. Insurgent groups secure outright victories against incumbents only about a third of the time (Fearon 2007). By contrast, a bit more than half of all coup attempts succeed (Powell and Thyne 2011). Probably for these reasons, more insurgencies have ousted colonial powers and foreign occupiers than domestic governments. In other words, insurgency is rarely the strategy of choice; it is used when no other strategy is available.

Popular uprisings also sometimes initiate authoritarian regimes, but this is not usually the intention of those who joined the uprising. When massive demonstrations persuade an incumbent to resign, power is handed to interim leaders to manage the transition. These leaders are supposed to oversee competitive elections to choose a new government, but they may opt to consolidate power in their own hands instead, initiating a dictatorship.

To summarize this section, the selection of means to overthrow governments is largely instrumental. The method of seizure reflects the resources and capacities that comprise the comparative advantage of different kinds of seizure groups. Most autocracies begin with coups because the command of men and weapons gives coup plotters a great advantage relative to other would-be seizure groups. Coups are the easiest and cheapest means available, unless the group bent on establishing a dictatorship already controls government as the elected incumbent.

BEFORE THE SEIZURE OF POWER

Many are called to the vocation of dictatorship, but few are chosen. The majority of seizure groups fail. Apart from groups that already control government at the time of authoritarianization, members of would-be seizure groups lead difficult lives. Some are jailed or killed by the governments they seek to overthrow. They also risk their careers, income, and liberty. These difficulties and dangers put strong evolutionary pressures on would-be seizure groups. Those we observe after the initiation of dictatorship are highly selected for traits that were useful in getting them to that point. Because this selection pressure weeds out much of the natural diversity among those who aspire to establish dictatorships, we can make some generalizations about those who succeed.

Centralization of authority within the group of plotters contributes to discipline and secrecy, both of which help seizure groups survive in a hostile environment. Nevertheless, successful seizure groups must usually also maintain a somewhat collegial internal organization in order to retain sufficient membership.[8] Seizure-group leaders cannot usually impose heavy costs on those who abandon the cause. Out-of-power leaders have little ability beyond moral authority and force of personality to enforce discipline. They usually have no police apparatus at their disposal and few means to intimidate. Individuals who disagree with a leader can simply leave the party or coup conspiracy. It is estimated, for example, that 90 percent of those who joined the Communist Party in the United States had left by the end of the first year. Leaving the party or coup conspiracy entails few costs for the one who leaves. In contrast, the loss of comrades can be quite damaging to remaining conspirators. They may be left with too few allies for effective action, and their former colleagues may turn them in to authorities. In short, if leaders demand too much obedience and subordination from adherents, they may simply desert, leaving the group too small to accomplish its goals – arguably the fate of all the western communist parties rigidly controlled by the Comintern.

To maintain the minimum support needed for effective action, plot leaders must therefore consult and be somewhat open to the ideas and interests of members of the group. As a result, successful seizure groups usually enforce norms of discipline and secrecy with respect to outsiders, but relationships within the group tend to be relatively collegial before seizures of power.

Seizure groups need some support from the populace as well and thus must be somewhat responsive to popular aspirations. A group bent on seizing power does not need majority support, but it needs some. Regardless of the mode of seizing power, groups need the "contingent consent" of the ruled (Levi 1997). To attract the support they need, military seizure groups typically promise things nearly all citizens want, such as public order, growth, and an end to

---

[8] We build on Kenneth Jowitt's (1975) argument about traits that help Leninist parties succeed at different stages. During the chaotic period of power seizure, according to Jowitt, collegial relationships within the party give cadres the autonomy and discretion to respond to changing conditions, thereby contributing to survival. A different set of traits contributes to survival during the post-seizure period.

corruption in their first broadcast informing the people of a coup. Other kinds of seizure groups make equally attractive promises.

Seizure groups are more likely to succeed when they (1) articulate goals that are attractive and intelligible to many ordinary people, such as peace, prosperity, and the end of corruption (Jowitt 1975) and (2) choose a moment to seize power when disgust with incumbents has spread through much of the populace. When both these conditions hold, seizure groups can attract broad, though often temporary, public support. Elite groups as well as ordinary citizens often support a dictatorial seizure of power simply because they want to oust the old order.

During insurgencies, the evolutionary pressures on seizure groups are even stronger. If the struggle is long and violent, the seizure group needs to draw manpower and other resources from the population, and it cannot do this entirely through coercion. Where the struggle to oust the old regime has been prolonged and the seizure group has needed to maintain popular support for some years and also to recruit fighters and extract resources from the population, successful groups have generally provided more than promises. As Samuel Popkin (1979) argues, change-oriented movements are more likely to succeed in attracting mass support if their leaders can provide real benefits to those they seek to mobilize. Since they have few material resources to hand out, they often provide goods such as land redistribution and organization for self-defense in the areas they control, along with individual benefits that require cadre labor but little money.[9] Literacy campaigns are a common strategy. These benefits are valued by recipients and create loyalty that ideology and promises alone could not elicit. Leninist parties in China and Vietnam relied on these strategies during the years of insurgency (Johnson 1962; Popkin 1979). Before the seizure of power, communist parties redistributed land to tillers. Only after they controlled the government, military, and security services did they carry out unpopular collectivizations of agriculture.

The point of this discussion of collegial relationships within potential seizure groups and groups' efforts to respond to popular demands is to highlight the contrast with the change in power relationships that occurs after seizures of power. The bargaining power of followers relative to leaders within seizure groups and of ordinary citizens relative to seizure group members is much stronger before the seizure of power than afterward.

The dependence of leaders on the led carries over into the immediate aftermath of the seizure, when the regime is still uncertain of its grip on power and reliant on much of the ousted incumbent's bureaucratic and military apparatus. The seizure group's responsiveness to citizens declines, however, as the new leadership gains control over the implementing arms of government, such as the

---

[9] See Mampilly (2011) for a study of how rebel groups provide public goods to citizens who live in territory they control.

police and tax authorities. The longer-term fate of collegial leadership in dictatorships is discussed in Chapters 4 and 5.

THE MORNING AFTER A SEIZURE OF POWER

Nonincumbent groups seize control of government in order to change public policies and redistribute the fruits of control of the state.[10] Even if personal ambition motivates participants, groups that lead seizures also expect to be able to advance public welfare by improving economic performance, restoring order, and achieving other widely shared goals, though these expectations arise more from inexperience and ideological commitment than realistic assessment. The fruits to be redistributed include status, power, and opportunities as well as material goods. Seizure groups expect to be able to redistribute away from the individuals and groups they believe benefited from the status quo and toward groups seen as having a legitimate claim to more, including themselves. The anticipated redistribution sometimes includes private property but invariably includes the direct benefits of controlling government. In short, many of the same goals motivate authoritarian seizure groups as motivate out-of-power parties competing in democratic elections.

Nonincumbent seizure groups, however, tend to lack experience in government, and they also often lack a detailed plan for what to do if they succeed in capturing power. Before the overthrow, seizure groups typically have developed a thoroughgoing critique of the government they hope to oust, which is needed to attract support, and they usually have a practical plan for how to force it from office.

For military officers, this usually means careful, detailed plans for which officers will order troops they command to surround or seize key government facilities.[11] Plotters have to include officers who actually command troops stationed near facilities to be taken. Depending on the kind of defenses the incumbent controls, plotters may need the cooperation of officers who command tank regiments or heavy artillery. They may have to coordinate with the police and air force. If plotters include highest-ranking officers, they can minimize opposition to their plans by retiring officers loyal to the incumbent before they attempt the coup. Much of the planning effort for coups goes into securing the support of other officers so that the ruler being ousted will not have an equally threatening armed force on his side (Potash 1969, 1980, 1996; Stepan 1971; Decalo 1976; Nordlinger 1977; Fontana 1987). One of the goals of careful coup planning is to minimize the chance of bloodshed or, worse,

[10] Dictatorships begun by the authoritarianization of a democratic government or elite rule changes are exceptions.

[11] There are of course exceptions. Sometimes barely planned coups succeed by luck. The 1981 coup in Ghana led by J. J. Rawlings and the 1980 coup led by Samuel Doe in Liberia are examples of barely planned coups.

protracted armed conflict (Potash 1969, 1980, 1996). Because of the obvious and credible threat posed by tanks and armies drawn up around the presidential palace, coups have been accomplished without bloodshed about two-thirds of the time.[12]

Party-based nonincumbent seizure groups have a more difficult task because, unlike officers, they cannot order others to participate. They must usually attract large numbers of other civilians to demonstrate, strike, or fight along with them. The leadership's main task beforehand is the persuasion and organization of supporters drawn from the initially uncommitted population. Great effort has to be put into gathering the resources and attracting and training enough militants to mobilize large numbers into the streets and keep them there beyond the first few days, or to recruit and supply an insurgent army and keep it alive and fighting for months or years.

In other words, for nonincumbent seizure groups – regardless of whether they are led by a party or the military – the plotting, planning, and organizing required for a successful overthrow usually take a lot of effort, attention to detail, and strategic thinking. The urgent need to get this part of the plan right limits the amount of attention that goes into planning what to do after the overthrow, and the need for secrecy can limit the seizure group's ability to consult experts and interest groups. Moreover, sometimes the details about who will rule post-seizure and what policies will be followed need to be kept vague in order to attract key support. After the 1958 Iraqi coup, for example, "Those in power lacked both experience and a shared ideology, with the result that fundamental issues of principle, such as who was in command, and what form of government and political system should be adopted, remained unresolved" (Farouk-Sluglett and Sluglett 1987, 52). Describing another Iraqi coup ten years later, the same authors say that "the coup had been carried out by a group of officers, each of whom felt equally entitled to play a, or *the*, key role in government" (119).

For all these reasons, nonincumbent seizure groups usually achieve office without a detailed policy plan. Those who carry out seizures of power typically have idealized goals they expect to accomplish, and they may have decided to initiate a few grand policy changes, such as nationalization of natural resources, land redistribution, or economic liberalization. Their lack of practical experience in government limits their ability to make detailed plans for how to implement their policies, however. Members of the seizure group may agree on the general direction of policy changes, but not on specific strategies for how to carry them out, elicit the cooperation of affected citizens, or impose the policies on those who will inevitably be damaged by them. They usually have not made decisions about priorities among desired changes, speed of

---

[12] This estimate was tabulated using the Center for Systemic Peace's "Coups d'Etat, 1946–2013" data set (available at www.systemicpeace.org), which provides data on the number of deaths associated with successful coups worldwide.

implementation, or the mix of coercion and cooptation that should characterize their interaction with different groups of citizens. Differences of opinion about these things cause conflict within the group.

After their accession, they face immediately all the economic and other problems that helped make their seizure of power possible, as well as the urgent need to make a large number of appointments and policy decisions quickly. They have to adapt the group's previous decision-making procedures to policy-making on the fly. They have to either create human structures for implementing policies and protecting themselves or make use of the perhaps disloyal public employees hired during the ousted regime. And they also have to create or adapt police and other agencies that interact with the public to prevent the mobilization of opposition.

While engaged in a frenetic effort to deal with problems, they must also devise methods for reaching policy decisions and find ways to resolve disagreements among themselves. Thus, the early days of dictatorship tend to be anxious, chaotic, and full of uncertainty.[13]

POST-SEIZURE ORGANIZATION

Regardless of how seizure groups achieve power, the starting point for assigning tasks and making decisions is the group's preexisting organization and its norms and procedures for choosing leaders, making choices, and maintaining internal cohesion. Preexisting organization and norms vary by kind of group. In this section we discuss characteristic differences among seizure groups.[14]

Coups tend to lead to the occupation of the top offices in the new dictatorship by officers, regardless of what civilian allies might have hoped. Because of strong hierarchical norms within the military, plotters often choose the top-ranked officer who cooperated with plotters as regime leader because other officers would balk at being led by a lower-ranked officer. Higher-ranked officers who opposed the coup tend to be retired (or jailed, exiled, or killed) in order to prevent potential destabilizing challenges to the chain of command. After the coup led by Qaddafi (a captain), 430 of Libya's 600 officers were retired, jailed, or posted abroad (Blundy and Lycett 1987, 64).

---

[13] Seizures led by incumbents face fewer challenges of course. Pushing rule changes through legislatures is less dangerous than insurgency or staging coups. Incumbent seizure groups may have filled the army and police with supporters before authoritarianization, eliminating one of the most urgent tasks facing other seizure groups. Seizure groups that authoritarianize an elected government also have more government experience than other seizure groups, and they can typically count on the loyalty of existing bureaucrats (many of whom they appointed). In addition, the gradual and subtle nature of some authoritarianizations can leave citizens without a focal point around which opposition might coalesce.

[14] We do not discuss monarchies in this section because foreigners handed control over to nearly all authoritarian monarchies that have ruled since 1946.

The clear formal hierarchy of command in military seizure groups tends to centralize decision-making within an inner circle of highly ranked officers. The wide dispersion of arms and command of troops across the officer corps, however, means that before making key decisions, military dictators must consult with other officers or risk a coup led by their colleagues. To deal with that basic feature of military rule, regime leaders include as many officers as they believe are needed to ensure the cooperation of all parts of the armed forces in the ruling inner circle. For highly professionalized militaries, this means a junta made up of the commanders of the branches of the armed forces and often also the commander of the national police. In more factionalized militaries, however, the ruling military council may include many more officers in order to ensure ethnic representation or to include all officers who command troops. In some, even representatives of noncommissioned officers and soldiers are included.

Uniformed members of the inner circle serve as representatives of their subordinates and thus facilitate consultation between the leader and the forces that serve as his primary support base. Officers in the inner circle are expected both to advocate for policies that serve their subordinates' interests or reflect their opinions and to ensure subordinates' loyalty to the leadership. The policies of dictators established by military seizure groups thus tend to reflect the views of their officer corps, leading to increased spending on the military (Bove and Brauner 2014), pay raises, immediate promotions of those involved in the coup and sometimes all officers, violent responses to minority demands for greater rights and autonomy (Nordlinger 1977), and the adoption of policies favored by other officers regardless of whether the dictator himself shares their ideas. For example, Mathieu Kérékou in Benin and Didier Ratsiraka in Madagascar introduced socialist rhetoric and policies, though neither had displayed much earlier leftism (Decalo 1979, 1986).[15]

The need to retain the support of other officers also constrains the dictator's discretion over personnel appointments. All dictators try to appoint loyalists to key posts, but the need to conform to military promotion norms in order to avoid alienating other officers limits the discretion of military dictators. Even after the murder of senior commanders during coups, "coup participants still [keep] up the normal command relationships between each other" (Luckham 1971, 31). As a result, military dictators often lack the full control of membership in the dictatorial elite enjoyed by some other dictators because they can only choose appointees from among candidates with the right rank and seniority.[16] Policy implementation can also be undermined because appointments to

---

[15] Decalo (1986) describes Ratsiraka as a "bourgeois technocrat ... with no previous ideological convictions" (129).

[16] For multiple examples, see Potash's (1969, 1980, 1996) careful descriptions of decision-making in several Argentine military dictatorships.

ministries and state agencies depend on the promotion and retirement norms of the armed forces rather than substantive competence (North 1983, 273).

At the time of the seizure, the military usually lacks an organized civilian network capable of mobilizing, or even reaching and gathering information from, ordinary citizens. Officers' training to obey and to give orders exacerbates this deficiency, as does their lack of training or experience in persuasion, bargaining, and compromise.

Civilian seizure groups are more heterogeneous than military seizure groups. Some are armed while others are not. We first describe those that seize power via armed insurgency. Successful insurgency leads to control of the dictatorship's inner circle by the leadership of the rebellion. Military and civilian roles tend to be fused in insurgencies, and that often persists in the post-seizure inner circle.

Insurgent seizure groups share some (but not all) of the characteristics of military seizure groups. Arms and command over troops are widely dispersed within insurgent groups, but military promotion norms do not constrain the leader's discretion over appointments, increasing his power relative to others in the inner circle. Successful insurgent groups develop strong discipline, but where regional commanders have led autonomous insurgent forces in different parts of the country, intense factionalism can develop. That is, discipline may operate within region-based factions, but not necessarily across them. The various factions will then need to be represented in the post-seizure dictatorial elite for the same reason that ruling military councils include many officers when the military is factionalized. Examples of factionalized insurgencies include the multiple armed forces that cooperated with difficulty during the Mexican revolution and the several separate regional Khmer Rouge armies in Cambodia, each led by its own party/military commander before the fall of Phnom Penh.

Since successful insurgency requires the maintenance of organized networks for recruiting fighters, extracting resources, training soldiers, and disciplining dissidents, insurgent groups often have much more of the organizational structure needed to reach most citizens and to incorporate them into the seizure group's project than do other seizure groups. Internal party institutions in dictatorships brought to power by insurgency thus tend to be stronger relative to society but weaker relative to the dictator than those of parties that achieved power via authoritarianization or popular uprising. Because they have often developed internal security services before the seizure, they can very quickly consolidate control over the population once the ruling group has control of the resources of the state.

Insurgents who have achieved power usually purge and reorganize, or replace, the armed forces and security services of the ousted regime. They may have sufficient trained soldiers and cadres to replace the incumbent army and part of the incumbent administration rather than having to retrain and monitor (or compromise with) them, as most other seizure groups do.

Former insurgents thus have less need to coopt opposition leaders and more ability to respond to opposition with coercion than do dominant parties that achieved power by nonviolent means. In short, their ability to penetrate both state and society, and thus to implement dramatic policy shifts, initially tends to be much greater than that of military or unarmed party-led seizure groups.

Because of the great costs and risks associated with joining insurgencies, those who become their leaders and most dedicated militants tend to have commitments to extreme ideologies or policies (DeNardo 1985). Only individuals who want radical changes would shoulder such costs.[17] Consequently, insurgent seizure groups often want to impose unpopular policy changes – for example, collectivization of agriculture or the exclusion of distrusted classes or ethnicities from government jobs. Because of the prior development of extensive cadre networks and security agencies, they may also have greater capacity to carry out such changes than do military or unarmed party-led seizure groups.

Unarmed civilian seizure groups, in contrast, tend to be more loosely organized. Intensive organization is not needed to win a democratic election, the precondition for authoritarianization, which is the most common way for civilian seizure groups to achieve power. Nor is much organization needed to mobilize people into the streets for a few days or weeks. There are a few well-known cases in which well-organized groups seized power by mobilizing ordinary people for a popular uprising (e.g., the Iranian revolution), but most of the time popular uprising is a tactic chosen by groups that lack the organization and resources to maintain insurgency or a multiyear electoral campaign against an authoritarian incumbent. In short, unarmed civilian seizure groups are usually loosely organized, partly because they did not need high internal unity in order to achieve power, but also because they so often include many different parties or groups that joined forces only to win an election or oust a previous incumbent.

Authoritarianization usually results in civilian leadership of the new dictatorship, with power centered in the hands of the incumbent. It involves a change in the relationship between the ruling party and the opposition, but often not in the composition of the government's inner circle. Parties that achieve control via authoritarianization very often coopt the leaders of other parties, thus reducing societal opposition at the expense of their own discipline and ideological coherence. They may also coopt military officers, but they rarely bring them into the regime's inner circle.

Paradoxically, loose party organization gives leaders more autonomy relative to the rest of the inner circle than military dictators initially enjoy. Both electoral and revolutionary parties have rules for choosing leaders, making strategy choices, and delegating tasks. Leaders of out-of-power parties can

---

[17] A seminal article by Kalt and Zupan (1984) developed the logic linking political activism with extremism in democracies. The logic is even more compelling when activism is physically dangerous.

usually be removed by followers. Relative bargaining power often changes after the seizure of power, however, and the members of the inner circles of dictatorships that achieved power via popular uprising or authoritarianization may have limited ability to constrain the dictator's policy choices because they lack unity and arms.

At the same time, the weak organization of such parties can also mean that the dictator cannot restrain or discipline party subordinates, which undermines policy implementation and efforts to limit corruption. At the beginning, such groups usually have very broad citizen support, but linkages with ordinary citizens tend to be superficial and ultimately depend on delivering benefits. In contrast to the military, such civilian seizure groups usually have little coercive capacity but a great deal of experience in persuasion and compromise. They are good at coopting opposition elites, but bad at delivering on their promises to ordinary citizens, which requires a disciplined and honest cadre of officials to implement reforms and distributive decisions.

These characteristics of the seizure group set in motion political processes that define the dictatorship initially. These features in turn affect who can become the leaders of the new dictatorship, how centralized power is within the dictatorial inner circle on the morning after the seizure, and how the new elite responds to citizen demands and opposition.

CONCLUSION

In this chapter, we have provided some basic facts about how dictatorships begin and who leads them. We also described the immediate aftermath of different kinds of seizures of power. We noted that most dictatorships replace earlier autocracies and that the regimes they oust are often incompetent, dishonest, or both, as well as repressive. Since World War II, military coups have established more dictatorships than other means of seizing power. Authoritarianization by a democratically elected incumbent, insurgency, and foreign imposition are the other common ways of establishing dictatorship.

Groups of military officers or civilian-led parties install most dictatorships. We see decisions about how to seize power as strategic and opportunistic. That is, military officers have a comparative advantage in using violence and threats of violence to take over governments, so that is what they usually use. Incumbent elected parties that decide to prevent future electoral defeats can most easily sustain their rule by using their control over the legislature and courts to change formal or informal rules in ways that prevent fair competition. Insurgency is a very costly and difficult way to gain political control, so it is only used when other means are unavailable, as, for example, against foreign occupiers. The initiation of new dictatorships by insurgents has become less frequent as foreign occupation has become less common and as more incumbent dictatorships have allowed semi-competitive elections, giving opponents a less costly way to challenge them.

Because of the difficulty and risk of trying to force out an incumbent government, groups that seek to do so focus their efforts on organizing the details of the physical overthrow, often at the expense of planning what to do post-seizure. In order to attract sufficient support, they may need to promise different things to different people or keep their policy goals vague. The need for secrecy during plotting means they cannot usually choose important cabinet officials, develop detailed implementation plans, or consult experts for policy advice before the seizure of power. Sometimes they have not even decided who will lead the new government. The lack of detailed planning about what to do post-seizure tends to make the first months after forcible impositions of dictatorship chaotic. Power struggles occur between supporters of different policies and different individual officeholders. Strategic skills not previously displayed in public and unforeseen events affect who wins post-seizure power struggles, which add to the difficulty of predicting what kind of policies will emerge after the establishment of a new dictatorship. It may take time for observers and even participants to figure out what kind of regime is being created.

3

What Do We Know about Coups?

In 1952, the arbitrary and corrupt Egyptian monarchy ended. Troops commanded by a group of young officers who had named themselves the Free Officers occupied the army's general headquarters and arrested twenty of the highest-ranking officers – the king's strongest military loyalists. Tanks simultaneously surrounded the broadcasting building, the telephone exchange, the railroad station, and the airports. This classic coup took only a few hours. Two guards were killed. No one else resisted. The Free Officers did not arrest the king or his ministers. Three days later, they asked the king to abdicate, and he left the country, ending the monarchy (Haddad 1973, 21–23).

King Farouk had ruled "comfortably for sixteen years and would have probably ruled longer if revolutionary action had depended on the people's initiative," according to George Haddad (1973, 10). The Free Officers' leader, Colonel Gamal Abdel Nasser, stated that the army was "'the force to do the job' because it had more cohesion, its men trusted each other ... and it had 'enough material strength at its disposal to guarantee a swift and decisive action'" (Haddad 1973, 15). The Free Officers had been plotting since at least 1949. Soldiers blamed Egypt's poor performance in the Palestine War of 1948 on senior officers, the king, and his cronies, which alienated much of the officer corps from the monarchy. A scandal involving the corrupt procurement of defective arms had become public and implicated the king. In short, much of the officer corps felt betrayed by the king and the officers he had promoted to the highest ranks, but most ordinary Egyptians appeared content with the monarchy. When violent conflict with the British over control of the Suez Canal led to a destructive riot in Cairo and a cabinet crisis, the Free Officers decided the time to end the old regime had come (Haddad 1973, 7–11). The plotters struck during a high point of cabinet disorganization and popular anger with the government's Suez policy in order to reduce the chances of bloodshed, effective opposition, and failure.

Coups, as noted in the previous chapter, are the most frequent means of initiating new dictatorships and also the most common way of ending them, as we show in later chapters. Yet we lack a good general understanding of why they happen. When insurgents seize control of a government or an elected ruling party authoritarianizes a democracy, it seems self-evident that providing benefits for themselves and their supporters motivates their actions. Analysts debate the motivations behind military seizures of power, however.

Some scholars have viewed officers as defending the interests of economic elites, and thus as more likely to seize power if popular mobilization becomes threatening to elites or if politicians responsive to popular interests propose redistribution (e.g., O'Donnell 1973; Acemoglu and Robinson 2001). In this view, officers are allied with economic elites and serve as their agents rather than pursuing their own interests, not only when plotting coups but also while they control governments. If this view is correct, officers' comparative advantage in overthrowing governments gives economic elites a powerful weapon to use in bargaining with incumbent governments whether democratic or autocratic.

Scholars such as Nordlinger have challenged this idea, however, noting that "the personal interests of officers – their desire for promotions, political ambitions, and fear of dismissal" (1977, 66) have motivated many coups. Nordlinger also observes that although some military-led governments choose policies that benefit existing economic elites, others expropriate private property and pursue redistributive policies. Svolik (2012) has proposed an interesting synthesis of these two views: he suggests that incumbent political leaders increase the funding of their military agents when organized mass opposition threatens their political control, but that then the military uses the additional resources to seize power for itself, rather than serving as a loyal agent.

In this chapter, we examine what currently available evidence can tell us about soldiers' seizures of power. We first discuss the various ways that coups are used to change the political status quo and why we might expect these different uses to be associated with different officer motivations, political contexts, or social forces. Next, we compare the conditions associated with coups that end democracies and those that replace one dictatorship with another. At issue is whether popular mobilization against economic elites or incumbent political leaders increases the likelihood of military intervention. Claims that the military intervenes to prevent redistribution usually assume implicitly that coups oust democratic governments sympathetic to popular demands, which leads to the expectation that the circumstances associated with coups differ for democracies and dictatorships. In the final empirical section, we retest Svolik's argument about the association between popular mobilization and coups. We find no relationship between various measures of mobilized popular opposition and *regime-change* coups. This finding indicates that coups have little to do with elite fears of redistribution or with the buildup of military resources in response to popular mobilization. Instead, we find that officers' grievances are associated with coups.

COUPS FOR VARIOUS PURPOSES

Investigating the conditions associated with coups requires some preliminary discussion because of the various kinds of change accomplished via coup. Coups are military officers' instrument of choice in several different situations, but here we are interested only in those coups that bring new dictatorships to power. Regime-initiating coups include the highly visible events that replace an elected civilian leader with someone who wears a uniform and carries a weapon, but coups also oust incumbent dictatorships. Such coups replace one dictatorship with another. The coups that ousted monarchies in Egypt (1952), Iraq (1958), and Libya (1969) are examples. Coups against incumbent dictatorships can oust any type of preexisting autocratic ruling group, even those controlled by rival ethnicity-based military factions. These coups result in new autocratic regimes.

Officers also use coups as a means of changing leaders in ongoing dictatorships, however, especially those led by the military. These leader-shuffling events are not military seizures of power because they replace one military dictator with another from the same ruling group; the basic formal and informal rules remain unchanged. The coups in Argentina during the early 1970s that replaced one general with another are examples. They did not begin (or end) the dictatorship, which lasted from 1966 to 1973 and ended in an election. Each coup replaced the junta leader but did not replace the group – in this case top military officers – that could select leaders and make key policy decisions. Other examples include the 1980 and 1984 coups in Mauritania, each of which sacked one member of the Military Committee for National Salvation and replaced him with another allied officer. We do not treat these leader replacements as military *seizures of power* because the same group of elites within the military continues to rule before and after the leader change.

We emphasize the difference between regime-initiating coups and leader-shuffling coups because available coup data sets do not distinguish the two, and most analysts have used these data without disaggregating.[1] In what follows, we show that lumping together leader-shuffling coups and those that initiate new dictatorships can blur our understanding of the causes of regime-initiating coups. To more accurately model the process by which a military faction ousts an incumbent government that did not include members of the plotters' faction, we exclude reshuffling coups from the sample used in the first tests below and focus only on regime-initiating military seizures of power. We explore the implications of doing so for previous research as well as for our own analysis.

---

[1] Aksoy, Carter, and Wright (2015) are an exception.

PRECONDITIONS ASSOCIATED WITH REGIME-CHANGE COUPS

We begin by examining two kinds of regime-initiating coups: those that replace democracy with dictatorship and those that replace one autocracy with another. We examine these separately to see if they have different causes. The first sample includes only incumbent dictatorships. The second sample includes only incumbent democracies. The second analysis is similar to research on the causes of democratic breakdown. We treat authoritarianizations by the incumbent democratic leadership – or what others call *power grabs* or *autogolpes* by the democratic incumbent – as right-censored events.[2]

We have good measures of popular mobilization (protest, violent protest, and civil conflict), which are needed to test arguments about the effects of widespread popular opposition on the likelihood of military seizures of power. A finding that popular participation in protests or civil conflict increases the likelihood of coups would support the view of officers as agents of civilian elites since widespread popular mobilization might be expected to lead to elite fears of redistribution or loss of political control.

We lack the kinds of measures of soldiers' specific grievances needed for careful tests of Nordlinger's argument about soldiers' reasons for seizing power. As an approximation of the latter, we use information about officers' past experiences and measures of ethnic representation that we believe might affect soldiers' grievances.

We first examine the factors that prior studies have most often linked to military intervention: level of development, oil wealth, growth, international and civil conflict, protest, and ethnic diversity.[3] We also include indicator variables to investigate the possible effects of earlier political experience. The first identifies countries that were democratic before the current dictatorship (in the sample of incumbent dictatorships); the second identifies countries that had previous experience with military rule. Earlier studies have found that a history of past military intervention increases the likelihood of coups. To account for unmeasured factors that vary by country, we estimate a model with country-level random effects and standard errors clustered by country.[4] All specifications include decade fixed effects and a logged measure of duration dependence.

---

[2] Authoritarianization is the other way democracies are replaced by dictatorship. We treat them as right-censored in order to avoid inadvertently treating them as surviving democracies.

[3] Level of development is measured as the log of GDP per capita, lagged one year. Oil wealth is measured as the log of oil income, lagged one year. Growth is lagged one year. These variables come from the Ethnic Power Relations data set (Wimmer, Cederman, and Min 2009). Data on international and civil conflict are lagged dummy variables for conflict exceeding 1,000 battle deaths in a calendar year, from Themnér and Wallensteen (2014). Data on violent and nonviolent protest movements are lagged one year, from the NAVCO2 project (Chenoweth and Lewis 2013).

[4] Variables for the manner in which the autocratic regime seized power, used in models 2 and 3, are from our data, http://sites.psu.edu/dictators/how-dictatorships-work/. They do not vary

For the sample of incumbent dictatorships, we also examine two character-istics of the incumbent regime that could influence the likelihood that officers develop grievances against regime elites: how the dictatorship came to power in the first place and the ethnic composition of the officer corps and government. We include the way the incumbent dictatorship achieved power as a proxy indicator of the congruence of interests between military officers and ruling elites. We expect more shared interests after insurgent seizures of power because new rebel governments often replace the existing officer corps with rebel officers.

We also investigate the effects of ethnicity because of literature linking ethnic exclusion with different forms of political instability, such as coups and civil wars. For example, Roessler (2011, 2016) argues that leaders who use ethnic criteria to exclude rivals within their initial support coalition may decrease the risk of coups but increase the risk of ethnic insurgency. To investigate the relationship between ethnic inclusion and coups, we include variables that measure ethnic fractionalization in the society and the share of the politically relevant ethnic population that is excluded from participation in the incumbent government.[5] This measure of ethnic exclusion focuses on the groups that share executive political power, not the military. To measure ethnic inclusiveness in the military, we include an indicator variable for whether the officer corps is ethnically heterogeneous, that is, whether it includes members of all larger ethnic groups. This variable, from our own data collection, exists only for the sample of incumbent dictatorships.

Figure 3.1 shows the results for models of regime-initiating coups against incumbent dictatorships. The shapes (diamond, square, and triangle) indicate the point estimates produced by different models, while the lines represent 90 (thick) and 95 (thin) percent confidence intervals. The first specification, shown as diamonds, excludes the seizure-of-power and ethnicity variables. The second, with square point estimates, adds the seizure-of-power variables, while the third specification (triangles) adds the ethnicity variables. Because the estimator is nonlinear, the estimates are not directly comparable across variables.

In these models, the only structural variables consistently associated with military seizures of power are the level of development and population size: the military is less likely to initiate a (new) dictatorship in wealthier countries, as also found in previous research (Londregan and Poole 1990). We find no consistent association between military seizures of power and oil income,

---

substantially within most countries, so we use a country random-effects estimator. Of the 118 countries, 65 have no variation in coup seizure, 100 have no variation in foreign seizure, and 97 have no variation in rebel seizure.

[5] Ethnic exclusion and fractionalization data, both lagged one year, are from version 3 of the Ethnic Power Relations data (Wimmer, Cederman, and Min 2009).

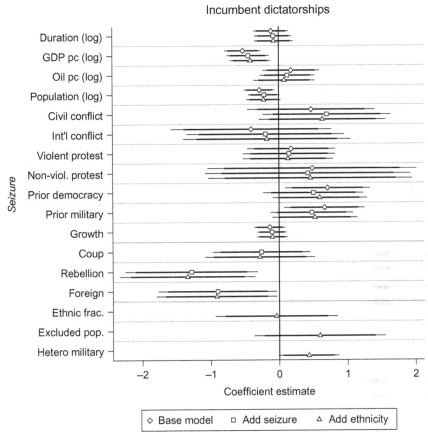

FIGURE 3.1 Regime-initiating coups against incumbent dictatorships.

economic growth, civil or international conflict, and protest, all of which have been suggested as causes of coups by other analysts. The lack of relationship between protest and coups means that our findings fail to support arguments that officers seize power in order to defend the interests of economic elites threatened by popular mobilization. Prior regime type, however, does appear to be correlated with coups: dictatorships in countries that had earlier experienced military rule or democracy are more likely to be ended by coups than dictatorships in countries previously ruled by civilian dictatorships.

Next, we consider some circumstances that might contribute to the development of officers' grievances against incumbent rulers. We expect the makeup of the dictatorship's inner circle and its relationship with military leadership to affect the congruence of interests between rulers and officers, and thus the likelihood of regime-change coups motivated by officers' grievances. We use the way the dictatorship first achieved power (coup, rebellion, foreign imposition, and nonviolent) as an indicator of the military's relationship to the dictatorial elite. The excluded category of seizure includes the less violent means of achieving dictatorial power (authoritarianization, elite rule changes, and popular uprising).

The variables for how the dictatorship initially seized power do not vary over time within individual dictatorships. Instead, they identify a characteristic of the seizure group measured prior to the initiation of dictatorship. This last point is important because the dictator cannot change this characteristic in order to forestall coups. That is, these characteristics of the seizure group are exogenous with respect to later attempts to prevent coups.

The coefficient labeled "Coup" estimates the chances of a regime-change coup in year N against dictatorships first established by coup relative to the left-out group, dictatorships that achieved power in less violent ways. We expect military dictators to consult more with other officers than do other dictators and to share many of their interests. Consequently, we might expect fewer grievances to develop in the officer corps during periods of military rule, leading to fewer regime-change coups. On the other hand, consultation does not eliminate factionalism or personal ambition, other causes of coups. The officer corps of newly independent countries were especially prone to factionalism for the reasons described later in the discussion of ethnic heterogeneity. As a result of these cross-cutting influences, we may see no difference in coup susceptibility between regimes initiated by coup and those initiated by less forceful means.

In contrast, we expect no cross-cutting influences in regimes initiated by rebellion. Successful rebellion leads to political control by the insurgents and often the replacement of the preexisting army by the rebel army. Consequently, the dictatorial elite and the new army share interests, ideas, experiences, and often friendship, which should reduce the seriousness of differences between officers and rulers and hence officer grievances.

Foreign imposition of dictatorship also often goes along with replacing, retraining, and reorganizing both the military and the internal security forces of the occupied country. These strategies aim at coup-proofing. The occupier may also station troops in the country for some years after the formal occupation has ended. For example, Vietnam kept troops in Cambodia for ten years after its replacement of the Khmer Rouge government in 1979. We expect military reorganization, improved internal security, and the stationing of foreign troops to deter coups against foreign-imposed dictatorships.

We test these expectations in the second model in Figure 3.1. We find that coups are unlikely to unseat dictatorships that come to power via rebellion or foreign imposition. The likelihood of regime-change coups in military-led dictatorships (initiated by coup) is not statistically different from their likelihood in regimes that came to power by more peaceful means. These results suggest an association between officers' grievances and regime-change coups.

Once we account for how a dictatorship seized power, the estimates for earlier democratic experience or military rule lose statistical significance, in part because military regimes differ systematically from other dictatorships in how they end (Geddes 1999). These earlier regime endings are the same events used to code the current regime's method of power seizure. Our estimates thus suggest that some of the explanatory power attributed by other research to earlier experience with military rule may simply reflect the fact that researchers have yet to examine systematically how characteristics of different autocratic seizure groups affect the likelihood of later coups.

The final specification in Figure 3.1 adds ethnicity variables to the model: ethnic fractionalization of the population (*ethnic fractionalization*), the share of the ethnically relevant population excluded from executive political power (*excluded*), and a measure of whether the officer corps includes members of the larger ethnic groups in the country (*heterogeneous military*). Ethnic fractionalization and the exclusion of representatives of significant ethnic groups from political influence do not correlate with military seizures of power against dictatorships. An ethnically heterogeneous officer corps, however, is associated with a higher likelihood of regime-change coups.

A heterogeneous officer corps means that men from several ethnicities have enough control over armed men to oust a government. Most colonial governments tended to recruit soldiers from relatively underdeveloped regions, with the result that the first officers at independence often came from one region and one or a few ethnic groups. Political leaders at independence usually came from more developed parts of the country, and thus from different regions and ethnicities (Horowitz 1985). When post-independence leaders took over recruitment of officers, they usually either recruited from their own regions (to ensure officer loyalty) or from all regions – to try to create a truly national army. This recruitment sequence led to a post-independence officer corps that was heterogeneous but nevertheless stratified by ethnicity. Top officers often came from one area and lower-ranking officers from others. As a result, we see quite a few coups carried out by junior officers from one ethnic cluster against ruling senior officers from another. These coups reflect the grievances of junior officers over slow promotions and their regions' share of federal spending.

We view the pattern of officer recruitment before and after independence as the underlying reason for the association between regime-change coups and an ethnically mixed officer corps. We note that coups carried out by officers from heterogeneous armed forces were much more likely during the years when the forces of newly independent countries still reflected colonial recruitment (1957–1974) than afterward. Indeed, we show (in the replication files) that regime-change coups in countries with heterogeneous militaries were most common in the first five years of a dictatorship's existence and quite rare afterward. This finding adds to the evidence that officers' grievances can motivate coups.

These empirical tests improve on the standard model of coups by adding variables that reflect characteristics of the autocratic leadership group that bargains with the military, as well as characteristics of the officer corps itself.

TABLE 3.1 *Area under the ROC for models of regime-change coups in dictatorships*

Model	Area under the ROC
Structural	0.748
Structural + Seizure Type	0.771
Structural + Seizure Type + ethnicity	0.776

As shown in Table 3.1, the model with standard variables has an area under the ROC – a measure of in-sample predictive power – of 0.748. Adding measures of the seizure type – a proxy for the relationship between the incumbent ruling group and the military – improves model accuracy, with an area under the ROC of nearly 0.771. The final model that adds ethnic variables again increases model accuracy, with an area under the ROC of 0.776. The difference in predictive accuracy between the first and third models is statistically significant at the $p<0.05$ level, indicating a substantial improvement in model accuracy. Equally important, the variables that capture the relationship between the incumbent leadership group and the military are exogenous to dictatorial attempts to retain power because they measure a characteristic that cannot be altered after the seizure of power, namely, how the incumbent ruling group seized power in the first place.

Figure 3.2 shows the results from a similar series of tests that investigate the factors associated with military coups against democratic leaders. In the baseline model, shown as diamonds, we find that the only significant correlates of such coups are the level of development, the Cold War (1947–1989) period, and whether the country had experienced an earlier military intervention.[6] As with coups that end dictatorships, there is no consistent association between coups that end democracies and oil income, conflict, or protest. Instead, the findings are consistent with those who argue that poor countries are likely to experience coups (Londregan and Poole 1990) and that democracies preceded by military rule are more vulnerable to coups (Cheibub 2006).

Next, we add to the model a set of variables that measures how the democratic regime came into existence. A large number of post-1946 democracies (31 percent) began with a competitive election (*election*) held by an outgoing dictatorship. An additional 22 percent of democracies arose in the aftermath of popular uprisings (*uprising*), while roughly 20 percent were formed by armed force, including those initiated after coups (*coups*), rebellions, or foreign invasions (*rebel/foreign*). The remainder were initiated by elite rule changes such as suffrage expansions, which is the reference category.

---

[6] We also find that longer-lasting democracies are less likely to end in coups. Without modeling potential nonproportional hazards, we cannot interpret democratic duration as "consolidation." See Svolik (2008) on modeling consolidation of democracy using a split-population estimator.

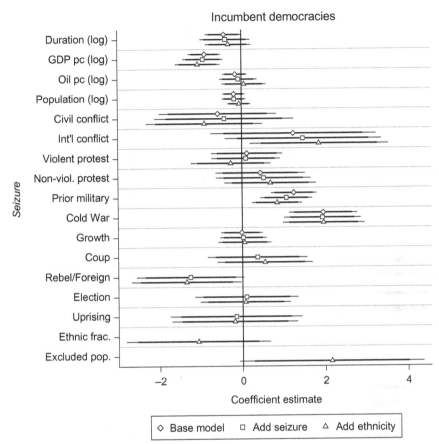

FIGURE 3.2 Coups against incumbent democracies.

We add these variables to keep the tests as similar as possible, but we do not interpret them the same way as in dictatorships. The events that usher in democracy often do not determine the identity of subsequent leaders and thus do not have the same implications for the later relationship between political leaders and military officers. That is, when coups or popular uprisings lead to democracy, the transitional leadership that takes power initially oversees a fair, competitive election that chooses who rules. Elite rule changes that initiate democracy also lead to fair, competitive elections. Since leadership during the democratic regime is chosen in elections regardless of how the democracy was initiated, we would not expect particular modes of initiation to be associated with later military grievances. Foreign or rebel initiation might, however, deter coups by reducing the likelihood that they would succeed.

Adding these variables does not change the findings for level of development and earlier experience with military rule. Democracies initiated after armed seizures of power by rebel groups or foreigners are less likely to be ousted in a coup than those initiated by elite rule changes (the reference category), though this relationship may be spurious. One-third of the foreign-initiated democracies arose after US liberation of Western Europe during World War II. None of the foreign-initiated democracies later fell to a coup. This probably has more to do with the past history and economic performance of these countries than with how democracy began. Initiation by coup, election, or popular uprising has no effect on the likelihood of succumbing to a later coup, as expected.

In the final model, we add ethnicity variables: ethnic fractionalization of the population and the share of the ethnically relevant population excluded from executive political power. We do not have data from democracies on whether the military is ethnically heterogeneous, so we cannot test this idea for the sample of democracies. While ethnic fractionalization per se is not associated with coups, ethnic political exclusion increases the likelihood of coups against democracies.[7] This suggests that the military is more likely to intervene against incumbent democrats when executive power is not shared widely across ethnic groups. This finding is consistent with the earlier argument that coups are more likely when dissatisfaction with the incumbent is widespread. It also seems likely that when a large part of the citizenry lacks representation in the executive, many officers also lack representation, leading to grievances.

INEQUALITY AND COUPS

In this section, we test Svolik's (2012) argument that threats from organized societal opposition against incumbent dictators increase their allocations to the military, which in turn heightens the military's ability to seize power for itself. Officers, in this view, are most likely to replace the incumbent regime when political elites face the threat of "mass, organized, and potentially violent opposition" (2012, 125). Figures 3.1 and 3.3 show the effects of violent and nonviolent protest as well as civil conflict on regime-change coups. These coefficients are not close to standard levels of statistical significance. These results thus fail to support the idea that widespread popular opposition increases the likelihood of military intervention, either directly or through the mechanism Svolik suggests.

Svolik's own tests, however, use income inequality as a proxy for mass, potentially violent opposition rather than direct measures of protest. So, our next tests assess the effect of inequality on coups. Svolik expects popular challenges to be most threatening at middle levels of income inequality. He then shows that middling inequality predicts coups in a data set that combines

---

[7] Adding seizure and ethnic variables to the model of coups against incumbent democracies does not substantially improve the predictive accuracy of the model, in part because the baseline model has high in-sample predictive power, with an area under the ROC of 0.88.

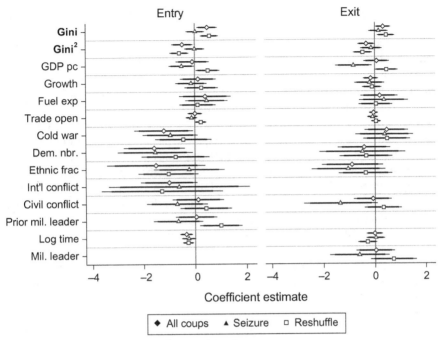

FIGURE 3.3 Causes of coups in dictatorships, by coup type.

leader-shuffling and regime-change coups. It is possible, however, that coups that initiate new dictatorships might be caused by factors different from those associated with leader-shuffling coups, particularly if the latter serve as a mechanism to maintain leader accountability to other elites. Some military regimes use reshuffling coups to replace leaders much the way parliamentary regimes rely on votes of no confidence. We investigate the possibility that the causes of regime-change coups differ from those of reshuffling coups in the later analysis.

To do this, we first verify the main finding from Svolik's analysis. The data he used separately identify coups that result in the initiation of an individual officer's tenure as dictator and coups that remove a dictator from power (meaning that reshuffling coups are included in both samples, along with regime-change coups). We then further disaggregate his data to distinguish regime-change coups from leader-reshuffling coups. We separate his leader-entry coup data into two groups: (1) those that correspond to military *seizures* of power, i.e. regime changes, and (2) *reshuffling* leadership changes in ongoing authoritarian regimes. Roughly 47 percent of Svolik's entry coups are military seizures of power, while 53 percent replace leaders in ongoing dictatorships. For coups that involve the exit of dictators, 39 percent initiate regime transitions. The other 61 percent are leadership reshuffles among members of the same ruling group. Altogether, the majority of coups in these data are reshuffling coups.

Figure 3.3 shows the results from this analysis. The left panel presents the estimates for leader-entry coups, while the right panel depicts the estimates for leader-exit coups.[8] The top coefficient estimate (diamond shape) for each variable comes from the specification verifying Svolik's results, and thus reflects data that include both regime-change and leader-shuffling coups.[9] The middle estimate (triangle shape) for each examines only regime-change coups, that is, coups that establish new autocratic regimes. The bottom estimate (square shape) for each comes from a model that examines only *reshuffling* coups.

The main variables of interest are the Gini coefficient (i.e., inequality) and the squared term that captures the nonlinearity in the hypothesized effect of inequality. For both entry and exit coups, the coefficients of interest are statistically different from zero in the verification model (top estimates, using a sample that combines regime-change and reshuffling coups) and the model that examines reshuffling coups only (bottom estimates). For regime-change coups – those in which an out-of-power military faction seizes power from the incumbent dictatorship and establishes a new autocratic regime – the estimates for the inequality variables are small and not close to statistical significance. Civil conflict, arguably a direct measure of "mass, organized, and potentially violent opposition," may *reduce* the likelihood of regime-change coups rather than raising it, as claimed in Svolik's argument, though it is not statistically significant for coups that establish new dictatorships (entry coups). It does not *increase* the likelihood of either kind of coup. Thus, we find no support for Svolik's argument with regard to regime-change coups.

These findings suggest that Svolik's empirical results depend primarily on reshuffling coups within ongoing dictatorships. Eighty-five percent of leader-change coups occur in military-led dictatorships, however. In other words, most of these coups replace one military dictator with another rather than replacing a civilian dictator with a military one, as would be expected if they reflect a transition from rulers with a comparative advantage in cooptation to rulers with a comparative advantage in repression, as Svolik argues.

CONCLUSION

Our findings on the causes of coups fail to support the claim that popular mobilization in protest or rebellion increases the likelihood of coups against

---

[8] We drop international conflict from the specification because there are no observations in which international conflict occurs in the same year as a regime-change exit.
[9] These reported results are not exactly the same as those reported in Svolik (2012) because the verification file does not include code setting the random seed for estimating a random coefficients model using the *gllamm* package. For substantive purposes, however, the top estimates we report are identical to those reported by Svolik.

either democratic or authoritarian governments. Instead, our results suggest that officers are motivated by their own interests. Coups that end democracies are less likely when the incumbent government includes representatives of all the country's ethnic groups, implying that all ethnic groups represented in the officer corps are represented as well.

Regime-change coups that oust dictatorships are less likely when the dictatorship originally achieved power by means of insurgency or foreign imposition. We interpret this result as indicating that officers who share experiences, values, ideas, and friendship (developed during the insurgency that created the regime or imposed by foreign occupiers) with regime leaders are less likely to develop grievances against them. We also find that ethnic heterogeneity in the army is associated with more regime-change coups. Ethnic heterogeneity predisposes the military to factionalism. The grievances of one ethnic faction can motivate coups against dictatorships led by other ethnic factions. This result suggests one of the mechanisms underlying the inability of factionalized armies to provide a stable basis for rule, which we analyze in Chapter 5.

In the retest of Svolik's (2012) argument about the effect of income inequality on the likelihood of coups, we show that his results depend on combining leader-shuffling coups with regime-change coups. When the two kinds of coups are looked at separately, we find that middling levels of inequality are associated with leader-shuffling coups in ongoing dictatorships, but not with coups that initiate new dictatorships. Leader-shuffling coups usually replace one military dictator with another, rather than replacing civilian dictators with military rulers, as Svolik theorized. *Regime-change* coups are unrelated to inequality. The direct indicators of threatening mass opposition (protest and civil conflict) also have no effect on the likelihood of regime-change coups. In short, we find no support for the idea that regime-change coups are motivated, either directly or indirectly, by elite fears of popular opposition or redistribution.

Instead, the variables associated with military seizures of power, especially those that end earlier dictatorships, reflect characteristics of the officer corps and the group of political leaders with which the military bargains. Although theoretical models of coups have focused on this bargaining relationship, to date there have been few empirical tests of the effects of characteristics of the *actors* doing the bargaining. We show that when dictatorial leaders share many interests and experiences with military officers – which we argue happens more often after seizures of power by armed rebellion or foreign invasion – their military forces are less likely to oust them.

These results justify treating the military as an interest group and organized political actor in its own right. In this book, we build on that result. We pay attention to the special capacities the military can deploy and the consequences of military organization for bargaining, both among officers and between them and other political actors. We treat officers as motivated by their own interests. They can ally with other groups just as any other political actor can, but they do not routinely represent any particular societal interest.

PART II

ELITE CONSOLIDATION

4

Power Concentration

The Effect of Elite Factionalism on Personalization

Islam Karimov, Soviet Uzbekistan's last Communist Party leader, remained in power after 1991, to become independent Uzbekistan's first dictator. The rest of the Uzbek political elite at independence had also spent their careers in the Communist Party. There had been no nationalist uprising in Uzbekistan. Russian-officered Soviet troops were still stationed in the country, and the KGB managed internal security (Collins 2006, 173). Indeed, many observers saw the Karimov regime as a simple continuation of Communist Party rule under a new name.

Yet, even before formal independence, Karimov had eliminated the Communist Party of Uzbekistan (CPU) as the institutional base for the regime and taken personal control of the security services and high-level appointments previously controlled by the party. Karimov retained the support of most of Uzbekistan's pre-independence elite despite destroying the formal underpinnings of their political power because the informal bases of their power remained intact. Regionally based loyalty networks, usually referred to as clans, continued to structure political bargaining and decision making as they had during communist rule.[1]

When first appointed, Karimov was weak; he was not a clan leader or an important figure in the ruling party (Carlisle 1995, 196, 255; Collins 2006, 118–23). The most influential Uzbek clans had consolidated their informal control during Soviet rule by infiltrating and coopting the CPU, which enabled them to take over party and government patronage networks along with different parts of the state-owned economy. Gorbachev's earlier efforts to clean up corruption and limit clan power had failed, and he had bowed to political

[1] Clans are "informal power networks mobilised to capture the state and its resources in the interest of the members and leaders of these networks" (Ilkhamov 2007, 70). Note the similarity between this definition and Downs's definition of parties as teams organized to capture government.

necessity in appointing a new CPU general secretary supported by the most powerful clans. Clan leaders backed Karimov because they distrusted one another. Karimov lacked an independent power base and needed the clan leaders' support to retain power, so he was expected to be responsive to their demands (Collins 2006, 122–23; Ilkhamov 2007, 74–76). Clan leaders "thought of him as their puppet" (Carlisle 1995, 196).

When Karimov was appointed first secretary, he "needed to demonstrate sensitivity to local elite interests, and to maintain a balance of power amongst the various significant clan actors … [E]ven though [he] did not trust certain clan or regional factions," he incorporated "at least token members of each regional elite into the new government" (Collins 2006, 128). He had to share the most with the clan leader most eager to replace him, whom he appointed first as prime minister and then as vice president (Carlisle 1995, 196, 198; Collins 2006, 129). Supporters of the vice president dominated the Supreme Soviet.

As of early 1991, Karimov somewhat precariously controlled the CPU and government by balancing and juggling competing clan interests. He lacked a Soviet patron, and the Communist Party of the Soviet Union was disintegrating. Karimov had to choose political and economic strategies to "retain all the major [clan] players in the pact" (Collins 2006, 193). One observer described his governing style as "consensual" (Ilkhamov 2007, 75, 78).

All clans included in the pact benefited from the regime, but they nevertheless competed fiercely over high-level posts and the opportunities to make profits and strip state assets that came with appointments. The clans' mutual antagonism provided Karimov with opportunities for power grabs at the expense of particular clans, despite his need to maintain the support of most of them. On the heels of the Soviet coup attempt, Karimov banned the CPU and seized its assets, in part to reduce the resources and power of the Supreme Soviet. Banning the party stripped many deputies of their privileged access to jobs as members of the *nomenklatura*.[2] He then created a new government-support party, the National Democratic Party of Uzbekistan, led by himself. It never controlled the resources the CPU had, however, or dominated politics and controlled appointments. In the future, legislative nominations would be vetted not by the party but by Karimov personally, reducing the power of the legislature (Collins 2006, 194–95, 253, 257). Outlawing the CPU shifted the balance of power between Karimov and others in the ruling elite sufficiently for him to abolish the office of vice president, arrest some of the vice president's allies, and

---

[2] In communist systems, high-level jobs in the bureaucracy, party, economy, education, and military were reserved for individuals approved by the Communist Party. The nomenklatura was the official list of individuals, nearly all of whom were party members, who could be appointed to jobs at different levels of importance. By ending the party, Karimov opened recruitment for these jobs to much wider competition.

thus rid himself of his most threatening supporter. Other clans did not defend those excluded or arrested.

"The result of [Karimov's] policies from 1990 through 1993 was the gradual transformation from a communist regime to an autocratic one, in which power belonged not to a hegemonic party, but to Karimov himself and the clique of clan elites who surrounded him" (Collins 2006, 198). A feature of the post-Soviet context that aided Karimov's power grab is that he was not threatened militarily. The clans had not penetrated the military stationed in Uzbekistan or the KGB because Russians controlled both, and none of the clans had its own militia.

In the wake of the Soviet coup attempt, Karimov increased his control of security forces. He shifted resources to the presidential guard and the Committee for Defense, which he had created a few months before to counterbalance the Soviet troops stationed in Uzbekistan. He also put Soviet military forces under the highest-ranking Uzbek officer's command (Collins 2006, 162) and appointed a close ally from his own clan to lead the internal security agency. From then on, Karimov kept the presidential guard, army, and internal security agency "under his close supervision and control" (Collins 2006, 274).

Through the early 1990s, Karimov continued juggling multiple clan supporters, mostly by distributing state-controlled economic opportunities among them. "[W]ith a tenuous political pact supporting him, Karimov had no choice but to engage in a negotiating process with various factions" (Collins 2006, 257). On the civilian side, he used his "political budget," funded largely by the export of cotton, gold, and oil along with the drug trade, to secure support (Collins 2006, 262–67; De Waal 2015). In contrast to the dictators described by De Waal (2015), however, he had a near-monopoly on the means of violence. Members of Karimov's clan staffed the internal security agency. In the military, Russian officers were purged and usually returned to Russia, while politically motivated promotions and dismissals solidified the loyalties of Uzbek officers (Collins 2006, 274).

In the mid-1990s, Karimov began incrementally eliminating some of his erstwhile allies from the inner circle. "Gradually, he consolidated power under his personal control and loosened his dependence on his previous allies and partners" (Ilkhamov 2007, 76). For example, the all-important head of cadre policy, a representative of one of the most powerful clans, was arrested in 1994. Karimov transferred the head of the Uzbek KGB, a man from his own clan, to a less important post in 1995, and created a second security service so that the two could report on each other (Collins 2006, 263).

Nevertheless, most clans continued to support Karimov in exchange for the vast economic opportunities made possible by continued state ownership of much of the economy. The Jurabekov clan linked to Samarkand, for example, controlled oil and gas, many of the bazaars, and the cotton complex. The Alimov clan from Tashkent controlled much of the banking system, the Ministry of Foreign Economic Relations, the tax inspectorate, the general procurator, a share of the dollar trade, and most import-export businesses. Less powerful clans controlled less, and a few were entirely excluded (Collins 2006, 264–68). The monopoly rents, black market currency dealing, asset stripping, and widespread corruption facilitated by clan control of the economy, however, led to slow growth, increased poverty, and rising inequality.

By the late 1990s Karimov was "locked in an ongoing struggle to maintain and increase his own personal autocratic control and to hold together powerful regional and clan elites without allowing them to strip the state of its capacity to survive" (Collins 2006, 170). He dismissed or demoted the prime minister, defense minister, and several members of the inner circle from the Ferghana network without political consequences. In 1998, Karimov dismissed Jurabekov, Uzbekistan's most powerful clan leader, along with many other members of his network. A few months later, however, Karimov reinstated Jurabekov after an assassination attempt attributed to him (Collins 2006, 170–71).[3] Though Karimov narrowly escaped assassination, the attempt demonstrated the Jurabekov clan's credible threat to oust the dictator if he failed to share with them, and he promptly reinstated them. However, the other clans did not make similarly credible threats and therefore could not prevent power grabbing at their expense.

As Karimov excluded important members of the original inner circle from office and benefits, members of his own family took control of key sectors of the economy. "Step by step, the major export resources were concentrated in the hands of the central government, under the President's personal control" (Ilkhamov 2007, 76). By the early 2000s, the family controlled the major state telecoms company, gold mining, and part of the oil business (Collins 2006, 170–71). In 2006, Radio Free Europe/Radio Liberty reported that Karimov had "chip[ped]" away at the political and economic might of some of Uzbekistan's most influential clans." Jurabekov was dismissed once more in 2004 and accused of corruption. This time he did not return to the inner circle. The defense minister was forced to resign in 2005 and tried for corruption and abuse of office. About 200 families had grown very rich under Karimov's original system of power sharing, but the circle of beneficiaries became smaller and smaller in the 2000s, as it narrowed to not much more than the Karimov family.[4]

Until his natural death in 2016, Karimov remained "a master at maneuvering among the various clans in Uzbekistan and playing them off one another" (Panier 2016). He retained control by balancing the clans, allowing no single one to become too powerful, and rotating ministers, governors, and other

---

[3] "Analysis: Uzbek Eminence Falls from Grace," 2005, *Radio Free Europe/Radio Liberty* (February 22), www.rferl.org/a/1057594.html; "Uzbekistan: Islam Karimov vs. the Clans," 2005, RFE/RL (April 22), www.rferl.org/a/1058611.html.

[4] "Uzbekistan: Karimov Appears to Have Political Clans Firmly in Hand," 2006, RFE/RL (August 31), www.rferl.org/a/1070977.html.

appointments frequently to prevent officials from building their own support networks from which to challenge him (Saidazimova 2005; Ilkhamov 2007, 77; Panier 2016). Nevertheless, "[c]ompeting regional and clan factions trusted Karimov more than they trusted each other, and hence preferred to have him at the center" (Collins 2006, 261).

Uzbekistan's experience raises the question: How can a political leader who seemed entirely dependent on the support of his country's most powerful political forces concentrate power at their expense and without forfeiting their support? In this chapter, we explain how this happens. We show how factionalism in the ruling group – in Uzbekistan, their division into multiple competing clans – undermines power sharing and thus facilitates the emergence of one-man rule. This happens for two reasons. First, disunited ruling groups have difficulty making credible threats to oust the dictator and therefore cannot constrain him. And second, most members of the support group remain willing to support the dictator even when he unilaterally reduces their access to benefits because they are still better off inside the inner circle than excluded from it. In contrast, a united seizure group can constrain the dictator's ability to concentrate power, as well as his policy and distributive discretion, because they can make credible threats to oust him if he fails to share.

The chapter begins with an overview of how bargaining works in dictatorships. It describes the central dilemma of new dictatorships: the colossal control problem caused by handing dictatorial power to one member of the ruling group. It explains our theory of how this problem affects bargaining between dictators and other members of the dictatorial elite and describes the central interests of both.

The second half of the chapter shows how preexisting characteristics of the seizure group affect its ability to make enforceable bargains with the new dictator. The dictator has little need to share or consult with his closest supporters if preexisting factions facilitate bargaining with them separately, as Karimov could with clan leaders. Bargaining separately induces competition among faction leaders, which drives down the price dictators have to pay for support. Based on these insights, we generate expectations about conditions that facilitate the concentration of power in the hands of one man, which we call "personalism." We then explain how these informal bargaining relationships, established during the dictatorship's first years, can become sticky over time. Last, we test these ideas using new data and show evidence consistent with our arguments.

ELITE BARGAINING IN DICTATORSHIPS

In autocracies, a small number of regime insiders, usually acting in private under informal rules, hammer out key decisions about leadership and policy directions even in regimes with stable, well-developed formal institutions.

The influence and authority of members of the dictatorial elite may be renegotiated frequently during the early years and subject to arbitrary and violent change. Dictatorial elites may ignore formal rules and institutions if they obstruct the drive to amass power. Losers in policy debates may be excluded from the inner circle, demoted, arrested, or even executed. Life in a dictatorial elite is thus insecure, dangerous, and frightening. Informal procedures may become institutionalized over time, meaning that they become both more predictable and costly to change, but for the first months or years after an autocratic seizure of power, bargaining within the dictatorial elite often occurs in an environment of contested, changing, and nonbinding institutions (Svolik 2012).

When making decisions about policy, leadership, and institutional choice, the dictator and members of his inner circle take into account expected effects of the choice on regime survival, but also how decisions may affect their individual power, influence, and access to resources. Members of dictatorial elites live in grim, dog-eat-dog worlds. Taking one policy position can provide the opportunity to take a bite out of another dog, while taking a different one could incite the pack to tear you apart. Autocratic policy makers, like democratic ones, may care deeply about the substance of policy, but they cannot afford to ignore how their decisions will affect regime survival and their personal survival as well.

To explain these decisions, we focus initially on the interests of members of the seizure group. Because the members of groups never share exactly the same interests, our theory begins with strategic interactions among them. We do not assume that seizure groups, or the regime elites that derive from them, are unitary actors because the empirical record shows that discipline among them is imperfect. How much discipline they can maintain requires empirical investigation. Consequently, neither the dictatorship's inner circle as a whole nor any subset of it larger than one member should be assumed to behave as a unitary actor.

We do assume that members of the dictatorship's inner circle want to maintain the dictatorship, which they expect to further their policy goals, as well as provide opportunities for personal advancement and often enrichment. However, they also want to increase their personal share of power relative to others in the inner circle. They must compete with each other for power, not only to improve their standing in the inner circle or their access to wealth, but also to maintain their current positions against lower-ranked regime supporters striving to replace them in the inner circle. An increase in power for one member of the inner circle comes at the expense of someone else. We see power as a rank ordering based on politically relevant resources, understood by insiders even when not perceptible to observers. One insider cannot move up the rank order without displacing someone else.

Because of the intense competition within the inner circle, we expect the dictatorship's most powerful decision makers to consider how all policy, appointment, and institutional choices might affect their own standing, as well as regime maintenance. The creation of new formal institutions benefits the individuals who will lead them and those who will work in new agencies associated with their implementation. Policy choices also often entail the creation of new agencies, which, again, benefits those chosen to lead and work in them. Policies also have distributional consequences that advantage some and disadvantage others. They thus affect the welfare of the constituents of inner circle members differently. Consequently, we expect inner-circle members to favor policies and institutions that both improve their own place in the hierarchy and increase the likelihood of regime survival. However, both are impossible for everyone in the inner circle since any change that increases the powers of one member decreases those of others. Bargaining over policy thus has a noncooperative dimension, and strategic considerations often affect substantive policy choices (just as in democracies).

In other words, the dictator and inner circle engage simultaneously in two kinds of strategic interaction: (1) a cooperative effort aimed at keeping all of them (the regime) in power and (2) noncooperative interactions in which different members/factions seek to enhance their own power and resources at the expense of others in the inner circle. Each individual strives to amass resources and capacities up to the point at which his efforts would destabilize the regime or lead to his own exclusion from the inner circle.

The dictator has a resource advantage because he has the most direct access to state revenues and an information advantage because he has access to the reports of all internal security services. Nevertheless, the dictator faces the same dilemma as other members of the inner circle: he wants to extend and consolidate his control up to the point at which other members of the inner circle would take the risk of trying to oust him. The struggle over the distribution of power in a new dictatorship can transform the seizure group from the cooperative near-equals who had plotted the fall of the old regime into competitors in a vicious struggle for survival and dominance.

We see these incentives as common to all dictatorships, but they play out in different ways, depending on concrete characteristics of the seizure group that pre-date the installation of the dictatorship. We argue that preexisting differences among the groups that initiate dictatorship lead to post-seizure differences in what kinds of individuals with what interests become members of the dictatorial inner circle, how the inner circle makes decisions, which policies and institutions they choose, how they seek to attract members of society as allies, and how they respond to opposition. Preexisting characteristics of the seizure group do not determine everything that happens over the course of a dictatorship, but they do affect the likelihood that regimes will display specific, often long-lasting, patterns of behavior. The institutions chosen by dictatorial elites *after* they take power also have consequences for subsequent bargaining and the way dictatorships break down. That is their purpose, after all. Preexisting characteristics of the seizure group, however, influence the choice of these institutions.

We thus share with Svolik (2012) the view that all dictatorships face certain dilemmas, such as the dictator's temptation to grab more power than his supporters want to delegate, but we emphasize that these dilemmas can have different outcomes, depending on characteristics of the seizure group that affect the bargaining power of different members of the group. In this chapter, we explain how one preexisting feature of seizure groups, their position on a continuum from factionalism to unity, affects authoritarian politics.

We provide greater detail in the sections that follow, beginning with the first decision seizure groups confront: selection of a leader.

HANDING POWER TO A LEADER

In order to govern, seizure groups must choose a leader (dictator).[5] They need a leader to speak on behalf of the new government, represent it to the populace and foreign actors, organize the implementation of policies made by the group, coordinate their activities across agencies and levels of government, mediate conflicts within the inner circle, act in emergencies, and make final decisions when opinions in the group are divided. The point of choosing a leader is to achieve the goals of the group. However, the delegation of the powers needed to fulfill these responsibilities in the largely institution-free setting of early dictatorship causes the interests of the dictator to diverge from those of his closest allies. While the dictator hopes to defang his allies' threats to oust him if he disregards their interests, they seek to hold the new dictator in check. This happens regardless of whether the dictator and his allies come from the same ethnic or other close-knit group. This divergence of interests creates the colossal problem of how to control a leader with dictatorial powers.

When the seizure group delegates powers to a leader, it does not intend to give him the capacity to choose policies most of them oppose, unilaterally exclude from the inner circle individuals who helped seize power, or dismiss, jail, or kill seizure-group members, their allies, and family members. These are highly visible depredations on the ruling group. The absence of binding limits and institutional checks on the dictator, however, mean that only credible threats to oust the dictator deter him from reneging on agreements and abusing his supporters (Magaloni 2008; Svolik 2012).

The dictatorial elite cannot costlessly dismiss the dictator. On the contrary, efforts to oust a dictator always involve a high risk of failure, followed by near-certain exclusion from the ruling group and possible exile, imprisonment, torture, and/or execution. And yet the dictatorial elite can limit the dictator's

---

[5] Literal leadership choice often occurs before the seizure of power. Regardless of the timing of original leadership choice, after the seizure of power groups "choose" leaders in the sense that if the support of enough members were withdrawn, the leader could not retain his position (Bueno de Mesquita et al. 2003).

depredations only *if* they can credibly commit to ousting him if he seizes more power or resources than they have agreed to transfer.

Seizure groups should anticipate the possibility that the man chosen to lead could escape their control, since the dictator cannot make credible promises not to use his powers. Before they take power, some seizure groups try to hem in the dictator by making rules about who should help him make policy, how these lieutenants should be chosen, the periodic rotation of leadership, and how they will handle succession. When plotters come from professionalized militaries, which tend to be legalistic and rule-bound, they may negotiate quite detailed arrangements for term limits and consultation over policy choice within the officer corps (Fontana 1987). These rules can be enforced at the time they are agreed to because power is dispersed within the group. The man who wants to be leader must agree to power-sharing arrangements such as regular consultation or term limits in exchange for the support of other members of the seizure group.

Most dictators, like Karimov, are weak the day they become regime leader. Karimov needed support initially from several clan leaders and the Communist Party to stay in power, and thus had to distribute state offices and the resources they controlled among them. Military dictators are sometimes weak because they have had to retire from active duty, and thus give up the ability to control others' promotions, postings, and retirements, in order to secure the support of others in the junta for their appointment as leader.

Bargains made when the dictator is weak, however, last only as long as they are self-enforcing because of the lack of third-party enforcement institutions in dictatorships (Barzel 2002, 257; Acemoglu, Johnson, and Robinson 2005, 429; Svolik 2012). The initiation of dictatorship creates immediate opportunities for changing the relative distribution of power within the seizure group. History is replete with examples of men who were invited to lead by plotters who believed they would be malleable figureheads, but who quickly marginalized and sometimes killed those who had expected to call the shots. Plotters sometimes consciously choose an individual considered uncharismatic and legalistic to reduce the likelihood of future concentration of power in his hands. It has been reported that Chilean plotters chose General Augusto Pinochet, a latecomer to the coup conspiracy, for that reason. He was quick to concentrate power in his own hands, however. Other examples include Major Mathieu Kérékou, who was invited by even more junior coup plotters to lead the 1972 seizure of power in Benin. Within three years, he had excluded the original plotters from government, apparently killing one and jailing several others (Decalo 1979; Allen 1988). After the 1975 coup in Bangladesh, junior officers and ex-officers released General Mohammad Zia ul-Hak from jail and appointed him Chief Martial Law Administrator because they feared the rest of the army would not acquiesce in the coup if a junior officer was appointed. Zia quickly excluded them from the ruling group, arrested those who tried to oust him for violating their initial bargain, and executed their leaders for treason (Codron 2007, 12–13).

This problem is not limited to military seizure groups. Malawi's Hastings Banda, recruited as a presidential candidate by young civilian nationalists, not only excluded his youthful colleagues but quickly transformed the elected government he led into a highly repressive autocracy. Banda, a doctor who had been working outside the country for more than twenty years, was invited to lead by young independence leaders who "assumed he could not conceivably harbor any long-term political ambitions" (Decalo 1998, 59). After the founding election, he dismissed his young allies from their cabinet posts, forced them into exile, and purged the ruling party of anyone suspected of challenging his "unfettered personal rule" (Decalo 1998, 64), which then lasted for more than thirty years.[6]

The frequency of this sequence of events suggests that control of the state, even as rudimentary a state as Malawi's at independence, gives the paramount leader a resource advantage over his erstwhile colleagues. The new dictator finds himself "almost immediately in command of all the financial and administrative resources of the state" (Tripp 2007, 143). Becoming head of state gives the new dictator access to revenues – especially from taxes, the export of natural resources, and foreign aid – far greater than he has had before and greater than other members of the seizure group can command. This control endows the new dictator with agenda-setting power when it comes to policy-making and distributive decisions. Revenues can be shared with the inner circle or spent by the dictator to buy personal support and security. Further, access to state revenues gives the dictator substantial control over appointments to state offices, which he can use to bring loyalists into decision-making positions and to create state agencies to pursue goals not shared by the rest of the seizure group.

These revenues can enable the dictator to outmaneuver his allies. In some circumstances, he can buy the support of some members of the inner circle for the exclusion of others. He may even be able to buy their support for changes that further enhance his power at the expense of theirs. In short, a dictator who was first among equals on the day he was chosen has substantial potential to grab additional resources and power later.

We refer to dictatorships in which the leader has concentrated power at the expense of his closest supporters as personalist. The defining feature of personalist dictatorship is that the dictator has personal discretion and control over the key levers of power in his political system. Key levers of power include the unfettered ability to appoint, promote, and dismiss high-level officers and

---

[6] Of course, the respectable senior leader does not always win these power struggles. General Naguib, invited by the youthful Free Officers to lead the government that would replace the Egyptian monarchy, was ousted two years later by Colonel Nasser, the plotters' original leader (Haddad 1973, 11–42). Regardless of who eventually emerges on top, however, these are examples of why struggles for power within the dictator's inner circle often begin soon after seizures of power.

officials, and thus to control the agencies, economic enterprises, and armed forces the appointees lead. In such regimes, the dictator's choices are relatively unconstrained by the institutions that can act as veto players in other dictatorships, especially the military high command and the ruling party executive committee. Personalist dictators juggle, manipulate, and divide and rule other powerful political actors. Like all dictators, they need some support, but they can choose from among competing factions which ones can join or remain in the ruling elite at any particular time.[7] Personalist dictators are thus powerful relative to other members of the elite, but not necessarily relative to society or to international actors.

Islam Karimov's rule exemplified personalism, especially in later years. His control of Uzbekistan's political system derived from his appointment powers. Initially, he had to bargain with several clan leaders over the composition of his government and the control of all important state-owned enterprises and government agencies. Over time, however, he achieved much greater personal discretion over appointments, and most important clans continued supporting him despite losing some of their influence and access to income.

We argue that discretion such as Karimov's arises from the dictator's ability to bargain separately with supporters, to play them off against each other, to ally with some in order to damage or exclude others, and to bring previously excluded groups into the dictatorial inner circle in order to tip the balance of power in his favor when needed. The concentrated power wielded by personalist leaders is thus not absolute but rather depends on the dictator's ability to use a changeable divide-and-rule strategy against supporters who could control or overthrow him if they could unite. The description of Yemen's Ali Abdullah Saleh as "dancing on the heads of snakes" captures this understanding of the personalist dictator as not necessarily the deadliest member of the ruling coalition but rather the one who can stay aloft by pitting some factions against others in an ever-changing balancing act (Clark 2010).

Personalism can rise and fall during a single dictator's tenure, for reasons we describe later. (The data we use to measure personalism are coded yearly to capture these within-ruler and within-regime changes. They thus differ from our older regime-type coding, which could not capture these real-world variations.)

---

[7] Some definitions of personalism emphasize informal alliances between the dictator and leaders of ethnic or other kinds of groups and personal loyalties maintained through patronage networks (e.g., Roessler 2016). We put less emphasis on informality for two reasons. First, personalist dictators distribute formal offices in government, the ruling party, and the military to their elite supporters. The bargains that keep the ruling group together could not be maintained without access to state revenues, and even rudimentary states have formal governing structures that provide the resources that hold alliances together. Second, personalized relationships and bargaining can occur within formal institutions such as ruling parties. For example, Stalin had nearly full discretion over appointments and decision-making during the last decade of his life, but most of those decisions were made in party committees and implemented by party cadres.

The Dictator's Interests

Since achieving the post of dictator requires great effort (as well as quite a bit of luck), we can infer that those who achieve it wanted it. Regardless of whether the job lives up to expectations, the danger inherent in giving it up predisposes dictators to try to hang on to power. Twenty percent of dictators are jailed or killed within the first year after losing office, while another fifth flee their native countries to avoid such consequences.[8]

Dictators must fear their closest allies. Their careers can end in two ways other than natural death: the overthrow of the regime or the ouster of the dictator despite regime continuity. Members of dictatorial inner circles often lead ousters even when they also involve popular mobilization. Figure 4.1 shows the frequency of the various events that end dictatorial *regimes*, a subject we return to in Chapter 8. More dictatorships end in coups, that is, overthrows by the officers who were entrusted to defend them, than in other ways. Formerly powerful members of inner circles, however, have also led many popular uprisings and opposition election campaigns, the other common ways that autocracies end.

Only about half of dictator ousters accompany *regime* failures (Geddes, Wright, and Frantz 2014). The rest of the time, dictators are replaced but the regime survives. Regime insiders cause nearly all dictator replacements in surviving autocracies. Coups cause about a quarter of these. Eighty-five percent of such leader-shuffling coups replace one military dictator with another. Deaths, party decisions, and term limits enforced by the dictatorial inner circle account for most of the remaining three-quarters of dictator replacements in

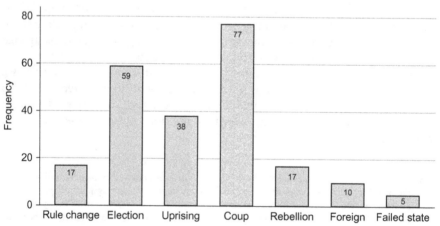

FIGURE 4.1 Frequency of events that end dictatorships.
Note: *Election* includes those in which incumbents lose or do not run.

---

[8] Calculated from Archigos data.

ongoing regimes. It is rare for popular action to oust a dictator without ending the dictatorship as well.

These basic facts about dictator ousters reveal the potential threat to the dictator posed by members of the inner circle (Svolik 2012; Roessler 2016). This threat gives the dictator an interest in closely scrutinizing his allies' activities and dismissing, jailing, or killing them if he begins to suspect their loyalty. The dictator's interest in limiting threats from the inner circle implies that members of the dictator's support coalition today cannot count on being included in it tomorrow.[9]

To sum up, the average dictator has good reasons for wanting to retain power since he cannot count on a safe, affluent retirement if he steps down. Nor can he count on his family being left in peace and prosperity. The individuals most likely to be able to oust him are members of his inner circle. The dictator thus needs their support. Because promises can never be completely credible, however, the dictator has reason to spy on his allies to try to assess whether they are plotting behind his back. The dictator has every reason to try to build his own political resources at the expense of his allies, as he can never fully trust them. In other words, he has strong reasons to violate the implicit leadership contract by aggrandizing his own power.

The Interests of Other Members of the Inner Circle

Exclusion from the dictator's inner circle can result in execution, torture, long imprisonment, property confiscation, exile, and poverty. Family members may have to bear these costs along with the target of the dictator's suspicions. Consequently, constraining the dictator's ability to exclude members from the inner circle ranks at the top of its members' goals. Members of the inner circle also want to influence policy choices and build their own clientele networks, which are needed to secure their influence and acquire wealth. Some of them yearn to supplant the dictator. To accomplish these goals, they need to retain influence on decision making, and they need to obtain posts and promotions that entail both some policy discretion and the ability to hire, promote, and do favors for others. The opportunities available to members of the inner circle vary with the kind of posts they occupy.

The members of the dictator's inner circle thus have strong reasons to want to maintain collegiality in decision-making and the dispersion of resources within the group, rather than allowing the dictator to usurp policy discretion and control over top appointments. These aims give members of the dictator's inner circle good reasons to create institutions that enforce constraints on the dictator, and thus to prefer some institutional arrangements to others.

For example, members of the inner circle may demand term limits for the leader as a way of both limiting his ability to amass powers over time and

---

[9] This statement of the dictator's interests thus conflicts with a central feature of the model proposed by Bueno de Mesquita et al. (2003).

increasing their own chances of occupying the top post in the future. In dictatorships led by a military officer, other officers in the inner circle also want him to retire from active duty, which establishes the credibility of his commitment not to use control over their promotions, retirement, and postings to concentrate power at their expense (Arriagada 1988; Remmer 1991). If the dictatorship is organized by a ruling party, members of the inner circle want party procedures for choosing its executive committee (politburo, standing committee) to be followed in spirit not just letter; they do not want the dictator personally to choose members of the party's decision-making body since that would mean that he can exclude anyone who might disagree with him.

Members of the inner circle also favor an institutional arrangement that limits the dictator's personal control over internal security forces. Preventing the dictator from gaining personal control over the internal security apparatus is important to the welfare of members of the inner circle. If a dictator controls the security police, he *cannot* credibly commit not to use it against his allies.

Conflict over the distribution of power between dictators and their supporters afflicts all new dictatorships. Many of the power struggles during the first months and years of dictatorship can be understood as efforts by the inner circle to control the dictator, efforts by the dictator to escape control, and efforts by both to institutionalize the relationship in order to reduce potentially regime-destabilizing conflict between them.

In this environment, everyone's actions are somewhat unpredictable, prompting both the dictator and his lieutenants to remain on guard and trigger-happy. Furthermore, the unreliability of information increases the likelihood of misinterpreting the actions of others, opening the way to paranoia. Despite his information advantage over others in the inner circle, the dictator's information about what they really think and what they may be planning remains limited and unreliable (Wintrobe 1998). For all these reasons, early periods in dictatorships tend to be unstable, conflictual, and sometimes bloody.

BARGAINING OVER THE DISTRIBUTION OF RESOURCES AND POWER

Earlier studies have emphasized the importance of whether the dictator can credibly commit to fulfill promises he makes (e.g., Magaloni 2008; Svolik 2012; Boix and Svolik 2013). Less attention has been paid to *how much* spoils and power the dictator really needs to share with his closest allies to retain their support. Here we ask: Assuming the dictator *could* credibly commit to sharing power, how much does he need to share? That is, how much power sharing does his personal survival require?

A dictator can reduce the amount he shares in two main ways: by reducing the number of supporters with whom he shares spoils and influence and by reducing the *amount* of power or influence he shares without decreasing the number of supporters. These two strategies often go together. Reducing the number of groups represented in the inner circle, and thus reducing the benefits received by the constituencies they represent, is easier for outsiders to observe than reductions in influence while the individuals who have lost some power remain part of the dictatorial elite. We discuss reducing the size of the ruling coalition first.

Seizure groups are often large when they take power. At the time of a coup, for example, many members of the officer corps must acquiesce in the seizure for it to succeed, even if they do not actively support it; "authoritarianization" can occur only after a party has attracted the support of most citizens in an election. A dictator may not need all this support to survive, however, because some members of the seizure group may lack the means to oust him.[10] This means that the inner-circle members linked to some constituencies can be safely shed, and the dictator can keep their "share" (Bueno de Mesquita et al. 2003).

Bargaining between the dictator and others in the inner circle over the distribution of power and spoils begins when the dictator decides whether to stick to arrangements initially agreed to or renege on the implicit or explicit commitment to share and consult. The dictator controls some amount of goods and powers that both he and other members of the inner circle value highly. These can include access to material goods, such as the revenues from state-owned natural resources, as well as control over various aspects of policy and the choice of personnel to fill high and low offices. These goods are valuable, both to have and to dole out to clients. The dictator makes an initial decision about how to distribute these goods to best secure the adherence of needed supporters. His lieutenants expect to be consulted about these decisions and to receive a share, but their expectations may not be enforceable.

The dictator's agenda-setting power gives him an advantage over those who can only react to proposals (Baron and Ferejohn 1989). Those whose only options are to accept or reject distributive proposals must make decisions about whether to continue supporting the dictator – based on a comparison between what the dictator offers and what they expect to receive if they withdraw from the ruling group. Once the dictator has demonstrated the way he intends to handle the resources he controls, other members of the inner circle can acquiesce in the distribution he proposes or contest it. If they could replace the dictator, they might do much better, but if they see the choice as lying between acceptance of what the dictator offers and exclusion from the ruling coalition (the consequence of rejecting the offer), they would be better off accepting even quite a small amount in exchange for their continued support. This logic leads to the counterintuitive conclusion that members of dictatorial elites may continue to support the dictator even if they receive only a little in return.

---

[10] Thus we focus here on the groups Roessler (2016) does not consider, those that it is safe to exclude precisely because they cannot threaten the dictator with overthrow.

The capacity of the dictator's allies to influence his distribution decisions (enforce their expectations) depends on the credibility of their threats to oust him. The dictator can always be removed by the united action of other elites. Sometimes he can be removed by small groups of them. Trying to remove dictators is risky, however, and no one plotting such a course can count on success. Terrible consequences can follow the discovery of plots. As a result, fewer allies plot than are dissatisfied with their share. The dictator thus reaps an additional bargaining advantage from the riskiness of plots. The more unlikely a plot's success, the larger share a dictator can keep.

To summarize these points, all dictators need some support, which they must reward, but they need to offer only enough to maintain the minimum coalition required to stay in power. The other original members of the seizure group, and the parts of its larger support coalition associated with them, can be excluded without endangering the regime. There is a strong incentive to exclude them because the dictator can then keep their "share" or give it to others whose support he needs more. Remaining inner-circle members want to share spoils and power, but they still have little bargaining power besides the threat to replace the dictator. These conditions mean that the dictator can often get away with keeping the lion's share for himself, just as the proposer in standard legislative bargaining games can (Baron and Ferejohn 1989).

This logic thus makes clear why members of authoritarian coalitions often acquiesce in the concentration of power and resources in the hands of dictators. Note that although Baron and Ferejohn's (1989) result does not fit empirical reality in democratic legislatures very well – that is, prime ministers do not generally keep the lion's share of resources – it is eerily similar to the reality of conspicuous consumption and Swiss bank accounts enjoyed by many dictators.

CHARACTERISTICS THAT INFLUENCE THE CREDIBILITY OF THREATS TO OUST THE DICTATOR

So far we have treated members of the dictator's inner circle as separate individual actors. A real inner circle might resemble this image if, for example, the leaders of multiple clans, parties, or ethnic groups, who had cooperated to throw out a previous regime or colonial power, formed the new ruling group. Militaries riven by ethnic, ideological, or personal factions may also contain many faction leaders who bargain individually rather than being subsumed in a single unified military bargainer. Parties colonized by clans, as in Uzbekistan, can also contain multiple faction leaders who bargain individually on behalf of their members. So can recently organized parties formed by coopting the leaders of older rival parties. In these circumstances, the dictator does in fact bargain with multiple separate actors, and threats to oust him are less credible because of the high risk of plots involving single factions and the difficulty of uniting the factions for joint action. As a result, the dictator can often concentrate resources and power in his own hands, as Karimov did.

Preexisting discipline and unity within the seizure group – from which the dictatorial inner circle is chosen – tilt post-seizure bargaining against the dictator, however. Internally cohesive seizure groups can bargain as something close to unitary actors over issues such as limitations on the dictator's personal discretion. They also face fewer collective action problems when it comes to organizing the dictator's overthrow. Disciplined unity develops in professionalized militaries and parties formed as "organizational weapons"[11] because these institutions transparently link individuals' future career success to obedience to superior officers or the party line. Officers are punished or dismissed for disobeying senior officers, thus ending their careers and livelihoods. In disciplined parties, ordinary party members can be excluded for criticizing the party line, and elected deputies who vote against it may be expelled from the party and lose their seats. Such incentives are needed to maintain unity within groups.

Many armies and ruling parties lack this degree of internal discipline. In armies factionalized by ethnic, partisan, or personal loyalties, officers' career prospects depend on their faction leaders' success in achieving promotions and access to other opportunities. In such a military, lower-ranked officers cannot be counted on to obey the orders of higher-ranked officers from rival factions. In parties that have achieved dominance by persuading the leaders of other parties to "cross the aisle" in return for jobs and other spoils, discipline also tends to be low. A party history of incorporating most major political interests into one party tends to result in party factionalization based on ethnicity, region, policy position, or personal loyalties.

Where dictators have to bargain with an inner circle drawn from a unified and disciplined party or military, the threat of ouster is more credible and the price of support higher. Dictators in this situation face groups that, like labor unions, can drive harder bargains than the individuals in them could drive separately (Frantz and Ezrow 2011). In these circumstances, dictators usually find it expedient to consult with other officers or the party executive committee and distribute resources broadly within the support group.[12] In short, the prior organization, unity, and discipline of seizure groups give dictators reason to maintain power-sharing arrangements with members of the inner circle.

---

[11] Selznick's (1952) term for communist parties characterized by "democratic" centralism and extreme discipline.

[12] In a bargaining model, commitment by the seizure group to make decisions as a unitary actor turns the negotiation between the dictator and his allies into a two-person game. In two-person games where exclusion from the game is not possible without ending the game (that is, the dictator cannot retain power if the unified support group turns on him or if he excludes them) and the cost of bargaining is the same for both players, the division of the pie will be equal (Rubinstein 1982).

If the original seizure group includes both a disciplined group and some additional allies, supporters affiliated with more disorganized groups pose weaker threats to the dictator and are thus less risky to exclude. As an example of this process, within months of the Sandinista rebels' victory over the forces of Nicaraguan dictator Anastasio Somoza Debayle in 1979, they had eliminated the democratic reformist (non-Sandinista) members of the broad coalition that supported the revolution (Gorman 1981, 138–42). Cold War observers noted that when broadly based coalitions that included a well-organized Marxist party ousted a government, the non-Marxist members of the coalition were shed soon after power was secured. The special perfidy of Marxist parties does not explain this phenomenon, however. It arises from the logic of the post-seizure situation. Military coup makers and well-organized non-Marxist parties also excluded their less unified and unneeded supporters once they had secured power. Non-Ba'thist officers from the intensely factionalized Iraqi military, for example, led the 1968 coup, supported by the Ba'th Party. To try to stabilize power sharing between these groups, the plotters chose a Ba'thist president (regime leader), and the non-Ba'thist coup leaders got prime minister, minister of defense, and command of the Republican Guard. Within less than two weeks, however, one of the non-Ba'thist coup leaders had been persuaded to join the party. The other non-Ba'thist coup leaders could then be excluded safely. They were forced into exile, leaving the Ba'th Party and its chosen leader able to consolidate a more narrowly based dictatorship (Tripp 2007, 184–85).

The dictator's drive to narrow his support base arises from minimum-survival coalition logic (Bueno de Mesquita et al. 2003). That is, the dictator wants enough support to survive in power, but no more because support must be paid for, even if at a low rate, in resources and shared power. The larger the number of individuals or groups over which resources must be spread, the less for each one. Because authoritarian governments need less support to remain in power after they have captured and transformed the state bureaucracy, courts, military, police, and taxing authority than for the initial seizure of power, they can get away with excluding some members of the seizure coalition and large parts of the population from the distribution of benefits.

The internal cohesion of seizure groups affects bargaining within the inner circle via two different paths. First, the dictator can bargain separately with each member of a factionalized seizure group, offering some special deals in return for siding with him on crucial decisions and inducing members of the inner circle to compete with each other for resources. If the dictator excludes a member of a factionalized inner circle, as Karimov did many times, remaining members are more likely to seize the resources of a fallen comrade and use him as a stepping-stone to a higher place in the hierarchy than rally to his support. Overall, members of factionalized seizure groups tend to get less from the dictator in exchange for their support because their competition with one another lowers the price they can extract.

Second, factionalism reduces the credibility of threats to oust the dictator if he fails to share. Factionalized support groups have difficulty organizing to oust the dictator, and most unarmed factions lack the capacity to oust him on their own. As we saw in the summary of recent Uzbek history at the beginning of the chapter, if one faction can credibly threaten the dictator with ouster, it can enforce its own sharing agreement, but most of the time unarmed factions cannot. Consequently, the dictator can concentrate more powers in his own hands.

In this section, we focused on one characteristic of seizure groups, which influences the credibility of threats by members of the dictatorial inner circle to oust the dictator: how much unity and discipline had been enforced within the seizure group before it seized power. When united militaries or disciplined parties lead authoritarian seizures of power, lieutenants are likely to be able to resist extreme concentration of power in the dictator's hands. When, instead, factions divide the officer corps or parties are recent amalgams of multiple jostling cliques, they cannot obstruct the dictator's drive to concentrate power. Our argument thus suggests an explanation for the personalization of power in many African countries noted by Africanists (e.g., Bratton and van de Walle 1997) after an initial seizure of power by the military or a transition from elected government to single-party rule. The newness of parties and the recent Africanization of the officer corps at the time of independence often resulted in factionalized party and military seizure groups in the first decades after independence.

MEASURING PERSONALISM

In the next section, we test the argument about why dictators can concentrate power in their hands at the expense of their closest supporters. Though anecdotal evidence supports the ideas we propose, the absence of a measure of personalism has hampered our ability to evaluate them systematically in the past. Here, we leverage new data we collected on various features of dictatorship to derive such a measure.

To capture the idea of personalism, we use eight indicators of dictators' observable behavior (assessed yearly) that we believe demonstrate power concentration at the expense of others in the dictatorial elite (Geddes, Wright, and Frantz 2017; Wright 2018). We create a time-varying index of personalism using these eight indicators: dictator's personal control of the *security apparatus*, creation of loyalist paramilitary forces (*create paramilitary*), dictator's control of the composition of the *party executive* committee, the party executive committee behaving as a *rubber stamp*, dictator's personal control of *appointments*, dictator's creation of a *new party* to support the regime, dictator's control of military *promotions*, and dictator's *purges* of officers.[13]

The first two reflect the dictator's relationship with security forces: whether he personally controls the internal security police (*security apparatus*) and whether he has created a paramilitary force outside the normal chain of military command (*create paramilitary*). Personal control of internal security agencies increases the dictator's information advantage over other members of the dictatorial elite as well as his ability to use violence against them. The dictator's advantage comes not only from his access to the information collected, which he can keep from other members of the inner circle, but also from his ability to order security officers to arrest his colleagues. Knowledge provided by security agencies can help the dictator identify members of the inner circle who might challenge him. Actions by the dictator that we code as indicating personal control of internal security include his direct appointment of the head of the security service (if this appointment appears to ignore the normal military hierarchy), his creation of a new security agency, and his appointment of a relative or close friend to lead a security force.

Dictators use paramilitary forces to counterbalance the regular military when they see it as unreliable. The creation of armed forces directly controlled by the dictator increases the concentration of power in that it reduces the regular military's ability to threaten the dictator with ouster if he fails to share or consult. In order to identify only paramilitary forces created by dictators to solidify their personal power, we exclude party militias and those created to help fight insurgencies. We code both the appointment of a relative or close friend to command a paramilitary force and the recruitment of a paramilitary group primarily from the dictator's tribe, home region, or clan as indicating his personal control. The forces coded as dictators' paramilitary forces include Kwame Nkrumah of Ghana's President's Own Guard and Saddam Hussein's Republican Guards.

The next indicator of personalism assesses the dictator's relationship with the ruling party's leadership. We code whether the regime leader chooses or vetoes members of the party executive committee (*party executive*) in dictatorships organized by a ruling party. The dictator has concentrated power, we argue, if he chooses top party leaders rather than party leaders choosing him. In communist Hungary, for example, the first dictator, Mátyás Rákosi, began the regime with a politburo composed of about equal numbers of close allies who had spent the war with him in Moscow and cadres who had spent the war underground or in jail in Hungary. Rákosi did not choose the leadership of the

---

[13] Adding to the index additional indicators of personalism that measure whether the dictator appoints his relatives to high office, rule by plebiscite, whether the military is ethnically homogenous, and whether the regime leader also leads the support party does not alter the findings reported below. A composite measure that includes these additional variables is correlated with the one used at 0.982.

underground party members, meaning that he did not initially control the composition of the Politburo. After the seizure of power, however, Rákosi gradually eliminated those with independent bases of support in Hungary – life-long dedicated communists who were accused of treason, subjected to show trials, and sentenced to long prison sentences or execution (Kovrig 1984). By the early 1950s, Rákosi fully controlled who joined or was dismissed from the Politburo, and thus the Politburo could not constrain him.

A fourth variable also captures information about the ruling-party executive committee. It identifies party executive committees that serve as arenas for hammering out policy decisions rather than as rubber stamps for policy and personnel choices made by the dictator (*rubber stamp*). We see discussion of policy alternatives and disagreements over choices, which are reported in the media and in secondary sources, as indications that the dictator has not concentrated policy-making power. The absence of policy disagreements indicates the opposite. In North Korea, for example, Kim Il-sung reorganized the Korean Workers' Party (KWP) leadership structure at the 1966 Party Congress; by 1968 "he faced no further challenges from within KWP" (Buzo 1999, 34). The party leadership had been transformed into a rubber stamp.

The variable *appointments* assesses the dictator's control over appointments to important offices in the government, military, and ruling party. To code this item, we rely on secondary literature such as this statement about Mobutu Sese Seko, dictator of what is now the Democratic Republic of Congo:

State-party personnel are completely dependent on him for selection, appointment, and maintenance in power ... Mobutu constantly rotates the membership of the highest organs of power. (Callaghy 1984, 180)

The variable *new party* identifies country-years in which autocracies organize new ruling parties. We consider the dictator's creation of a new support party a strategy for adding personal loyalists to the dictatorial inner circle. Bringing new members into the dictatorial elite dilutes the power of existing members (usually those who helped seize power) and increases the weight of the faction supporting the dictator. We code a new support party if the dictator or a close ally created a new party after the seizure of power or, in a few cases, during an election campaign before authoritarianization.[14] When a dictator organizes a ruling party, he chooses its leadership. Such parties rarely develop sufficient autonomous power to constrain the dictator.

The last two indicators of personalism assess the dictator's relationship with the military: whether he promotes officers loyal to himself or from his tribal, ethnic, partisan, or religious group (*promotions*) and whether he imprisons or kills officers from other groups without fair trials (*purges*). Dictator-controlled promotions and purges demonstrate the dictator's capacity to change the

---

[14] Once the dictator or close ally creates a support party, all subsequent years for that leader are coded as having a new party that was created to support the dictator.

command structure of the military, and thus the composition of military decision-making bodies. If the dictator can control the composition of the officer corps, the military cannot make credible threats to oust him if he fails to share power.

There is substantial overlap among these indicators, both because dictators who use one strategy for concentrating power in their own hands often use others as well and because one piece of historical information can sometimes be used to code more than one indicator. The information that Saddam Hussein appointed relatives to the military high command and to head the security apparatus and Republican Guard, for example, demonstrates that he controlled the internal security forces (*security apparatus*), personalized a paramilitary force (*create paramilitary*), and controlled military promotions (*promotions*).

Using these eight indicators, we create a composite measure of personalism from an item response theory (IRT) two-parameter logistic model (2PL) that allows each item (variable) to vary in its difficulty and discrimination.[15] We transform the scores from this latent trait estimate into an index bounded by 0 and 1, where higher levels of personalism approach 1 and lower levels of personalism approach 0.

The personalism index differs from the categorical regime-type variables used in past research (e.g., Geddes 2003). The old measure classified differences across *regimes* (that is, spans of consecutive country-years), but the new one is coded every year in every regime to measure changes over time in the dictator's concentration of power. Importantly, this time-varying measure is coded for all dictatorships – not just those with powerful leaders – to capture differences between regimes, between leaders in the same regime, and over time during any individual leader's tenure in power. This allows us to investigate the gradual concentration of power by individual dictators (the most common pattern) as well as occasional reversals.

Figure 4.2 shows the personalism scores for six dictatorships: three communist dictatorships in Asia, all identified by Levitsky and Way (2013) as revolutionary regimes, and three coded as hybrid regimes by Geddes (2003) and not considered revolutionary. This latter group has features of personalist rule as well as features of military and party-based rule, which is the reason they were coded as hybrids of the three pure types. The personalism scores show how the concentration of power in the hands of paramount leaders varied over time in these long-lasting dictatorships.

In the left panel, we see that the personalism score for China (solid line) reflects the ups and downs in power concentration since the Chinese Communist Party took power in 1949. The highly collegial communist leadership immediately after the revolution was followed by the modest concentration of

---

[15] As an alternative, we used principal component analysis (PCA) to extract the first dimension from these variables. This factor, with an eigenvalue greater than 3, is correlated with the personalism index employed throughout at 0.99.

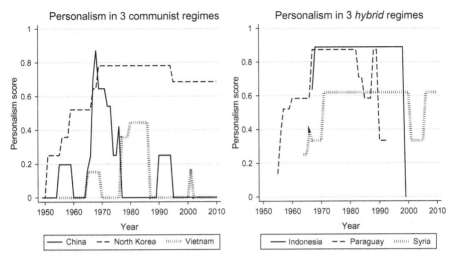

FIGURE 4.2 Illustration of personalism scores.

power in Mao's hands during the 1950s, Mao's loss of power after the failure of the Great Leap Forward, and then Mao's rapid concentration of power in the 1960s during the Cultural Revolution.[16] The concentration of power dropped again as Mao's health failed and normalcy was reestablished in the 1970s. Chinese leadership then became unusually collegial again except for a short time during Deng Xiaoping's dominance.[17] The North Korean regime (dashed line) was moderately personalist during its first years in existence under Soviet tutelage, but Kim Il-sung dramatically increased his control relative to other ruling party elites in the late 1950s and even more during the 1960s.[18] His son and grandson maintained the extreme personalization of power in North Korea.

In contrast, Vietnam's (hatched line) first dictator, Ho Chi Minh, never concentrated great power in his hands. The uptick of personalism in the late 1960s reflects the exclusion of the faction opposed to escalating the war in the south as Lê Duẩn consolidated his position as successor to Ho Chi Minh in the years before Ho's death (Vu 2014, 28–30). The larger surge in personalism scores from the mid-1970s to mid-1980s reflects the post-war consolidation of

[16] Changes in the graph appear slightly later than real-world changes because the data are coded as of January 1, meaning that if a dictator increases the concentration of power in his hands in one year, it will first appear in the data set the following year.

[17] As we write, China specialists suggest that the current leader, Xi Jinping, is concentrating greater power in his hands. (See, for example, Lee, 2015.) The data on which the personalism score depends extend only to 2010, however, so Xi's term is not shown.

[18] To reflect this, the Communist regime in North Korea was classified as a hybrid, dominant-party-personalist, in the old regime-type coding (Geddes 2003).

power by Lê Duẩn and a handful of close supporters at the expense of other veteran communists. Lê Duẩn's appointment of his son to head the secret police, appointment of other relatives to other important posts, and the purge of pro-Chinese factions from the party elite that enabled him to control promotions in the military demonstrate his concentration of power (Nguyen 1983, 70–72). The decline in Vietnamese personalism in 1986 coincides with Lê Duẩn's death.

In the right panel, we note first that the early years of the dictatorships in Syria and Paraguay show a pattern similar to that in North Korea and China while Mao was alive: an initial period of relative collegiality followed by the rapid concentration of power in the dictator's hands. This is the average pattern we find in the data. Note that in all three of these hybrid regimes, first dictators began their rule with more power than any of the communist leaders because none of them had to bargain with well-developed, unified party institutions.

Suharto of Indonesia (solid line) faced remarkably little constraint from other political elites even at the beginning. Not only did he lack a support party until creating one a few years after seizing power, but the upper ranks of the officer corps had been decimated by assassinations during a violent uprising not long before the coup that brought him to power. Consequently, Suharto did not have to negotiate with other highly ranked officers as most dictators from the military do. The precipitous drop in the personalism score for the last year of this dictatorship reflects Suharto's resignation and his replacement by a weak protégé who lacked a support base in the military.

In Paraguay (dashed line) and Syria (hatched line), military dictators allied with preexisting but highly factionalized parties, which they reorganized, purged, and molded into effective instruments of personal rule over their first years in power. The Colorado Party in Paraguay was especially useful because, although hopelessly factionalized at the elite level and thus unable to exert much constraint on the dictator, it had a well-organized mass base that Stroessner coopted to use for both spying and mobilization against challenges from fellow officers. The steep drop in personalism followed by reconcentration in the 1980s reflects the development of competing factions within the Stroessner ruling group as he aged and members of the inner circle began to battle over succession. Stroessner briefly reasserted himself, but was then ousted by a member of his inner circle. The dramatic decline shortly before the regime ended reflects the tenure of this less powerful successor.

In these cases, the dictator who concentrated great personal power lived for several decades longer and maintained a high level of personalization, followed by a precipitous drop when he died, resigned, or was ousted. In Syria, we see a drop in personalization when Bashar al-Assad succeeded his father in 2000 and then an upswing as Bashar consolidated his hold on the system. In the other two, successors were unable to reconcentrate personal power or maintain the regime. In all cases, the personalism score seems to track historical events well.

Importantly, these time-varying indicators of personalism reflect observed behavior after the seizure of power. The indicators of factionalism within the seizure group that we employ below in the analysis to *explain* personalism reflect characteristics of what *later* became the seizure group measured *prior* to the seizure of power. They are thus not endogenously determined by dictators' strategic behavior aimed at remaining in power.

PATTERNS OF PERSONALISM

In this section, we use our measure of personalism to describe typical patterns of power concentration in dictatorships. Personalism scores tend to be low during the year after seizures of power, as would be expected if most dictators are weak, like Karimov, relative to other members of the ruling group when dictatorships begin. Where the dictator can take first steps toward power concentration soon after seizures of power, however, we expect him to then use his increased resources to eliminate from the inner circle individuals who have the greatest ability or disposition to challenge him in the future – as Karimov did. In this way, he can concentrate more power in his own hands. This strategy is associated with longer tenure in office for the dictator. First dictators – that is, those who are the first to assume power after the initiation of dictatorship – with higher personalism scores during their first three years in office retain their positions nearly twice as long on average as first dictators with low early personalism scores. First dictators with high personalism scores (top third of the personalism index) during the first years in power survive 14.7 years on average, while first leaders with low personalism scores (bottom third) survive only 7.8 years on average.[19]

Changes in the relative power of inner-circle members can become long lasting through the replacement of individuals who might potentially have challenged the dictator with others who lack independent support bases and are thus more dependent on him. Whatever resolution arises from the earliest conflict between the dictator and his closest allies increases the likelihood of a similar resolution to the next one. In other words, if the dictator gains more control over political resources as a result of the first conflict with other members of the inner circle, he then has a greater advantage in the next conflict with them.[20] In this way, where steps toward personalization occur soon after the seizure of power, it is likely to progress further.

In contrast, initial reliance on collegial institutions reduces the chance of later personalization. Where members of the inner circle have developed the expectation of participating in key decisions, attempts by the dictator to reverse

[19] The median tenure for first leaders with low personalism scores is 4 years; for those with high personalism scores, the median is 11.5 years. Note that this comparison pertains only to first leaders who survive at least three years in office, since scores during the first three years were used to create the comparison groups.

[20] Svolik (2012) shows how greater leader power enables the dictator to defeat regime insiders who try to use rebellion to deter further power grabs.

their policy choices or postpone regular meetings of the collegial decision-making body become focal points around which it is relatively easy (though never easy in absolute terms) to organize collective action against the dictator.

In short, we expect the deal agreed to by the dictator and members of the seizure group in the early months after the seizure of power to shape later interactions. Whatever pattern of power aggrandizement is established during the first years of a dictatorship tends to be perpetuated until the first dictator dies, sickens, or is overthrown.

The replacement of one dictator by another during a single regime often involves renegotiation of the distribution of power within the inner circle. Those who yearn to replace the dictator, whether after his death or via violent overthrow, must promise their colleagues a larger share of power in order to attract their support, but as with the first dictator, such promises are unenforceable unless members of the inner circle can both oust him if he reneges and credibly commit their subordinates to refrain from overthrowing him if he sticks to the bargain. The main differences between subsequent struggles and the first one is that members of the inner circle have learned from earlier struggles and may have developed disciplined, within-regime networks that allow them to bargain more credibly and effectively with the new dictator. In dictatorships that last beyond the tenure of the first leader, power relationships between the dictator and the inner circle thus tend to become somewhat more equal under subsequent leaders.

We assess these expectations in two ways. First, we examine how levels of personalism change over time for a regime's first leader relative to subsequent ones. The first dictator has an advantage in bargaining relative to later ones because of the inexperience of members of the ruling group. That is, they are experienced as military officers, insurgents, or party militants, but they have not usually had experience in the rule-free and dangerous context of bargaining within the inner circle of a dictatorship. The day after the new regime seizes power, the new dictator can begin using state resources, appointing officials, establishing procedures, and issuing decrees. It can take some time for other members of the inner circle to grasp all the implications of some of the dictator's initiatives. This implies that, on average, first dictators have advantages over later ones in parlaying initial gains in personal power into further increases over time.

Figure 4.3 compares levels of personalism over time for initial regime leaders with the personalism scores of subsequent dictators in the same regime. The horizontal axis marks the first three full years each dictator rules, while the vertical axis shows the predicted level of personalism from a regression model in which the dependent variable is the measured level of personalism:

$$Personalism = \alpha_0 + \beta_1{}^* Duration_t + \beta_2{}^* FirstLeader_i$$
$$+ \beta_3{}^*(Duration_t{}^* FirstLeader_i) + \gamma_t + \varepsilon_{it} \qquad (4.1)$$

In this equation, *Duration* is the natural log of leader years in power; *First-Leader* is a binary indicator of whether the dictator is the first one after the

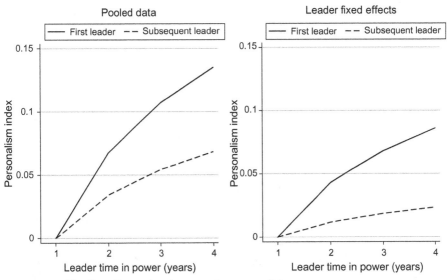

FIGURE 4.3 The first dictator's advantage in personalizing power.

regime seizes power; γ_t are five-year time period effects; and i indexes leader and t indexes years in power. Time-period effects ensure that measurement error correlated with historical time is not driving the estimates of interest.[21] The figures below report the substantive effect of the linear combination of β_2 and β_3, which estimates levels of personalism for first regime leaders; and of β_1, which estimates levels of personalism for subsequent leaders. By design, the approach simply shows the average levels of personalism as years in power increase, setting the average level in the first year as the baseline (set to zero on the vertical axis). The right panel of Figure 4.3 shows the result from a similar model specification but adds one crucial set of controls: an individual-level fixed effect for each dictator (δ_i). This allows the model to isolate the changes over time for each leader, net of any baseline differences between leaders in different countries or regimes.

The left panel shows the pooled data. During his first three years in office, the first regime leader, on average, increases the level of personalism nearly 0.15 points on the (0, 1) scale. For subsequent regime leaders, the gains in personalism are less than half of this. The right panel shows a similar pattern: the first leader increases personalism in the first three years by almost 0.09 points, while later leaders increase it by less than 0.02 points. The size of these effects is smaller in the right panel because the model accounts for all

---

[21] If we can better observe manifestations of personalism for more recent periods (e.g., post-2000), for example, this could systematically bias estimates.

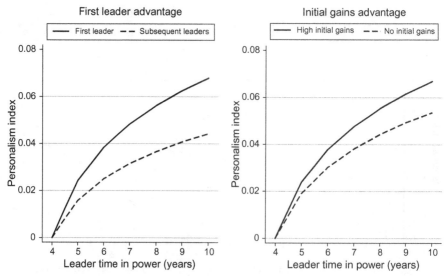

FIGURE 4.4 Personalizing power after the first three years.

differences in the average level of personalism for each individual leader and thus looks only at each *dictator's* time-trend in personalism. The descriptive patterns in Figure 4.3 are consistent with the expectation that first regime leaders have advantages in accumulating power. In the early years of dictatorship, the first dictator concentrates power faster than leaders who follow him.

Next we examine what happens after an initial three-year period of regime consolidation. In this exercise, we look at how personalism evolves in years four to ten for different groups of dictators. Figure 4.4 shows the pattern of personalism across all dictators who survive in power at least four years, using the average level of personalism at the start of year four as the baseline level (set to zero). The left panel of Figure 4.4 reports the estimates for a model similar to Equation 4.1 but with leader fixed effects (like the right panel of Figure 4.3). After a period of initial power concentration, first leaders continue to have an advantage in accumulating power relative to subsequent leaders: first dictators, on average, boost personalism scores by a further 0.07 points between years four and ten, while subsequent leaders increase their power by half as much during these years. These increases are smaller than those reported in Figure 4.3 because power concentration is more rapid during initial periods of regime consolidation than during later years.

Another way to analyze personalization after the initial period of consolidation is to compare leaders who successfully personalized during the first three years with those who did not. For each leader, we construct a variable that measures whether his score on the personalism index increased a lot during the first three years he ruled (*high initial gains*).[22] Then we test a regression model similar to those used above (with leader fixed effects), but compare leaders with *high initial gains* in personalism scores with leaders who did not concentrate power during their first three years. The right panel of Figure 4.4 shows that leaders who concentrate personal power in their first three years further increase their personalism scores by more than 0.06 points from years four to ten. Leaders who failed to accumulate personal power in their first three years do not make this up later; their gains after the initial period are smaller than those of leaders who amassed personal power from the outset. This evidence is consistent with Svolik's (2012) model of power concentration in which initial successful power grabs beget more successful power concentration over time.

THE EFFECT OF FACTIONALISM ON THE PERSONALIZATION OF POWER

Next we test our explanation of *why* some dictators can concentrate more power than others. We look at the effect of the degree of factionalism in the seizure group before the initiation of dictatorship on how personalism evolves over time after the group takes power. We expect more unified seizure groups to bargain more successfully, and thus to limit the accumulation of power in the dictator's hands.

Though we lack direct measures of seizure-group unity, we investigate the effects of two proxy measures. The first is the pre-seizure history of the group that becomes the dictatorship's ruling party after the seizure. We posit that a support coalition organized as a political party either to contest elections or to lead a revolution before the seizure of power has greater organizational unity, and can thus more successfully bargain with the dictator, than a support coalition not organized as a party before the seizure.[23]

The second proxy for coalition unity is intended to capture the pre-seizure unity of military seizure groups. For dictatorships that seized power in coups, we use the first dictator's military rank before the seizure of power as a proxy measure of factionalism. The logic is as follows. Junior and mid-level officers carry out many coups. In countries with relatively unified and disciplined military forces, however, lower-ranked coup leaders hand *regime* leadership to a senior officer after the coup because they do not expect other senior officers

---

[22] Of the 312 leaders who last more than three years in power, 28 percent have *high initial gains* during their first three years in power. About half (53 percent) of the 312 leaders are first regime leaders.

[23] Parties organized to contest elections ran candidates in one or more elections in an earlier authoritarian or democratic regime. We do not include the parties that were organized as vehicles for the dictator's election campaign prior to authoritarianization (e.g., Cambio 90, organized by Fujimori to manage his presidential campaign in 1990). Vehicle parties are centered on the leader from their creation and often have little independent organizational existence.

to follow orders issued by junior officers. In factionalized armies, however, multiple hierarchies exist, some of which junior officers lead. When senior officers lead dictatorships, we cannot be sure whether the military that backs them is unified, but when junior officers such as Captain Moammar Qaddafi of Libya or Sargent Samuel Doe of Liberia lead dictatorships, we know that the military that backs them was factionalized before the coup. The indicator we use here groups regime leaders ranked major and below in one category and all those ranked higher in the other.[24] It thus distinguishes the most factionalized cases (only the top 9 percent) from all others.

Seizure of power via popular uprising is another indicator of a factionalized army. Because popular uprisings are defined as unarmed seizures of power, they occur only when the country's military has refrained from using its advantage in violence to quell the upheaval. When the army is united, either it backs the incumbent to prevent popular demonstrations from ousting him or it replaces the incumbent itself. The overthrow of a government by popular uprising suggests an army divided between government supporters and opponents just before the regime change, and possibly along other dimensions as well.

We can thus use both seizure of power by popular uprising and the first dictator's rank before seizure via coup as indications of pre-seizure factionalization in the military coalition that supports the dictatorship.

The data indicate that more than one-third (37 percent) of dictators are supported by an *inherited* revolutionary or electoral party when they seize power (a sign of unity). Only 15 percent of dictators are supported by a highly factionalized military.[25] These two features are almost mutually exclusive: of the 280 regimes in the data, only seven have both an inherited party and a factionalized military.

We expect leaders who bargain with supporters organized in inherited (electoral or revolutionary) political parties, which should on average be more united than newly created parties or informally organized coalitions, to be less capable of personalizing power. By the same logic, leaders who bargain with a more unified military should be less likely to concentrate power in their own hands than those who negotiate with a more factionalized officer corps.

---

[24] Colonel was the highest rank in many armies at the time of coups, especially in the 1960s and 1970s, so the meaning of this rank is ambiguous.

[25] Note that each of these measures creates a more homogeneous set of cases on one side of the dichotomy than the other. Dictators in cases with *inherited* parties must all bargain with inner circles organized by inherited parties. In the cases that lack inherited parties, some dictators bargain with newly created parties that tend to lack organizational coherence, but others lack parties and bargain instead with officers from a disciplined, professional officer corps. In other words, the cases that lack inherited parties are a mix of cases with factionalized ruling groups and cases with united ruling groups. Our proxy measure of military factionalism implies that the militaries identified here as less factionalized include a mix of factionalized and unified military forces, so we can show the effect of high factionalism but not of high levels of military unity.

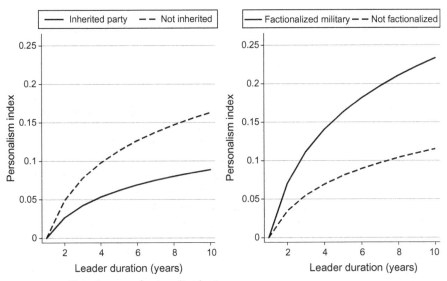

FIGURE 4.5 United versus factionalized seizure groups.

A first look at the raw data provides some evidence consistent with these expectations. While roughly 41 percent of first leaders increase personal power in their first three years, this figure differs considerably depending on the type of group with which the leader bargains. Less than one-third (32 percent) of first dictators who face an inherited support party concentrate power in their own hands, but nearly half (47 percent) of those who do not bargain with an inherited party do so. Fifty-four percent of first dictators who face a highly factionalized military concentrate power, while only 38 percent of those who face a more unified military do so.[26]

The left panel of Figure 4.5 compares the increase over time in personalism levels for first leaders who bargained with an inherited party (a more unified support coalition) and those who bargained with a new party or with supporters not organized into a party.[27] First leaders who do not bargain with an inherited party personalize by 0.098 points on average during the first three years; those who negotiate with an inherited political party, however, increase their personalism score by much less (0.053 points). By the end of the first decade in power, those who do not face an inherited party have increased personalism scores by 0.163 points, and those who bargain with an inherited party do so by a little more than half that amount (0.089 points). This suggests

---

[26] These differences for inherited party and factionalized military are both statistically significant at the 0.05 level. Figures are for first regime leaders, excluding subsequent ones.

[27] The estimates on the vertical axis reflect the predicted change in the level of personalism from a regression model similar to Equation (4.1) but with leader and year fixed effects.

that dictators who must bargain with a unified support group can less easily concentrate personal power than leaders whose supporters are less organized.

The right panel of Figure 4.5 shows the average level of personalism for first leaders who face a highly factionalized military and those who do not. We see an even stronger pattern: those who bargain with very factionalized militaries boost personalism by 0.14 points in their first three years, while those who bargain with more united militaries increase personalism by only 0.07 points, on average.[28] After a decade in power, dictators facing more unified officer corps have increased their power by 0.12 points, on average, while those whose military supporters are more factionalized increase it by twice as much (0.23 points). We interpret this evidence as suggesting that leaders who initially bargain with a highly factionalized military have a clear advantage in personalizing power.

To summarize, our empirical analysis shows that first dictators have an advantage in concentrating power in their own hands relative to later ones. Moreover, initial gains in power tend to make further gains easier. Dictators whose efforts to grab power are blocked early on are likely to concentrate power more slowly if at all later, even if they survive long in office.

We also show that dictators who have to bargain with a more united seizure coalition face stiffer resistance to concentrating personal power than those who do not. Inherited parties, we show, limit dictators' gains in personal power, as do more unified militaries. In contrast, dictators who bargain with factionalized military or civilian supporters have great advantages in concentrating personal power.

CONCLUSION

All members of the inner circles of dictatorships have common interests in regime survival but compete with each other over power and resources. Each individual member, including the dictator, has strong reasons to try to increase his power and access to resources at the expense of the others. Even if some individual members do not yearn for the dictator's job, they must compete in order to maintain their positions against ambitious regime supporters below them in the hierarchy. The competition within the inner circle means that for most purposes dictatorships should not be analyzed as unitary actors. Instead, we see members of the inner circle as continuously engaged in simultaneous cooperative strategies aimed at regime survival and noncooperative strategies aimed at increasing personal power.

The choice of one member of the inner circle as dictator (or the elected leader's acquisition of dictatorial powers if the seizure of power is accomplished via authoritarianization) results in the central political dynamic of authoritarian politics: conflict over the distribution of power within the regime's

---

[28] Remember that "more united" is a mix of fully united and fairly factionalized since we have no indicator for fully unified.

leadership group. Once the dictator is chosen, his interests diverge from those of his lieutenants. Dictators who had been first among equals in a collegial conspiracy before the ouster of the old regime gain reasons to concentrate power and resources in their own hands in order to increase their security at the top. Other members of the inner circle, meanwhile, have good reasons to try to limit the dictator's resources and policy-making discretion in order to protect their own positions and maintain their own influence and clientele networks. This conflict plays out in different ways, depending on the ex ante factionalism of the seizure group.

Characteristics of the seizure group that pre-date the establishment of the dictatorship influence the initial distribution of resources within the inner circle and what kinds of bargains can be enforced among them. In this chapter we focused on one ex ante characteristic: the unity or factionalism developed within the seizure group before they gained power. By unity, we mean that members of the inner circle can bargain with the dictator as a unitary actor and thus drive a harder bargain with him. Some military forces are unified by virtue of enforced discipline and the hierarchical command structure, but others are factionalized. The same goes for parties. Where the dictator's supporters are divided into factions, they are unlikely to be able to make credible threats to oust the dictator if he fails to share power and spoils. Where, however, they can behave as a unitary actor, they can more easily act together to oust him and thus the dictator's promises to share are credible.

The focus on bargaining highlights the logic behind coalition narrowing in dictatorships. We argue that if the members of the seizure group have been able to develop ways of enforcing their own internal unity, dictators' efforts to concentrate power tend to fail. In the real world, enforced internal unity develops in professionalized military forces and highly disciplined parties. In contrast, where a conspiracy drawn from a factionalized officer corps or party seizes power, the dictator's supporters often fail to resist the personalization of rule.[29]

Authoritarian regimes differ enormously from each other in levels of repression, distribution of costs and benefits across societal groups, policies followed, and ideological justification. Nevertheless, the impulse toward personalization seems to be common in all. The elite bargaining described in this chapter explains why these processes occur in such apparently different kinds of dictatorship.

In this chapter we have focused on how the factionalism or unity of the seizure group affects its ability to oust the dictator and thus the credibility of the dictator's promises to share power and spoils. In the next, we focus not on what

[29] Analysis in the replication files shows that dictatorships in the past two decades are increasingly likely to seize power with a factionalized military and less likely to seize power with an inherited political party. Together, these trends may explain why we observe an increase in personalist regimes since 1990 (Kendall-Taylor, Frantz, and Wright 2016).

makes the lieutenants' threats to oust the dictator if he fails to share more credible but rather on whether their promises to *refrain* from ousting him when he shares are credible. Allies' promises of *support* are credible only if their subordinates obey orders because dictators can be overthrown or assassinated by small numbers of armed men. We then consider the options available to the dictator when the promises of support from other members of the ruling group are not credible. In the process, we explain why seizure groups that did not need an organized civilian support base to achieve power sometimes later create mass parties.

5

Dictatorial Survival Strategies in Challenging Conditions

Factionalized Armed Supporters and Party Creation

When Benin became independent in 1960, three parties dominated politics, each rooted in a region and its ethnic groups. The same regional loyalties factionalized the newly created army. Most officers came from the south. They had started in the ranks during French rule and were promoted rapidly in order to indigenize the officer corps at independence. Most enlisted men came from the north (Decalo 1976, 55–57). As of 1965, when Benin's second coup occurred, the army was a few years old and had only 1,700 men. It had 43 indigenous officers and 12 French ones (Bebler 1973, 12–13). During the first decade after independence, divisions between older officers, who were rapidly promoted as the new nation built its army, and younger ones trained in military schools, whose promotions were soon blocked by budget crises, reinforced and overlaid regional factionalism within the army (Decalo 1976).

After the first coup in 1963, soldiers replaced the civilian president with a different civilian and returned to the barracks. Officers themselves took power after the1965 coup. Factionalism undermined Benin's first military dictatorship, which ended with a coup in 1967 that brought to power a new military regime of mid-ranking officers from a different ethnic group. The second military dictatorship attempted to deal with army factionalism by appointing an ethnically balanced cabinet. The new cabinet included captains, lieutenants, and NCOs in the dictatorship's inner circle to make sure that all army interests were represented. The leadership also dismissed some southern senior officers and promoted some from the north in an effort to equalize opportunities (Bebler 1973, 20–23). Nevertheless, another faction-based coup ousted this regime two years later. Officers then tried to reunify the military around an inclusive decision-making body with collegial leadership, but were unsuccessful. They returned power to civilians in 1970 because they could not find a successful formula for power sharing within the officer corps.

Benin's history in the 1960s is a story of military dictators' repeated failure to consolidate their rule because the factionalized officer corps could not provide stable support. Decalo describes the army as a "patchwork of competing personalist/ethnic allegiance-pyramids centered around officers of all ranks in which superior rank or authority was only grudgingly acknowledged" (1979, 234).

A seizure group that includes many members with control over armed force should be able to achieve an especially advantageous power-sharing arrangement with the leader because their threats to oust the dictator are highly credible. Responding to these threats, early military dictators in Benin agreed to oversight by broadly representative groups of officers, but to no avail. These strategies failed because officers included in the regime's inner circle could not prevent rogue coups led by other officers formally subordinate to them. Despite successive dictators' efforts to secure stability by consulting with representatives of many military factions, some officers always remained dissatisfied and quick to oust the current dictatorship. These failures were caused not by the inability of dictators' allies to make credible threats to oust the dictator if he fails to share, but rather by their inability to make good on promises of support when he *was sharing*. In that situation, a dictator cannot make himself safe by sharing more and more because dictators, like all other political leaders, face budget constraints.

This destructive game of musical chairs among military factions ended a few years after the 1972 coup that brought Major Mathieu Kérékou to power. Kérékou initially followed the same strategy as earlier military dictators. He dismissed all senior officers, appointed a cabinet of junior officers, and consulted a military ruling council representative of major military factions. Despite Kérékou's effort to consult all factions, the military remained unable to provide a stable base of support. Kérékou survived several coup attempts during his first two years in power (Decalo 1976, 76–84). Then, in 1974 Kérékou began creating an organized civilian support base, the Benin People's Revolutionary Party (RPB), to counterbalance the military and help stabilize his rule. Six "close friends of the president" made up the new party's politburo (Martin 1986, 68). Over time, Kérékou gradually increased civilian participation in inner-circle decision-making. Their support enabled him to remove the most threatening rival officers from posts from which armed challenges could be launched (Martin 1986, 68–75). Adding a loyal civilian support group to balance the factionalized military stabilized Kérékou's rule. He retained control until 1990, when widespread popular opposition forced him to democratize.

In this chapter, we explore two theoretical ideas highlighted by Benin's history. First, armed supporters can drive a hard bargain with the dictator when they maintain unity but not otherwise; factionalism prevents *them* from making credible promises to support the dictator if he shares. To be viable, a power-sharing bargain between the dictator and his allies must be credible on *both* sides: allies must believe the dictator's promise to share, and the dictator must believe the allies' promises to support him if and only if he shares. The allies' promise of support is not credible, however, if they cannot commit their own subordinates to honor the bargains they make. The second theoretical idea is that dictators can in some circumstances change the balance of forces within the ruling group by empowering new political actors. Kérékou did this when he organized a new support party and brought its leaders into the inner circle of the dictatorship.

In Chapter 4, we analyzed how and why dictators exclude rivals from their inner circle. Here we focus on the dictator's strategic *inclusion* of new players he expects to be more malleable and less dangerous than the original members. We also consider the conditions under which he has the ability to exercise this option.

In the first part of this chapter, we describe the especially difficult situation facing dictators whose power initially depends on an armed support base, or what Alex De Waal (2015) calls specialists in violence. In the next, we spell out our argument about how the interaction of dispersed armed force and factionalism in the seizure group can limit the dictator's options for bargaining with these supporters.[1] The third section considers the dictator's incentives to bring into the inner circle political actors who are more dependent on him for benefits and protection than are specialists in violence (military officers or others who command armed subordinates). It explains why civilian support groups are less dangerous to dictators than armed factions, and it discusses party creation as a strategy for mobilizing organized civilian support to counterbalance unreliable armed supporters. The fourth section provides evidence that party creation in dictatorships that lack support parties when they seize power contributes to a strategy designed to concentrate more power and resources in the dictator's hands, reducing his need to rely on members of the original seizure group. The last sections show evidence that fewer coups against dictators occur after party creation and that dictatorships that create parties post-seizure last longer than otherwise similar regimes lacking party organization.

THE STRATEGIC CONTEXT

Dictators who achieve power through armed force face an especially difficult survival problem. Consider the dilemma faced by a dictator who comes to power in a coup.[2] Besides the support of fellow plotters, he probably has the

---

[1] De Waal (2015) focuses on factions based on ethnicity and cases in which all relevant players are specialists in violence. We analyze the more general situation in which the seizure group is divided into factions for any reason and some potentially powerful political players lack easy recourse to violence.

[2] A large majority of the dictators who achieve power by force do so via coup, but sometimes officers are handed power during popular uprisings; insurgencies bring some armed groups to

initial support of some civilian elites who were fed up with the ousted incumbent but who would lack the capacity to save the new leader from ouster if his armed supporters turned against him.

At the outset he often has quite a bit of popular support as well, and for the same reason: dissatisfaction with the overthrown incumbent. This popular support, however, is unorganized, opportunistic, and superficial. "The people" or "the street" may support a coup in order to rid themselves of an incompetent, brutal, or disreputable leader, but that support will evaporate if the economy fails to improve quickly or if any other disaster strikes. Much of the citizenry can swing rapidly from support to opposition. Egypt's recent experience illustrates the volatility of unorganized popular support: Egyptian protestors forced a military-supported dictatorship from power in 2011, but in 2013 helped oust a democratically elected president and return the military to power.

The coup leader needs widespread support from other officers to survive in power when popular opposition arises, as it inevitably does. Military dictators have the support or acquiescence of many other officers at the time of seizure (otherwise their coup would have failed), but no way of guaranteeing that support in the future. Even at the beginning, support from the rest of the military might be quite superficial. As shown in earlier work (Geddes 2003), the incentives facing military officers when their colleagues initiate a coup create a first-mover advantage similar to that in "battle of the sexes" games. This means that if a small group of officers makes a successful first "coup move," such as seizing the airport and presidential palace, the rest of the military tends to go along, whether they sincerely want the intervention or not. So, the fact that a seizure of power has occurred implies temporary acquiescence by the rest of the officer corps but very little in terms of sincere or long-term support. In short, military dictators cannot count on the support of fellow officers tomorrow even if they have it today, and today's support may be shallower than it appears at the time the military seizes power.

Within the dictatorial inner circle, support for the dictator may also be short lived. Even though the dictator was a brother officer – and often a longtime ally and friend of other high-ranking officers – the day before he was selected as supreme leader, their interests diverge after his selection just as those of civilian dictators and their supporters do. Officers in the support group want to ensure large military budgets and their continued monopolization of force. They do not want their budget reduced in order to hire more security police or provide

power; and a few are imposed by foreigners. After insurgencies or foreign impositions, the new ruling group usually replaces the incumbent officer corps with its own supporters. Thus, when we speak of officers, we refer not only to the armed forces of an ousted regime that achieved power for themselves via coup or popular uprising, but also to those who replaced incumbent officers after insurgent seizures of power. Once the old officer corps has been replaced, "the military" is the new one imposed after regime change.

patronage jobs for civilian supporters of the dictator. They oppose the creation of presidential guards or people's militias to protect the dictator because such forces challenge their own monopoly of force and the credibility of their threats to oust the dictator if he fails to share, as well as depleting the budget. They have an interest in consultation within the officer corps before major policy decisions. They want to avoid the concentration of power, resources, and discretion in one man's hands, as well as the favoritism and deprofessionalization within the military that often accompany it. Dictators who succeed in concentrating resources and discretion in their own hands, that is, in personalizing power, threaten both the military as an institution and individual officers, since they control promotions, postings, forced retirements, and access to profit opportunities (both legal and illegal). At the extreme, such dictators control life and death through their personal control of the security apparatus, and military officers have no special immunity from security police. The same logic applies to other dictators brought to power by specialists in violence.

Since coups have ousted most dictators, especially those who come from the military, it is obvious that officers can be dangerous. Weapons, know-how, and the command of troops are widely dispersed in armies and in some insurgencies. This reality creates a hazardous environment for dictators, because coups require only a small number of individual plotters to execute them. Indeed, coups involving fewer than twenty men have occasionally succeeded.[3] Only a minority of coups involve consensus among the whole officer corps. Instead, small conspiratorial groups of officers carry out most coups using the first-mover strategy (Nordlinger 1977). In short, many different small groups of officers could stage a coup with reasonable prospects for success.

THE INTERACTION OF DISPERSED ARMS AND FACTIONALISM

Though much of the literature on autocracies has emphasized dictators' credibility problem,[4] it is not the main impediment to successful sharing bargains when arms are widely dispersed within the ruling group. *Military* dictators can increase the credibility of their promises to share in some ways not available to civilians, for example, by retiring from active duty.[5] Once they no longer command other officers, do not determine promotions, and cannot decide which officers will command which garrisons, leaders' ability to deter coups depends almost entirely on their ability to satisfy the rest of the military's policy

---

[3] For example, Master Sergeant Samuel Doe and seventeen men ended the dictatorship of William Tolbert and the long reign of the True Whig Party in Liberia (Thomson 1988, 44); sixteen NCOs carried out the 1980 coup in Surinam that ousted then-President Johan Ferrier (Hoefte 2013, 133).

[4] For example, Acemoglu and Robinson (2005); Magaloni (2008); and Svolik (2012).

[5] Sometimes officers are required by the rest of the military to retire before becoming junta president for exactly this reason (Remmer 1991).

and budget demands. This makes their promises credible. Military dictators can also increase their credibility by leaving internal security services within the military chain of command, thus limiting their ability to spy on, intimidate, and murder other officers.

The more serious impediment to successful power-sharing bargains is that armed supporters' promises *not* to oust as long as the dictator shares are never completely credible because they cannot always prevent "rogue" coups or armed ouster by other specialists in violence.[6] These are coups by factions, often led by lower-ranked officers, that *could* be defeated if the rest of the armed forces mobilized against them, but the dictator cannot count on the rest of the army doing so. The first-mover advantage built into the incentives facing officers means that a faction that makes a credible first coup move without being met by violent opposition can overthrow the government because the rest of the armed forces will acquiesce to this coup just as they did to the one that brought the current leader to power.[7] All dictators face some risk from armed supporters, but the less control commanding officers have over lower-ranked officers – that is, the less disciplined and unified the armed support group is – the less ability officers in the inner circle have to make enforceable bargains with the dictator that would reduce the risk.

An alternative way to express this problem is to note that militaries and other armed groups are not unitary actors, though some more closely approximate unity than others. In more professionalized militaries and unified insurgent groups, individuals' future career success is inextricably bound to following the orders of their commanders. Professional success depends on obedience to orders from the day that youths enter military school. Subordinates obey superiors regardless of personal, ethnic, or political loyalties. The likelihood of a rogue coup succeeding is low in unified militaries, and the cost of a failed attempt very high because serious breaches of discipline end careers. Coup leaders can also face court-martial, jail time, or execution. In this kind of military institution, commanding officers can count on lower-ranked officers to obey orders, which transforms a large group of individuals into something approximating a unitary actor. Unitary actors can make credible promises.

Factionalized militaries were common between 1946 and 2010, however, especially in newly independent countries. A factionalized army, "far from being a model of hierarchical organization, tends to be an assemblage of armed men who may or may not obey their officers" (Zolberg 1968, 72). In factionalized forces, discipline is less predictably enforced because personal, partisan, or ethnic loyalties can cross-cut military hierarchy. "[S]oldiers often [have] a

---

[6] Thus, for dictatorships with an armed support base, we see the supporters' credibility problem as the opposite of that emphasized by Svolik (2012). He sees their threat to oust a dictator who violates power sharing as lacking credibility, but we believe it is supporters' promise to refrain from ousting a dictator who shares that most often lacks credibility.

[7] See Singh (2014) for an elaboration of which actions make the first move of a coup credible.

stronger sense of commitment to their unit commander than to the army" (Crouch 1978, 27). Promotion and protection for lower-ranked officers, NCOs, and soldiers depend on faction leaders, not just on compliance with orders and military norms. Routes to higher rank other than the slow but predictable rise via increasing seniority are more available. Consequently, lower-ranked officers may disobey the orders of higher-ranked officers if they conflict with those of faction leaders. Support for coups can be a short-cut to rapid promotion, and punishment for coup attempts is not always severe. Some coup attempts result only in demotion, apparently because dictators fear the consequences of imposing harsher punishments in factionalized militaries. Others result in dismissal, but when changes at the top occur later, as they often do in countries with factionalized militaries, dismissed officers may be reinstated.

Officers included in the inner circle in this kind of setting cannot commit their subordinates to abide by the sharing bargain as they would be able to in a more unified military institution because faction leaders command the obedience of their members but do not offer unconditional obedience to hierarchical superiors. If factions become dissatisfied with their share or oppose a policy decision, they have a reasonable chance of bringing off a successful coup.

If the dictator has reason to doubt higher-ranked officers' ability to prevent factions from launching rogue coups, it makes little sense for him to share and consult because doing so will not protect him. Instead, he will renege on sharing agreements and use the resources saved to pursue other strategies for deterring coups.

THE STRATEGIC CREATION OF NEW POLITICAL ACTORS

Dictators facing a factionalized armed support base use several strategies for trying to deter coups and thus reduce their vulnerability. They spend heavily on the military. They promote loyal officers and retire opponents or appoint them as ambassadors to faraway places. They resist resigning from active service so that they can maintain personal control of promotions and command assignments. They strengthen security police and try to take personal control of them. They create paramilitary forces and presidential guards led by relatives and recruited from their home regions to counterbalance the regular military.

These strategies show how much dictators fear military supporters. Though these strategies may sometimes be useful, they can also backfire because other officers try to defend their own positions of power, which depend on the credible threat to oust the dictator. Officers resent and sometimes resist policies that undermine that threat. Promotion of the dictator's friends over the heads of competent officers violates military norms and leads to anger. Officers who have been passed over for promotion, dismissed, jailed, or exiled have led many coups and insurgencies. Officers may also resent the creation of paramilitary forces. In other words, these strategies are not risk free. They are highly visible to officers and may trigger the outcome they were designed to prevent.

Bangladeshi dictator General Mohammad Zia ul-Haq, for example, created a paramilitary force soon after achieving power and remained active duty chief of staff for several years to try to control the officer corps, but every time he intervened in promotions, mutinies broke out. He frequently transferred officers, sent them for new training, and raised salaries (Codron 2007, 14). Despite these measures and many executions of rebellious soldiers, he "did not manage to make the military a safe constituency to back his rule" (Codron 2007, 15). He began organizing a support party "to create a civilian power base when he failed to achieve the united support of the armed forces" (Rizvi 1985, 226).

Creating a civilian support organization, as General Zia did, is a subtler and often safer strategy for counterbalancing the military. Paul Lewis (1980) interprets Paraguayan dictator General Alfredo Stroessner's reorganization of the Colorado Party into a support vehicle in exactly this way. After describing Stroessner's lavish spending on the military and attempts to manage its factions, Lewis notes:

Other Paraguayan presidents [also] tried to buy military support and surrounded themselves with trusted officers. In the end, however, they failed to keep the greedier or more ambitious soldiers in line. Stroessner ... achieved a real advantage over his predecessors [by] fashioning ... a dominant single-party regime, based on a purified and obedient mass organization ... This instrument ... makes it risky and unprofitable for [officers] to conspire against him. (1980, 124–25).

Samuel Decalo describes the civilianization of the military regime in Niger similarly: "Faced with continuous factionalism within both the Supreme Military Council (CSM) and his cabinet, Kountché progressively disencumbered himself of his most threatening ... officer colleagues" (1990, 277). Kountché could not afford to challenge other officers openly. "[H]e was forced rather to 'work his way around them by mobilizing the masses'" (p. 278).[8] Egyptian military dictator Gamel Abdel Nasser established the National Union party "to strengthen his personal power and weaken the RCC [Revolutionary Command Council, dominated by the Free Officers]" (Perlmutter 1974, 143).

Organizing civilians aims at reducing the dictator's dependence on the military. A civilian support base can change the calculations of potential coup plotters by reducing their chances of a credible first coup move. Civilian support for dictators, even if superficial and manipulated, can deter coups because officers do not want troops on their way to encircle the presidential palace to confront crowds of fellow citizens. As a Guatemalan officer explained to an interviewer after an aborted attempt to overthrow a military dictator, "with civilians standing in front of the artillery tanks, the commander didn't want to cause civilian casualties" (Schirmer 1998, 218).

---

[8] The quote within the quote is from *Jeune Afrique*, April 28, 1982.

Many coups are bloodless. That is because potential coup leaders choose times when they expect little opposition. Since the Russian Revolution, officers have understood that asking troops to fire on their fellow citizens can lead to indiscipline, desertions, and mutiny.[9] The military can of course defeat unarmed or lightly armed civilian demonstrators, but orders to beat or fire on civilians risk provoking defiance among troops, which would undermine the military institution and officers' political power base, so officers exercise caution in what they demand of soldiers. The strategy of organizing a mass civilian support base – a new support party – helps dictators survive because of officers' strong preference for unopposed coups. The "fear of having to deal with massive civilian opposition" deters military plotting (Brooker 1995, 111).

As an example of how deterrence can work in practice, consider this sequence of events in Paraguay. Two top officers central to General Stroessner's military support base publicly criticized his decision to sign a treaty, which they claimed would compromise Paraguayan sovereignty. Such open criticism was extremely rare during Stroessner's rule. Insiders interpreted it as a sign of widespread military disaffection, indicating danger of a coup to replace Stroessner. In response, Stroessner mobilized his civilian support vehicle, the Colorado Party, in a massive campaign. Letters supporting Stroessner poured in to the newspapers. The party organized a pro-Stroessner demonstration in the capital. They used posters, fliers, full-page newspaper ads, and sound trucks in every neighborhood to publicize the event. Local party activists contacted people in person. The party assembled more than 1,400 cars and trucks to transport people in and out of the capital. On the day of the demonstration, the vehicles deposited people at party headquarters where they were all given red party T-shirts and large pictures of the dictator to brandish during the demonstration. The party provided free lunch. All public officials and their families were required to attend. In these ways, a demonstration of 50,000 people, "enormous by Paraguayan standards," turned out to support the dictator (Lewis 1980, 148). The military dropped its opposition to the treaty and made no coup attempt (Lewis 1980, 148–50).

The ability to mobilize mass demonstrations and overwhelming votes in support of the dictator makes organized civilians useful to dictators. Dictatorships provide organized civilian supporters with access to mass communications and government-controlled transportation, as in the Paraguayan example above. They supply party cadres with the carrots and sticks to make sure that ordinary people turn out for big demonstrations or vote when told to. Some

---

[9] During the 1956 Hungarian Revolution, "Army units dispatched to the scene not only refused to attack the demonstrators but handed over their weapons ... [T]he bulk of the military either remained inactive or joined the insurgents" (Kovrig 1979, 300–301). Soviet troops had to be used. Even at Tiananmen Square, where soldiers did fire on demonstrators, troops from the countryside had to be brought in because officers and troops stationed nearby had expressed sympathy with the demonstrators.

autocratic parties also earn popular support by distributing benefits to ordinary citizens, providing good economic policy, and making opportunities for education and upward mobility available to people whose futures looked bleak before.

Parties' usefulness to dictators does not depend on supplying benefits to citizens, however. Many of the toothless parties created after armed seizures of power are incompetent, abusive, corrupt, or simply inconsequential for most people. Cadres may sell the things they are supposed to distribute, and they may use their party positions to exploit their fellow citizens. According to Mobutu Sese Seku's Commissioner of Political Affairs, for example, cadres of the party created after Mobutu's seizure of power "treat the population with arrogance ... [and] love to threaten [people] with arrest for any reason at all, large or small" (Callaghy 1984, 168). Nevertheless, these party cadres can turn out masses of citizens for votes and demonstrations of support by threatening to block their future access to important services or to turn the names of those who fail to participate over to security police. One of the main tasks of Mobutu's party was organizing mass marches to demonstrate the people's "unfailing attachment and support for the Father of the Nation" (Callaghy 1984, 324).

Party militants develop a vested interest in the dictator's survival since the dictator supplies them with benefits in return for support. The dictator's control of state revenues makes this strategy possible. Party officials and activists often draw salaries. They have preferential access to jobs in the state bureaucracy and schooling for their children. They have insider opportunities to form businesses subsidized by the government and to manage or even take ownership of expropriated businesses and land. Their connections help them to get lucrative government contracts and profit from restrictions on trade. They have the possibility of rising in the party to achieve the political power and, usually, wealth associated with high office. Party militants' stake in regime maintenance derives from these advantages. Even where party activists enjoy no current benefits, their connections open up future possibilities for rewards and upward mobility (Svolik 2012). These benefits explain why dictators never have difficulty recruiting civilians into their support parties.

Dictatorships often also task party members, especially local party officials, with reporting suspicious behavior, hostile attitudes, and the presence of strangers in villages or neighborhoods. Party militias can be used to set up roadblocks to impede the movement of weapons and to patrol at night looking for clandestine meetings and other suspicious activity. The effectiveness of such mass spy networks varies a lot from one dictatorship to another, but in some, the pervasiveness of spies and informers makes it very hard for potential plotters to find ways of meeting and communicating with each other. In this way as well, civilian support parties can reduce the likelihood of coups.

Although many dictators who achieved power without party support create one after the seizure, most do not. About 40 percent of groups that established dictatorships after 1946 were organized as parties beforehand. If monarchies are excluded, military officers led about four-fifths of the nonparty seizure groups. Of those cases in which groups not organized as parties seized power, 38 percent of the time a party was later created to support the dictatorship and 9 percent of the time the dictator coopted and allied post-seizure with an existing party that had been organized during an earlier regime. In the latter scenario, the dictator often reorganized and purged the party, refashioning it into a personal support machine. In the other 52 percent of cases, the dictator never created or coopted a party – as would be expected if party creation is attractive to dictators who depend on the support of an officer corps riven by factions but not to those whose military support base is more unified and thus more stable.

EVIDENCE THAT POST-SEIZURE PARTY CREATION AIMS TO COUNTERBALANCE FACTIONALIZED ARMED SUPPORTERS

The argument that dictators create parties after seizures of power in order to counterbalance factionalized armed support groups unable to make credible sharing bargains implies that a number of relationships should be observable in the real world. If authoritarian party creation is a strategic choice by dictators to protect themselves from armed rivals, we should see that dictators themselves initiate most party creations. We cannot observe that directly because public announcements may be untruthful or may not make clear who sought to create this new institution. We should, however, observe the following:

> *Most newly created dictatorial support parties should be led either by the dictator himself or one of his relatives or close allies.*

If dictators create parties to counterbalance their armed rivals, we should also find that party creation brings with it lessened military influence on policy-making. As an example, consider events in the Somalian dictatorship led by Major General Siad Barre. When a group of colonels ousted the elected government in 1969, they formed the Supreme Revolutionary Council (SRC) of twenty-five officers to rule the country and invited Barre to lead it. Barre had to consult with other officers on the SRC to formulate policy. After surviving several coup attempts, in 1976 the dictator created a new ruling party (the Somali Revolutionary Socialist Party, SRSP).[10] Decision-making was formally transferred from the military SRC to the seventy-five-man executive committee of the party, which included Barre's civilian supporters as well as some of the officers from the SRC. The SRC was disbanded, ending Barre's formal

---

[10] Barre's Soviet allies pressed their standard blueprint, which included a ruling party, on him. He may have created the party to please Soviet aid providers rather than to consolidate power, but it nevertheless functioned as other post-seizure dictatorial parties do to help stabilize his regime.

consultation with the military but retaining the most powerful officers in the party executive committee. After this first step toward military marginalization, the military had to share decision-making with selected civilians. Barre then further concentrated power in the party's five-member politburo, which included Barre and his son-in-law, who headed the internal security service. Over time, Barre replaced officers in the politburo with civilians, further marginalizing the military. Though the SRC was revived in 1980, it functioned thereafter as a parallel structure to the SRSP, with Barre very clearly the key regime decision maker (Adibe 1995, 8). In general, we expect that:

> *Dictators create authoritarian support parties as part of an effort to marginalize armed supporters from policy-making.*

Elections to confirm the dictator as president of the nation help to strip armed supporters of their role as king-maker and -breaker. Elections create an appearance of popular support aimed at undermining the feeling among officers that what the military gives it has the right to take away. Parties help incumbents "win" such elections even if no opposition candidates are permitted. Party activists, who are often public employees, spread the regime's messages, distribute T-shirts and benefits, hold campaign events, and make sure that citizens turn out to vote and vote for the right candidate (if they have a choice). When legislatures have the task of anointing the president, the selection of legislative candidates achieves high importance. Ruling party executive committees typically choose candidates, usually in consultation with the dictator himself. Because parties help dictators control elections, we should expect party creation to predate elections to confirm the dictator.

> *Parties should be created before elections that confirm the dictator as national executive.*

If the military were unified and able to bargain effectively, the dictator would be unable either to redistribute resources toward new civilian supporters unilaterally or to add new actors to the dictatorship's inner circle at will. Consequently, dictators infrequently propose party creation in countries with unified armed forces.[11] It is instructive therefore to observe one of the few times when a dictator misunderstood the strategic situation and tried to create a party despite the existence of a fairly unified army. General Gustavo Rojas Pinilla, the leader of a military regime in Colombia (1952–58), announced the creation of a new party, the Third Force movement. The idea received an unenthusiastic response from other officers, and languished unimplemented until the following year,

---

[11] In the small number of instances in which dictators have created post-seizure parties despite relatively unified and disciplined militaries (as in Brazil during military rule), enforced leader rotation and term limits have usually accompanied their creation. These institutions serve as an insurance policy for other officers to prevent the concentration of power in the dictator's hands that a party might otherwise facilitate.

when Rojas brought it forward again. But after meeting for several hours with an incensed group of more than a hundred other officers, Rojas let the party quietly disappear (Szulc 1959). They had made the threat to oust credible.

If more united seizure groups have greater ability to resist the personalization of rule, and hence party creation, then in military-led regimes, we might also expect to see more parties created in dictatorships led by junior officers compared with those led by senior officers. If the military is united and its hierarchy intact, junior officers who lead successful coups will turn power over to a senior officer immediately. This happens because a senior officer can command the cooperation of officers who do not share the goals of those who led the coup and because many officers would object to the violation of military norms involved in a junior officer becoming president and thus commander-in-chief of higher-ranked officers. The ability of junior officers actually to take power after a coup suggests severe factionalism. It indicates that factional loyalties have undermined the military's conventional emphasis on hierarchy and discipline.

Military dictatorships led by junior officers should create more support parties than those led by higher-ranked officers.

Finally, we think it unlikely that party creation would be the only effort a threatened dictator would make to try to safeguard himself from coups. We expect that a dictator who fears rogue coups would also invest in internal security agencies to spy on possible plotters and that he would create new, more loyal armed forces to protect himself from army attempts to oust him. If party creation is part of a broad strategy for reducing reliance on the military as a base of support, then we might expect to see that dictators who create parties are also more likely to take personal control of the security forces and to establish paramilitary forces to counterbalance the military than are dictators who can rely on a united military support base.

Dictator control over internal security services should be more likely in dictatorships that create a new support party than in those that do not.

The establishment of new paramilitary forces to protect the dictator should be more likely in dictatorships that create a new support party than in those that do not.

In what follows, we use our data set (unless otherwise noted) to examine whether these expectations match empirical reality.

Is Party Creation Usually Initiated by the Dictator?

In three-quarters of dictatorships in which a party was created after the seizure of power, we find that the dictator or a close relative led the newly created party, as would be expected if he controls party creation. The dictator always delegated the leadership of the new party to a close ally if he did not keep the post for himself or a relative.

Is Post-Seizure Party Creation Part of a Military Marginalization Strategy?

If dictators initiate party creation as part of a strategy to concentrate power, then party creation should be part of a process of marginalizing other officers from policy-making. To examine whether the process visible in Somalia is more general, we investigate how the creation of a new support party influences bargaining between the dictator and other officers by examining three related measures of military marginalization: leadership rotation within the military ruling group, consultation with other officers about policy decisions, and military representation in the cabinet. Because this argument pertains to military-led regimes, we test these expectations on dictatorships that gained power through armed seizures of power (coup, rebellion, uprising, or foreign imposition) in which the military selects the dictator. We further restrict the analysis to regimes that did not inherit a regime support party so that we can examine the extent to which the creation of a new party influences military marginalization. Among these regimes, 42 percent create a new support party, while the majority rule without a political party.[12]

The strongest indicator of collegial decision-making is the regular rotation of the presidency among officers. We expect party creation to be associated with less leadership rotation since it helps the dictator to reduce the power of his armed supporters. Regular leadership rotation is relatively rare: it occurs (at some point) in only 9 percent of military-led regimes that came to power in armed seizures (and lacked an inherited support party). We test the relationship between party creation and leader rotation using a model with regime-case fixed effects to isolate the influence of creating a new support party.[13] The model thus controls not only for cross-country variation in factors such as level of development and colonial legacy, but also for regime-specific features such as how the regime seized power, the prior experience of regime elites, and the institutional environment in which elites operate. We also control for two factors likely to influence the creation of new parties: whether the current dictator is the first leader of the regime, and the change in the international environment after the end of the Cold War to encourage the creation of "democratic-looking" political institutions such as parties. Figure 5.1 shows

---

[12] These percentages differ slightly from those above because the universe of cases in which the percentages are calculated is different. Because military-led regimes that create a new support party last longer than those that do not, the number of regime-years with a new support party is larger: 55 percent of military-led regime-years have new parties.

[13] This means we are comparing periods before and after new party creation within the same regime, and then pooling these estimates.

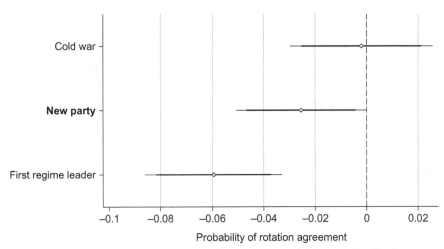

FIGURE 5.1 Post-seizure party creation and the rotation of dictatorial leadership.
Note: Estimating sample is military-led regimes with an armed seizure of power and no
prior support party.

that post-seizure party creation (*New party*) reduces the likelihood of the
regular rotation of the presidency by roughly 2.5 percent for military leaders
who seized power without a party.

We next look at two other measures of military marginalization: lack of
consultation with officers about policy decisions and civilianization of dictatorial policy-making. We capture the former using country specialists' assessments
of whether the dictator consults regularly with other officers. We measure the
latter by looking at the composition of cabinets. Military representation in the
cabinet is measured as whether the most important members of the cabinet –
other than the defense minister – are active duty or recently retired military,
police, or security officers. We define the "most important" ministries as the
prime minister (if one exists), the ministry of interior or state (which in most
countries controls the police, internal security agencies, and voting), and others
that are particularly important in the country context (e.g., the ministry
that deals with oil in oil-exporting countries). These forms of military marginalization are quite common: in more than half of these military-led regimes
(56 percent) the dictator makes most decisions without regular military consultation; and in most (77 percent), cabinets have little military representation.

To analyze the effect of party creation on these measures of military marginalization, we again estimate a linear probability model with regime-case fixed
effects, and controls for the Cold War period and first regime leader. This
approach compares *periods prior to party creation* with *periods after
party creation* within the same regime, and then pools these comparisons
into one average estimate. It accounts for cross-country variation in economic
and cultural factors as well as regime-specific features that affect elite

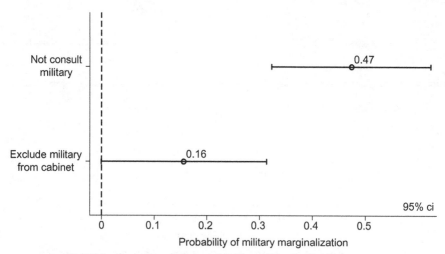

FIGURE 5.2 Post-seizure party creation and military marginalization.
Note: Estimating sample is military-led regimes with an armed seizure of power and no prior support party.

decision-making. Figure 5.2 reports the results, showing that party creation is associated with increases in both the probability that dictators eschew consultation with other officers and the likelihood that officers are excluded from the most important cabinet posts.

We also expect that if dictators create parties as part of an effort to marginalize the military, they should often be established in the run-up to elections that confirm the dictator as national leader, either directly or through the election of a legislature tasked with doing so. To assess this, we again restrict our analysis to dictatorships that came to power via armed force and lacked a support party when they seized power. In order to model the *creation* of a new support party, the sample includes only the observation years in which the dictatorship lacked a support party in the previous year.

We use data on national-level elections in which the incumbent, his party, or his chosen successor appears on the ballot to identify election years. We test the likelihood of party creation in the year before or year of elections relative to other years of the same regime.[14] As shown in Figure 5.3, we find that dictatorships are much more likely to create parties in the year of or before leader elections (31 percent) than at other times (4 percent). We also tested this prediction in a logistic regression model with control variables (Cold War, seizure type, a polynomial of years with no new party, and first leader), with

---

[14] Election data are from NELDA3. We examine only national-level presidential and parliamentary elections in which the office of the incumbent was contested (NELDA 20) and in which the incumbent or his chosen successor ran (NELDA 21).

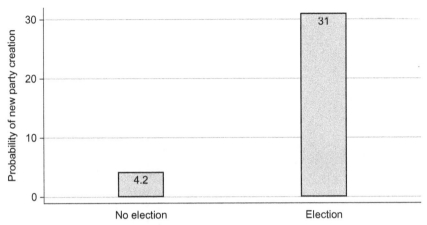

FIGURE 5.3 Post-seizure party creation before the leader's election.
Note: Military-led regimes with an armed seizure of power and no prior support party.

a similar result. Finally, we tested a linear model with regime-case fixed effects to isolate variation over time within dictatorships. Again, we find that dictatorships are more likely (18 percent) to create new parties in the run-up to elections.

Can More United Militaries Deter Party Creation?

To test the hypothesis that a more unified officer corps can better deter party creation, we use two individual traits of autocratic leaders as proxies for factionalism/unity within the officer corps: their age when they seized power and their rank just prior to the seizure of power.[15] As explained above, we think that the pre-seizure rank of the first dictator can be used as a proxy measure for factionalism. We reason that dictatorships led by highly ranked officers may depend on either factionalized or united officer corps for support (since a faction may be led by a high-ranked officer), but that those led by junior officers all rely on a factionalized military base. The future dictator's rank before the seizure of power is exogenous to promotions and other decisions made by the dictatorship. We use a parallel logic with regard to the age of the first dictator. Youthful military dictators are either low-ranked officers or higher-ranking officers in newly created armies. We expect new armies to have more problems with factionalism and indiscipline. We restrict the analysis to first leaders in regimes that came to power in armed seizures of power after 1945; there are 135 dictators in this group.

---

[15] Data on leader age from Horowitz and Stam (2014), with updates by the authors to fill in missing data.

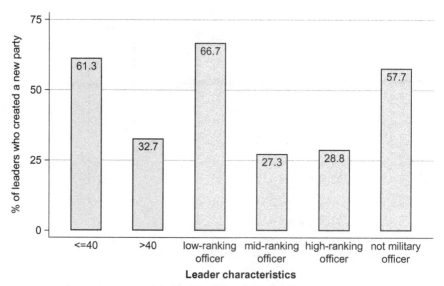

FIGURE 5.4 Post-seizure party creation, age, and rank of first dictator.

Figure 5.4 shows the share of dictators in each category that created a new party. The left two bars show that dictators forty years old or younger at the time they seized power were almost twice as likely to create a new party as those older than forty.

Next, we divide these dictators into four categories: civilians before seizing power and military officers of different ranks.[16] The four bars on the right show that two-thirds of low-ranking military dictators create new parties, while just over one-quarter of mid- and high-ranked officers do. Just over half of the civilian dictators to whom officers delegate power create post-seizure parties. In other words, young or low-ranking military dictators, who reflect factionalism in the armed forces, are even more likely to create parties than civilians.

Next, we examine whether these patterns persist when we control for potential confounders. To do this, we estimate a model that compares first regime leaders with one another, while controlling for seizure type (rebellion, uprising, and coup, with foreign imposition as the baseline category), indicators for whether the regime before the one being coded was a democracy or a military regime (with nonmilitary dictatorship as the reference category), and a variable measuring whether the dictator seized power before 1990. We cannot test dictator age at the time of seizing power in the same model as

---

[16] High-ranking officers are either generals or colonels in a military where colonel is the highest officer rank. Mid-ranking officers are colonels in a military with generals; and low-ranking officers are majors and below. Civilians are simply nonofficers. The cases include some civilian dictators because occasionally military officers delegate power to a civilian leader.

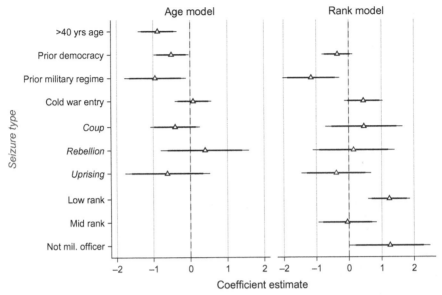

FIGURE 5.5 Effect of age, rank, and previous regime on post-seizure party creation.

variables for officer rank because age and rank are highly correlated: more than 80 percent of low-ranking officers who seize power are aged forty years or younger, while almost 90 percent of mid- and high-ranking officers are older than forty.

Figure 5.5 shows the results. The estimates in the left panel show that older dictators are less likely to create new parties than younger ones, while the right panel shows that low-ranking officers are more likely than high-ranking officers to do so. If leader age and officer rank are good proxies for military factionalism, then these findings suggest that dictatorships launched by factionalized militaries are more prone to personalization. Previous democratic experience reduces the likelihood that a new dictatorial support party will be created, as does earlier experience of military rule, relative to earlier experience of civilian-led autocracy.

Finally, as another proxy indicator of less professionalized military forces, we look at the newness of the military institution, the idea being that discipline and norms about hierarchy probably take some time to develop. In most previously colonized countries, the officer corps was created at around the time of independence, so we might expect to see more post-seizure party creation in new nations with new indigenous officer corps. To investigate this possibility, we examine the calendar time trend in post-seizure party creation by estimating a nonlinear model with a cubic calendar time polynomial and controls for how the regime seized power (coup, rebellion, and uprising, with foreign imposition as the reference category), leader's time in office (log), and whether the dictator is

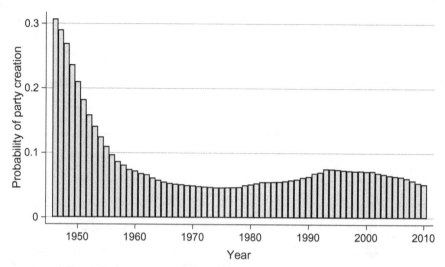

FIGURE 5.6 Post-seizure party creation over time.
Note: Sample is military-led regimes following an armed seizure of power, with no support party.

the regime's first leader.[17] Figure 5.6 shows that early in the post–World War II period, when indigenous militaries in many countries were still quite new, dictators had the highest propensity to create new parties. Party creation drops to a low point in the mid-1970s, once the period of decolonization was largely finished, and remains low for the next forty years, with a slight rise as the Cold War ended and newly independent countries emerged from the Soviet Union. Some of these countries lacked indigenous officers and had to create new officer corps at independence just as the earlier wave of newly independent countries did, and leaders in some of the post-Soviet dictatorships created new parties.

Is Party Creation Part of a Strategy to Reduce the Dictator's Vulnerability to Coups?

If dictators organize new support parties as part of a broad strategy to reduce the likelihood of coups, as suggested above, we would also expect them to engage in other coup-proofing strategies. Coup-proofing could include taking personal control of internal security in order to monitor potential plotters. It could also include establishing paramilitary forces such as presidential guards, which are often recruited from dictators' home regions. Such paramilitary forces help to defend dictators by remaining loyal during coup attempts by regular military

---

[17] For this analysis we want to model variation in party creation among countries in different time periods, so we do not include country fixed effects.

officers. In the dictatorships in which a party was created after the seizure of power, the dictator also takes personal control of internal security 72 percent of the time, compared with 27 percent of the time for dictators of regimes never supported by a party. Dictators who establish new support parties are three times as likely to establish paramilitary forces to protect them (52 percent) than are dictators who do not form post-seizure parties (17 percent).

As in the tests above, these relationships hold after we account for cross-country variation in a model with fixed effects: creating new parties is associated with a 25 percent increase in the probability of personalizing the security apparatus and a 33 percent rise in the chances of forming a paramilitary force loyal to the dictator.

These relationships indicate that dictators initiate party creation as part of a strategy to reduce dependence on the regular military when their original armed support base was too factionalized to make commitments of stable support in exchange for power sharing credible. Party creation after armed seizures of power thus paradoxically contributes to the personalization of dictatorial rule. Parties originally organized to lead a revolution or the struggle for independence may develop enough internal unity and discipline to constrain the dictator, but parties created by sitting dictators rarely do so because the dictator himself chooses and dismisses their leaders and controls the resources they need to maintain themselves.

POST-SEIZURE PARTY CREATION AND DICTATORIAL SURVIVAL

We concur with other analysts in seeing dictatorial ruling parties as autocratic survival tools (Gandhi and Przeworski 2007; Gandhi 2008; Magaloni 2008). We believe that post-seizure parties, like inherited parties, prolong dictatorial survival beyond what it would have been without them, but we see parties created after armed seizures of power as playing a quite different role in bargaining among elite actors than that played by parties that lead seizures of power. Post-seizure parties reduce intra-elite conflict by helping the dictator to concentrate power at the expense of armed supporters. The reduction in elite conflict increases dictatorial longevity.

Beatriz Magaloni's (2008) influential argument suggests that parties extend the life of dictatorships because they make possible credible intertemporal promises by the dictator to continue sharing spoils if allies continue supporting him. She suggests that parties can solve dictators' credibility problem *if* the dictator delegates control over appointments to high offices, including the dictatorship itself, to the party. When the party controls access to office, the dictator has reason to fulfill his promises because he knows he can be ousted, and his allies have reason to remain loyal because they can expect higher offices in the future. She refers to this form of power sharing as delegation by the dictator to the party, which implies that the dictator's own interests are served by it.

That seems a dubious assumption. Such agreements prolong regime survival while limiting both the dictator's time in power and his resources while in power. Thus, they do not appear to serve the dictator's interests. We suggest that dictators agree to such arrangements when they are weak relative to the rest of the dictatorial elite. That is, they agree to limit their own discretion when their choice is between becoming dictator under constraints and not being dictator at all. We can identify two empirical conditions that contribute to the dictator's relative weakness: (1) very recent accession to leadership, which we discuss in greater detail in Chapter 8 and (2) the wide dispersion of armed force among factions within the ruling group. Weakness forces the dictator to grant this form of power sharing. If power has already begun to be concentrated in the dictator's hands when the party is created, or if creating a new party helps the dictator reduce his dependence on armed supporters, he has less reason to delegate powers that may increase regime survival but not his own time in office. After most seizures of power through force, the dictator does *not* delegate control over highest offices to the party.

With the notable exception of the PRI regime in Mexico, nearly all dictatorships in which the dominant party actually controls access to high office were brought to power by parties originally organized before the seizure of power to win elections, lead revolutions, or fight for independence. In very few cases in which parties were created *after* the seizure of power does the party control access to high office.

Instead, as shown above, the dictator himself or one of his relatives leads the newly created party most of the time. In 45 percent of regimes in which the dictator creates a post-seizure support party, he also controls appointments to the party executive committee.[18] Controlling appointments to the party executive committee is symptomatic of much broader control. A contemporary observer of Mobutu (who created a post-seizure support party), for example, reports: "He controls and distributes all offices, all the posts, all advantages linked to power. All revenue, all nominations, all promotions ultimately depend on presidential good will."[19] Where the dictatorship's support party pre-dates the seizure of power, by contrast, the dictator controls appointments to the party executive committee in only 28 percent of cases.

The dictator who controls appointments to the party executive committee not only *cannot* make credible promises to share; he does not want to do so. Instead, he tries to keep his supporters insecure about the future so that they will compete with each other and work hard to demonstrate their loyalty. In Rafael Trujillo's Dominican Republic, for example, all officials had to sign undated letters of resignation before taking office. Legislators who displeased

---

[18] This and the following figure refer to dictatorships in which the regime gained power in an armed seizure (coup, uprising, rebellion, or foreign imposition).

[19] Jean Ryneman, "Comment le régime Mobutu a sapé ses propres fondements," *Le Monde Diplomatique*, May 1977.

Trujillo simply disappeared from the legislature and sometimes from the world of the living without anyone seeming to notice. Multiple legislators "resigned" within a month after nearly every election (Galíndez 1973). Cabinet ministers could find out they had lost their jobs by reading it in the newspaper (Hartlyn 1998). The statutes of the party Trujillo created after seizing power gave him the unilateral right to make decisions about who occupied these posts (Galíndez 1973). Under Mobutu, "state-party personnel are completely dependent on him for selection, appointment, and maintenance in power ... The powers of appointment and dismissal that Mobutu wields create constant uncertainty for all officials, which helps to maintain their loyalty to him" (Callaghy 1984, 180).

In many of the regimes in which the dictator's intertemporal commitment problems have *not* been solved, both dictators and dictatorships nevertheless last a long time. Mobutu lasted thirty-seven years in a very turbulent political environment, and Trujillo for thirty-one. Dictatorships that achieved power by force but then later created post-seizure parties last more than twice as long on average as otherwise similar regimes without support parties. To sum up our argument, even parties that do not deliver benefits beyond a relatively small group and do not control access to highest offices can still prolong both dictator and regime survival.

Next, we compare the effect on dictatorial survival of ruling parties established before and after seizures of power. We test a linear probability model with country and year fixed effects, controls for regime duration, and indicator variables for party history: pre-seizure electoral party, pre-seizure rebel party, no party (reference category), and new party (post-seizure creation). This analysis accounts for the fact that some regimes were still in power at the end of the sample period in 2010. The results show the following average yearly regime collapse rates: 10.1 percent probability of breakdown for dictatorships without a support party; less than half that, 4.5 percent, for those in which a party was created post seizure; 3.8 percent for regimes led by parties first organized to run in elections before the initiation of dictatorship; and only 1.9 percent for regimes led by parties organized to lead insurgencies. Comparison between the breakdown rate for regimes lacking support parties and those that create a party post-seizure provides compelling evidence that party creation prolongs survival because regimes that lack support parties and those that create one post-seizure have similar origins: both typically achieved power by force (most often via coup).[20] Apparently, autocracies supported by parties that have not solved the dictator's commitment problem – that is, parties that we

[20] Regimes that lacked a support party at the time of seizure but later created parties came to power via a coup in 65 percent of cases; those that did not create a party seized power in a coup in 60 percent of cases. In contrast, only 17 percent of regimes supported by a preexisting party achieved power via coup.

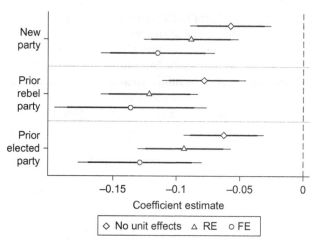

FIGURE 5.7 Parties and regime survival.
Note: Negative coefficient estimates interpreted as a decrease in the likelihood of collapse, relative to the comparison group: regimes that *never* have a support party.

know did not control the dictator's access to office because he achieved it before the party came into existence – nevertheless last quite a long time.

Figure 5.7 displays these same relationships as comparisons among regimes without support parties and regimes supported by parties created at different times for various purposes. In all models, dictatorships with support parties are less likely to end. In models that include fixed effects (circle symbol), post-seizure party creation is associated with a bit more than a 10 percent decrease in the likelihood of regime collapse compared with having no support party. Parties originally created before the seizure of power to run in elections or lead insurgencies reduce the likelihood of regime breakdown even more, but not by a great deal more.

These comparisons show that armed forces by themselves often do not provide a reliable support base for autocracy. Consequently, dictators who are delegated power by a seizure group that did not need to be organized as a party in order to achieve power can improve the odds of retaining it by creating a support party to counterbalance the potential volatility of military support.

THE EFFECT OF POST-SEIZURE PARTY CREATION ON THE LIKELIHOOD OF COUPS

If our argument about party creation is correct – that it is pursued by dictators propelled to power by factionalized armed seizure groups in order to lessen their risk of ouster by force – then we should see fewer coups and coup attempts in regimes that create parties than in those that opt not to. To evaluate this expectation, we look at the incidence of coups in dictatorships *without support*

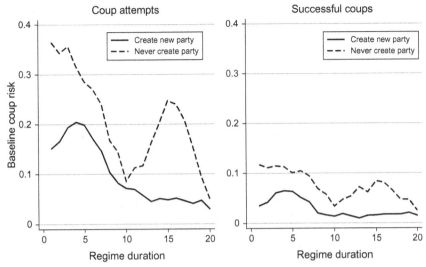

FIGURE 5.8 Coups in dictatorships with post-seizure parties or no parties.

parties at the time of the seizure of power. We compare the likelihood of coups in dictatorships that initially lacked a support party but later created one with those that never organized supporters into a party at all.

We begin by looking at the differences in the baseline rate of coup attempts – both failed attempts and successes – between regimes that had created parties and those that never did.[21] Coup risk declines on average during the first few years in all kinds of dictatorships, as dictators try to remove their least reliable supporters from troop commands, and the least stable dictatorships collapse and exit the sample. Figure 5.8 shows that during the first two decades in power, regimes that never create a party are at greater risk of both coup attempts (shown in the left panel) and successful coups (shown in the right). This implies that dictatorships that never create a party are particularly susceptible to coup conspiracies.

Because we have argued that the creation of a mass-based civilian support party deters officers from staging coups, we expect to see a larger difference in coup attempts than in successful coups. A comparison of the left and right panels of Figure 5.8 shows larger differences between the two lines for attempted than for successful coups. Both panels also show that the coup risk for dictatorships that have created support parties remains stably lower for more than a decade after party creation.

[21] The baseline coup rate is the five-year moving average of the number of coups and coup attempts, by regime duration year, divided by the number of regime-years at risk of having a coup (for each regime duration year).

In contrast, there is a large spike in coup attempts after the first decade in power for regimes that never create a party. Typically, armed seizures of power are followed by retirements of officers ranked above those who take power and a purge of officers who supported the ousted government. Rapid promotions for the cohort of the active coup plotters and those just below them follow. These changes in the officer corps create a cohort of coup beneficiaries, but over time many of these officers will retire or be dismissed, creating opportunities for younger officers to gain command of troops. Coups depend on troop command, and these junior officers become the coup plotters of the future. In this way, the normal seniority-based promotions inherent in military careers interact with the ambitions and criticisms of junior officers to produce the spike in coup attempts that begins after about ten years in power unless a well-established support party deters them.

The difference in trends for regimes with and without ruling parties is important for showing that party creation has consequences. If the trend lines moved in similar ways in each set of regimes, we might wonder if preexisting differences accounted for the difference in coups. However, the trends diverge, suggesting the limitations in the coup-proofing strategies that can be deployed by dictators dependent on all-military support bases.

For further evidence that dictatorships with parties created post-seizure are less vulnerable to coups, we note the success rate for coups conditional on attempts: while 22 percent of coup attempts in regimes with post-seizure parties succeed, nearly 29 percent succeed in regimes that never established a support party. After five years in power, the difference is greater: only 20 percent of coups in regimes with post-seizure parties succeed, while the share that succeeds in regimes with no party increases to 35 percent.[22] This suggests that once we account for all the factors that lead to coup attempts in the first place, dictators who have created a new support party have greater ability to thwart them. This result most likely reflects the strong correlation between post-seizure party creation and investment in other coup-proofing strategies, especially the dictator's establishment of new paramilitary forces recruited from especially loyal regions. Republican guards, presidential guards, and other kinds of specially recruited paramilitary forces are usually stationed near the presidential palace and tasked explicitly with defending him from armed challenges.

Next, we test a series of parametric models to evaluate whether creating a party reduces coup risk. We employ a nonlinear estimator with random effects for each regime. First, we test a specification with a minimum of control variables: time since last coup (logged), whether the dictator is civilian

---

[22] These differences are statistically significant. During the first five years, however, the difference in success rate is not statistically significant. Remember that these are the success rates for coup attempts against dictatorships that achieved power without the support of a party, most of which are led by the military. The higher success rate found in other studies refers to coups against democracies and other dictatorships as well (e.g., Singh 2014).

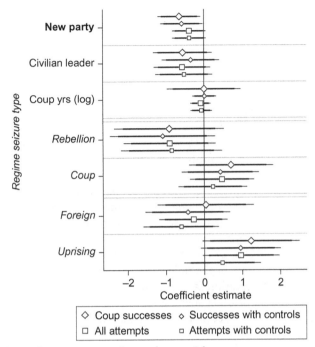

FIGURE 5.9 Post-seizure party creation and coup risk.

(as opposed to military), and how the regime seized power (coup, rebellion, foreign imposition, or popular uprising).[23] The top set of estimates in Figure 5.9, shown as large diamonds, is from this model, with successful coups as the dependent variable. Next, we add a set of standard control variables often thought to affect coup risk: GDP per capita (log, lagged), economic growth (lagged two-year moving average), oil rents (log, lagged), military expenditure (log, lagged), civil and international conflict (lagged), and protests (lagged). In the third specification we return to the minimal model but use *all coup attempts* (failed and successful ones) as the dependent variable. In the final model, we add controls to the *all attempts* model. In all four tests, post-seizure party creation is associated with a lower incidence of successful coups; however, the estimate for *New Party* is only statistically significant at the 0.10 level for the *all attempts* models.

To further explore how the creation of new support parties influences coup risk, we estimate a conditional logit model that compares the coup risk of individual leaders before and after new party creation.[24] This analysis looks only at the

[23] The reference category for seizure type is nonviolent, which includes family seizures, authoritarianization, and rule-change seizures.
[24] The specification includes the time since last coup (logged) and a binary indicator for the Cold War period.

sixty-seven leaders in dictatorships that initially lacked a support party but later created one; that is, it looks only at rulers who held power during periods both with and without a support party. Importantly, by focusing on the variation over time for individual dictators, we can rule out alternative explanations based on differences between leaders, regimes, and countries. The results from this test (not shown) also indicate that coup risk is lower after new party creation.[25]

Thus far in this chapter, we have combined reshuffling and regime-change coups when examining how party creation protects the dictator from ouster. Our theory about why dictators who achieved power by force later create parties to organize civilian supporters, however, claims that party creation helps the *dictator* concentrate personal power over other members of the ruling coalition. That idea leads to the expectation that new parties should lengthen dictators' time in power by deterring coups aimed at replacing leaders (reshuffling coups), but not necessarily those aimed at ending the regime. Members of the ruling group who want a change in leadership but not the end of the regime organize most leader-change coups. Regime-change coups, however, are usually organized by factions of the military excluded from the inner circle of the dictatorship. If party creation is a dictator's strategy for increasing his own power relative to that of other members of the dictatorial ruling group, as we have argued, it should protect him from leader-shuffling coups but not necessarily from regime-ending coups.

Figure 5.10 shows the results from a series of random effects models similar to those in Figure 5.9. The first two estimates are from models of leader-shuffling coups that treat regime-change coups as right-censored events, while the latter two estimates are from models of regime-change coups that treat reshuffling coups as right-censored events. These tests indicate that post-seizure parties are associated with fewer leader-shuffling coups but not with fewer regime-change coups.[26]

This evidence is consistent with our theory that post-seizure party creation is a strategy to protect dictators from their erstwhile allies in the armed forces. That is, party creation protects dictators from coups led by ambitious regime insiders eager to take the dictator's place without ending the regime. Post-seizure party creation is less reliably helpful for deterring coups aimed at ending the regime. We know from the findings reported in Figure 5.1 that the creation of new parties contributes to the survival of regimes as well as individual

---

[25] This result is statistically significant only at the 0.10 level. We also test similar models that divide the newly created parties into two categories: those led by the regime leader (or close relative) and those led by someone else. We find that, as expected, only those newly created support parties led by the regime leader are correlated with lower coup risk. These are the cases in which party creation contributes most to the personalization of rule. This finding is highly significant and persists in a similar model that isolates the temporal variation within regimes.

[26] These results also hold in a conditional logit model and in linear probability models with regime-case fixed effects.

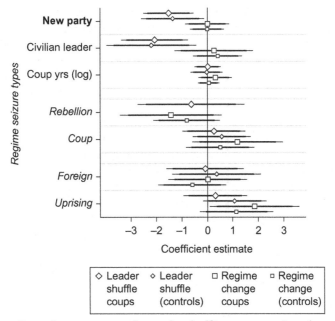

FIGURE 5.10 Post-seizure party creation and reshuffling versus regime-change coups.

dictators, but the results shown in Figure 5.10 imply that the extra *regime* durability associated with party creation comes not through coup deterrence but through some other mechanism. We discuss this other mechanism, the civilian side of how newly created parties contribute to regime durability, in Chapter 6. Those coups that do end the entire regime – rather than just replace the dictator – occur most often when junior officers from excluded ethnic groups successfully oust the regime leader and allied senior officers. Thus, the evidence from differentiating regime-change from leader-shuffling coups suggests that the kind of parties created by dictators post-seizure do not successfully coopt ethnic groups excluded from executive power and the senior officer ranks.

To conclude this section, dictators who organize post-seizure parties are less vulnerable to coups than dictators in regimes unsupported by a ruling party, as our argument detailing the motivations for post-seizure party creation implies. Further, the evidence suggests that post-seizure party creation helps deter coups emanating from regime insiders rather than those plotted by groups of soldiers excluded from the ruling group.

CONCLUSION

Dictators who achieve power through force of arms can face special difficulties in consolidating their rule because many of their supporters control sufficient weapons to oust them. This chapter has focused on the consequences for intra-elite bargaining of the interaction between the dispersion of armed force across members of the ruling group and the group's division into multiple factions. When many members of the seizure group – and the ruling coalition it becomes – command armed forces sufficient to threaten the dictator with ouster, they can achieve an effective power-sharing bargain with the dictator *if* they can maintain their own unity. If, however, deep factions divide an armed seizure group, those included in the dictator's inner circle cannot credibly commit their subordinates to support the dictator if he shares power and spoils. Consequently, power-sharing bargains cannot be maintained.

When the dictator cannot secure his hold on power by agreeing to share with the rest of the seizure group, he is better off keeping a larger share of the spoils and other benefits of office so that he can invest in other strategies. We suggest that dictators who depended on armed supporters to achieve power, but who cannot count on those supporters for holding onto it, often try to counterbalance their armed supporters with unarmed ones. To accomplish this, they organize civilian support networks and appoint their leaders to the dictatorial inner circle. The addition of civilian supporters to the ruling group changes bargaining within the group by increasing the diversity of interests and further reducing the unity of the inner circle; this in turn undermines the bargaining power of members of the dictatorial inner circle relative to the dictator. It thus contributes to the personalization of dictatorial rule. These civilian support organizations are usually called parties.

The evidence shown in this chapter is consistent with the argument that factionalism within an armed seizure group increases the likelihood of post-seizure party creation. We also offer evidence that post-seizure party creation usually reflects a dictator's interest rather than the collective interest of the ruling group: dictators usually assume a new party's leadership themselves; new parties tend to be established in the run-up to elections that "legitimize" the dictator's occupation of national executive office; and dictators often control appointments to the executive committees of ruling parties created post-seizure. We further show that post-seizure party creation is associated with the marginalization of military influence within the dictatorial inner circle.

Finally, we provide several kinds of evidence that post-seizure party creation is an effective dictatorial survival strategy. It is associated with both longer dictator tenure in office and longer regime survival. Party creation seems to protect dictators from coups, as would be expected if it were a strategy for reducing the dictator's vulnerability to ousters launched from an unreliable military force. After controlling for other factors known or believed to affect the incidence of coups, post-seizure party creation is associated with a reduced incidence of both coup attempts and successful coups.

Further investigation shows that post-seizure party creation affects the incidence of leader-change coups but not regime-change coups. This is what would be expected if party creation is a strategy used by dictators to safeguard *themselves* from armed insiders rather than a group strategy for *regime* defense. The findings in this chapter thus explain how party creation extends the survival of individual dictators: it is associated with a reduction in the likelihood of coups that would replace one dictator with another insider. They do not, however, explain how new dictatorial support parties contribute to regime survival. We turn to that question in the next chapters.

Post-seizure party creation thus seems paradoxical within the usual way political scientists think about authoritarian parties and support coalitions. The creation of a mass party through which some benefits are channeled from the political center to ordinary citizens seems to imply the broadening of the dictator's support coalition. At the same time, however, such broadening among the mostly powerless accompanies a disorganization and eventually a narrowing of the support coalition among the powerful, as threatening military supporters are replaced by less powerful civilian ones. In most cases, much of the military becomes marginalized after post-seizure party creation. Civilian party leaders handpicked by the dictator replace military members of the dictatorial inner circle, but they have much less ability to constrain or oust the dictator than do armed supporters. Post-seizure party creation thus transforms the dictator from a relatively equal bargainer within a group of others similar to himself into an arbiter among competing support factions, reducing his dependence on all of them and enhancing his individual discretion over resources and policy.

PART III

RULING SOCIETY

Implementation and Information Gathering

6

Why Parties and Elections in Dictatorships?

IMPLEMENTATION, MONITORING, AND INFORMATION GATHERING

As the initial conflicts within the inner circle become resolved, and elite decision-making becomes somewhat predictable, the ruling group must turn its attention to the rest of the country. Most dictatorships face some very basic problems when it comes to trying to rule the places they have taken control of. One ordinary problem is the need to motivate the implementation on the ground of decisions made in the inner circle, especially in new dictatorships when local officials may have owed their jobs to the ousted government.

Policy implementation requires the cooperation of local officials, who must be converted to the new order after regime change or recruited afresh, and then monitored to assure collaboration and prevent abuse of office. Without effective monitoring, local officials can sabotage policies, abusive ones can motivate popular opposition to the new regime, and resources extracted from citizens may stick to officials' fingers rather than reaching central coffers. Direct monitoring requires expertise and resources, however. Many dictatorships lack the trained and loyal manpower needed to do it and the revenues needed to pay them.

Information shortfalls are another and related ordinary problem (Wintrobe 1998). The dictatorial elite needs information about who opposes them, how their policies are working, and what disasters and difficulties afflict people in different parts of the country. Central leaders have difficulty acquiring needed information. Local officials engaged in sabotage, theft, or abuse of power will not provide accurate reports on local conditions. Even loyal and honest local officials dread being blamed for problems if they reveal them, and everyone fears retribution for bearing bad news. The potential for violent and arbitrary punishment in dictatorships distorts and disrupts the information reaching regime elites.

Cadres and officials whose futures depend on successful performance of tasks assigned to them by regime leaders have incentives to report successes and to hide policy failures and popular opposition. Writing about the last years of the East German dictatorship, which fell to popular opposition in 1989, Peter Grieder (2012, 91) reports:

The heavily varnished reports sent to the centre by district and local party officials only fortified the rarefied fool's paradise in which party leaders cocooned themselves. Most functionaries dared not submit truthful reports lest they be blamed for the problems identified in them. In 1988 and 1989, almost all failed to inform the Politburo accurately of the deteriorating situation.

Several of the most horrific dictatorial policy failures, such as the famine caused by the Great Leap Forward in China and the mass starvation during Pol Pot's rule in Cambodia, resulted partly from local cadres' unwillingness to report appalling policy failure on the ground (Kiernan 1982; Manning and Wemheuer 2011).

To solve some of their problems with policy implementation, monitoring, and information gathering, dictatorships establish seemingly democratic institutions, such as elections, mass parties, and legislatures, as we detail later. In order to engage ordinary people, institutions dependent on popular involvement must distribute benefits to motivate citizen participation. In return for access to benefits, help, and opportunities, citizens join the ruling party, vote, and demonstrate regime support in other ways. Mass organizations also facilitate mostly nonviolent forms of coercion and social control. The monitoring of local officials and information gathering are by-products of the more visible distributive and mobilizational functions of popular institutions.

In this chapter, we discuss some of the institutional arrangements used in dictatorships to enmesh, coopt, and gather information from ordinary citizens. We first describe the uses of ruling parties to routinize the exchange between the political elite and citizens of benefits for loyalty and service, while solving some of the dictatorial elite's implementation and monitoring problems. Next, we discuss how legislatures fit into the system of local information gathering and distribution of resources to citizens. Then we show the way elections incentivize the extension of patron–client networks down to the village and neighborhood level and the transfer of information from the grassroots to the center. We demonstrate that elections, even elections without choice, increase the benefits that reach the grassroots. This chapter thus focuses mostly on the deployment of positive incentives to encourage information gathering, monitoring, and citizen support.

We also explain the staying power of these institutions once they have been established. The institutions that engage citizens tend to stabilize and become costly to change, as large numbers of individuals develop an interest in maintaining them. The tendency of mass institutions toward stabilization contrasts with the fragility of agreements made within the ruling group, where temptations to renege on agreements are ever-present. The stability of mass institutions contributes to regime routinization.

ELITE COMPETITION AND INSTITUTIONS THAT ENGAGE CITIZENS

As members of the inner circle strive to improve their standing relative to others in the elite, they seek new sources of information and new ways to bolster the clientele networks that support and depend on them. Formal political institutions that reach, engage, and collect information from ordinary citizens can contribute to achieving these goals. Besides newly created ruling parties, explained in Chapter 5, such institutions include inherited ruling parties, elections, and legislatures. The institutions that extend distributive, mobilizational, and information-gathering capacity to the grassroots are run by, and report to, particular members of the dictatorial elite. They increase the power of the members of the inner circle who control them because they create resources that are useful in inner-circle competition. Institution creation generates jobs for supporters and thus helps the individuals who lead them to build their individual clientele networks. Institutions also generate new information streams that benefit those with access to them.

Besides these advantages to particular individuals, outreach institutions are expected to help secure the regime,[1] which is the reason members of the inner circle who do not benefit directly from them agree to their creation. These institutions can contribute to regime persistence by distributing benefits to ordinary citizens – and thus reducing their likelihood of joining opposition campaigns or uprisings – by increasing the likelihood of discovering plots and by reducing predatory behavior by local officials.

PARTIES

In Chapter 5, we focused on the use of newly created parties to counterbalance factionalized military support. Here, we emphasize other uses of parties: their information-gathering, mobilizational, and distributive activities.

The obvious function of dictatorial ruling parties is to distribute benefits to the nonelites on whom the dictatorship's survival depends. The party routinizes the exchange of material benefits (such as salaries, profit opportunities, favors,

---

[1] A number of studies have shown that dictatorships supported by parties last longer than those that lack a support party (Geddes 1999; Gandhi 2008; Magaloni 2008). All members of the dictatorial elite benefit from this.

special access, various kinds of goods, and services) for the loyalty, effort, and time of party activists and members. The ruling party organization monitors the performance of party cadres to make sure the dictatorial leadership is getting its money's worth from those to whom it provides benefits – in theory if not always in practice.

If the party led the seizure of power, then members of the party need to be rewarded for the risks they took and the privations they suffered to make the seizure possible. Regardless of how the dictatorial elite achieved power, however, the dictatorship continues to need active effort by loyalists to handle policy implementation, monitoring both officials and society, and information gathering as well as the organization of winning votes and the other displays of support that deter overt opposition.

Demonstrations to support dictators are rarely spontaneous. They require the work, organization, and logistical skills of many people, and these people have to have already developed their links to the rest of the community. It thus makes sense for dictatorships to use ruling-party networks to orchestrate support demonstrations. Such demonstrations serve serious purposes. Like election victories, they signal strength. Outsiders often respond to obviously orchestrated displays of popular support with puzzlement or ridicule because they assume the demonstrations aim to fool people about the dictatorship's popularity. We think this reaction reflects a misunderstanding. Such demonstrations show the strength of leaders and the regime in that they demonstrate the resources and organizational capacity to turn out huge crowds, choreograph their activities in minute detail, and prevent unwanted demands or unruliness from arising during mass actions that bring many thousands of people into face-to-face contact where they could potentially share grievances and plot unrest.

We interpret the over-the-top displays of grief and gargantuan demonstrations after Kim Jong-Il's death and his son's succession in North Korea,[2] for example, as a costly signal aimed at two different audiences during a time of regime weakness. One signal aimed to show foreigners that the population would defend the regime if it was attacked. The other signaled the resources and commitment of the faction supporting Kim Jong-Un to members of the elite who doubted the wisdom of choosing a politically inexperienced twenty-something as regime leader.

The need to organize demonstrations and election victories makes intermittent demands on party activists, but policy implementation, monitoring, and information gathering are their everyday tasks. Central leaders expect to solve the implementation problem by appointing party members to administrative jobs. Leaders assume that people who helped put them in power share

---

[2] "North Korean Leader Kim Jong-il Dies 'of Heart Attack,'" 2011, BBC News (December 19), www.bbc.co.uk/news/world-asia-16239693 (accessed November 20, 2015).

their ideas and interests and will therefore be loyal. The ruling group tries to assure the loyalty of officials and policy implementation on the ground by limiting government jobs and official posts to party members. They hope that shared dependence on the ruling party will align officials' incentives with their own and thus prevent sabotage and noncompliance with central directives.

If the party lacks sufficient educated members, they must continue to rely on some of the ousted government's employees but use party militants to monitor as much of their behavior and performance as they can. Monitoring is not limited to officials whose loyalty is suspect, however. Ruling parties also try to monitor their members who hold official positions to prevent shirking, stealing, incompetence, and other human frailties.

Cadres assigned to locations outside the capital are also expected to monitor local conditions and local people for signs of disgruntlement or opposition. Local officials are the main source of information about the grassroots for leaders in the capital. Officials are required to report on local affairs, expressions of opposition, strangers visiting, movements of people through the area, and anything else central authorities might consider signs of impending danger as well. In this way, they contribute to the information available to leaders. Leaders may also use party loyalists as "a network of unpaid spies and informers [in order] to keep all potential enemies under surveillance" (Lewis 1980, 150).

Central leaders assign party cadres many other tasks as well, for example, explaining policy choices to other citizens, and thus building support and compliance with them. The dictatorial elite expects party activists to "persuade the masses to … fulfill obligations to the state as well as to comply with laws and party resolutions. At the same time they are expected to give higher-level party authorities accurate feedback about both basic needs and concerns of the population and its reactions to party policies" (Porter 1993, 71).

The ruling party usually controls local governance through its control over the choice of local officials. Local administration can include law and order, provision of social services and emergency aid, hiring in local offices and schools, and allocation of basic infrastructure like electricity and piped water. If parties are well developed enough to control so many things of importance in daily life, citizens have strong reasons to cooperate with the ruling party and to refrain from overt opposition.

Party cadres are supposed to provide sufficiently good local governance and distribute enough to ordinary people to prevent the mobilization of opposition. Some mass parties also incorporate large numbers of ordinary people in networks that distribute smaller or intermittent benefits. Typically, party networks distribute whatever benefits the dictatorship makes available to nonelite supporters during election campaigns and via party control of local government. Party activists trade material benefits to citizens in return for political support, just as in democracies.[3] Regime leaders want their parties to develop clientele networks down to the grassroots in order to make sure goods reach the masses and information is collected.

These are important and time-consuming tasks. Doing them well requires effort and skill as well as loyalty. Party cadres must be paid for their time and effort. The payment of salaries and other kinds of benefits to party cadres builds and maintains a fairly wide network of people who receive something of value from the dictatorship and therefore tend to support it. Public employees and officials, who are ruling-party members in most dictatorships organized by parties, often form the core of popular support for dictatorships. Those employed by the party tend to be the dictatorship's most committed supporters because their own well-being depends on regime survival.

The Limitations of Dictatorial Ruling Parties

Dictatorial ruling parties often come up short with regard to accomplishing all the tasks central elites assign to them. Many of the reasons for their failure to perform well lie in human nature. The dictator himself may cause additional problems with the quality and motivations of party cadres, however.

Because parties have so much mobilizational potential, dictators exercise vigilance to make sure the party support base remains their own rather than being used by those with the responsibility for day-to-day party leadership or their allies. To prevent other members of the inner circle from using party-organized mass mobilization on their own behalf, dictators often interfere with party leadership. Most of the time (80 percent),[4] the dictator himself leads the ruling party.

The party strategy of General Francisco Franco of Spain provides an example of such vigilance and its consequences. Franco delegated the task of creating a support party from the civilian groups that backed his military uprising to his brother-in-law, making certain that the party did not become a challenging center of power during the early days when a chaotic political environment made that most possible. After its first years, when the regime had stabilized, Franco selected new leaders, reduced the importance of the party, and halved its budget (Payne 1987). Throughout the long years of his rule, Franco used the party to counterbalance his military support base, carefully preventing either one from becoming the dominant force in the dictatorial inner circle. By the 1950s, "no one belonged to the party who did not in some way make a living from it" (Payne 1961, 262). Franco, however, repeatedly

---

[3] Although most dictatorships use a party to organize distribution, dictators who have chosen not to organize a party can instead use administrative officials to distribute state resources to buy the cooperation of citizens. Several Middle Eastern monarchies have used this strategy.

[4] This number differs from the one noted in Chapter 5 because it refers to the proportion of all dictatorial ruling parties, not just those created after seizures of power.

resisted party leaders' efforts to rebuild it into a more engaged organization that could attract idealistic adherents and thus potentially increase its political heft. The instrumental nature of most party members' loyalty did not hinder the party's ability to turn out huge, cheering crowds for Franco to harangue, an activity he enjoyed (Payne 1987).

The Spanish example also illustrates a very common reason for the failure of dictatorial ruling parties to carry out all the tasks assigned to them. People join them for instrumental reasons. Once dictatorships are established, opportunists typically swamp even the parties that attracted very idealistic and committed members before seizing power. Some dictatorships, notably those controlled by communist parties, invest heavily in screening applicants and monitoring members' behavior, but most do not. Parties need not be all-encompassing or highly disciplined organizations in order to be useful to dictators, and most dictatorial ruling parties are not. Even if the party cannot be used as an organizational weapon, it still builds robust patron–client networks linking regime insiders to party members. The delivery of benefits via these patron–client networks creates vested interests in regime survival.

These vested interests, however, often fail to reach all areas of the country because many real-world ruling parties have lacked the number of trained and disciplined cadres needed to penetrate society effectively, especially during the first years after seizures of power or following post-seizure party creation. As a result, the number and location of people incorporated into the dictatorship's support network can be quite limited. Moreover, central regime leaders often lack the ability to monitor the behavior of local party cadres. The task of distributing goods to citizens creates opportunities for party cadres and local officials to steal, embezzle, and abuse their power. As we explain below, elections help to reduce abuses that most dictatorial ruling parties could not otherwise control.

Why Dictatorial Ruling Parties Persist

Despite these limitations, all dictatorial ruling parties control the allocation of some benefits that citizens value. Even those that have not successfully developed grassroots networks create strong attachments with those people whose jobs or other benefits depend on the ruling party. As a result, if parties are established, they tend to become self-sustaining. Organizing a ruling party, allocating resources to it to pay employees and distribute some benefits to others, and building the networks needed to link the regime inner circle to local leaders create widespread vested interests in the party's persistence. Citizens want to continue receiving whatever benefits the party delivers. Elites who occupy high offices in the ruling party would be alienated by losing their posts, which might lead to efforts to unseat the dictator.

In dictatorships organized by parties, all members of the ruling group – whether officers or civilians – derive some benefits from the party, but one member leads it, and a few control key party resources, most importantly, appointments to government jobs and party offices. Whoever controls the party has some influence on membership in the inner circle itself, as well as lower levels of leadership and vast numbers of jobs in both government and party. Nor would the dictator usually want to eliminate a counterbalance to the military. Disbanding the party would leave the military unchecked, and thus a greater threat to him.

Consequently, once in existence, regime support parties are rarely disbanded. Indeed, only 10 percent of dictatorships with support parties later dissolve them. Where they are disbanded, regime insiders often replace them with a new party led by many of the same people.

To sum up, parties seem to be an effective way to organize regime supporters and to routinize the distribution of benefits to them and the gathering of information from them. From a dictator's point of view, a party that organizes quotidian, largely instrumental support may be safer than one that can mobilize great activism and idealism, unless the dictator himself feels confident about his ability to control and direct it. Many dictators, like Franco, talk the talk of heroic party activism, but in practice rely on the government bureaucracy for making policy and allot to the party only humdrum tasks. Even where ruling parties have little real capacity to affect policy and leadership choice,[5] they tend to persist because they deliver benefits both to the dictatorship's inner circle by increasing regime stability and to party activists and members.

DICTATORIAL LEGISLATURES

Some analysts have argued that dictatorial legislatures serve as arenas for policy bargaining (Gandhi and Przeworski 2006; Gandhi and Przeworski 2007; Gandhi 2008; Malesky and Schuler 2010). Case studies and interviews with deputies often suggest a different picture, however. The Indonesian parliament during the long Suharto dictatorship, for example, "never drafted its own legislation and ... never rejected a bill submitted by the executive branch. It has no say in cabinet appointments [and] little influence over economic policy" (Schwarz 2000, 272). In Guinea Bissau, the assembly provided "pro-forma electoral acclamation of those appointed by the [ruling] party to government posts. It also [served] as a public forum for the airing of party propaganda and for the routine yes-voting on party policies" (Forrest 1987, 113). During the Diori dictatorship in Niger, "the assembly never served as a serious forum for debate" (Decalo 1990, 257). Ellen Lust-Okar argues that in dictatorial legislatures "competition is not over policy-making. Many (and in some cases most) policy arenas are off-limits to parliamentarians ... Rather ... [legislatures]

---

[5] See Brooker (1995) for a comparison of the ruling parties in a number of party-based autocracies with regard to how large a role they play in policy choice.

provide an important arena for competition over access to state resources" (2006, 459).

Interviews with deputies reinforce Lust-Okar's claim. In response to the question "To what extent do you believe that the parliament is able to influence the government?" only 7 percent of Jordanian deputies thought parliament played a large role (Lust-Okar 2006, 470). An Ivoirian deputy responded to questions about his activities as follows: "Individual deputies have no business trying to discuss [policies made by the ruling party politburo] in the Assembly because rhetoric is a waste of time and could even be harmful" (Zolberg 1964, 282). Another reported that deputies are "concerned mainly with gaining access to ... tangible benefits for their constituents" (Zolberg 1964, 283).

Our reading of the evidence is that most authoritarian legislatures play a role in the allocation of private benefits and local public goods to citizens, but that they have little influence on policy (Truex 2016).

The most valuable function of legislatures to dictatorships may be that they incentivize competition among regime supporters for the opportunities the legislature makes available to deputies themselves. The ruling elite's decision to elect a legislature creates highly desirable plums to be distributed to party militants by the dictator or those to whom he delegates the task of choosing candidates. Deputies usually receive salaries and other perquisites such as the use of cars and subsidized housing, as well as access to many kinds of opportunities and favors that can be used to help their friends, further their careers, and accumulate personal wealth.[6] So, ambitious people have strong reasons to compete for nominations and office. Ruling elites use this competition to motivate deputies to extend their distributive networks to the grassroots and transmit information to the center from the grassroots, as we describe in the next section.

ELECTIONS

Most dictatorships led by parties have regular popular elections. Until about 1990, most held single-candidate or single-list elections that gave voters no choice at all. Even elections without choice involve substantial costs because a campaign has to be organized to reach all parts of the country, and in most dictatorships, elites want to be able to claim high rates of voter participation. The frequency of elections in dictatorships, especially choice-free elections, raises the question: What are they for?

The dictatorships that held regular choice-free elections included the communist regimes and a number of one-party dictatorships in developing countries. Before the end of the Cold War, only about one-quarter of party-led

---

[6] See Zolberg (1964, 192–93), Lust-Okar (2006), and Blaydes (2011) for discussions of the benefits of elective office.

autocracies allowed opposition in legislative elections. The proportion that allows some opposition has risen to nearly two-thirds (61 percent) since the end of the Cold War.

When voters have some choice but the regime outlaws important parties, restricts suffrage to prevent substantial numbers of people from voting, or tilts the electoral playing field in ways that give the ruling party substantial advantages, we label elections semi-competitive. Dictatorships have inventive ways to bias election outcomes. Current semi-competitive electoral systems include those that:

- Permit all opposition parties to compete but use control of the media, interference with opposition campaigning, fraud, violence, and large-scale state spending to bias outcomes
- Permit some parties to compete but not others (e.g., regimes that outlaw popular Islamist parties while allowing secular opposition)
- Permit no opposition parties but allow independents to contest elections
- Permit competition among ruling-party candidates but not opposition parties.

Terms such as electoral authoritarian, competitive authoritarian, and quasi-democratic refer to dictatorships that hold regular semi-competitive elections, or sometimes a subset of such systems.[7] Since the end of the Cold War, international donors have tied foreign aid and other resources to holding elections that allow some competition. Many dictatorships also receive help in paying for elections. Indeed, some observers have suggested that aid offered to induce holding multiparty elections has become an important source of illicit wealth for the dictator's cronies in some regimes.[8]

Figure 6.1 shows the per capita amounts of aid (in constant US dollars) going to dictatorial regimes in which the paramount leader had won a semi-competitive multiparty election (solid line), a one-party election (dashed line), or no election (dotted line).[9] The last category includes regimes such as communist dictatorships, where ruling party elites choose regime leaders (though legislatures were usually elected in single-party elections); about half of military-led regimes; and monarchies. Until the early 1990s, dictatorships that held uncontested executive election rituals, such as Egypt during much of the time after 1952, received the most aid per capita. Post–Cold War, however,

---

[7] See Ezrow and Frantz (2011) for a review of the terms used to capture different types of electoral dictatorships.

[8] Wiseman, for example, sees "a real danger that foreign assistance for elections can simply become a new avenue for personal accumulation by state elites; in practice a new type of 'rent'" (1996, 940).

[9] Aid per capita is measured using a three-year moving average. We show the median instead of the mean level to reduce the influence of outliers. Substantial Western (US) aid flowed to Afghanistan, Iraq, and Pakistan from 2001 to 2010.

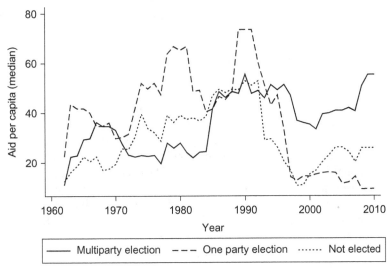

FIGURE 6.1 Foreign aid and the election of dictators.

dictatorships that hold semi-competitive executive elections, and can thus claim to be taking steps toward democracy, receive the most aid.[10]

This pattern reflects two changes that occurred in the late 1980s and early 1990s: donors withdrew aid from dictatorships that refused to hold multiparty contests, and many autocracies held multiparty elections for the first time. Substantial research suggests that changing donor behavior prompted many dictatorships to allow multiparty contests.[11] Sometimes these elections led to electoral defeat for the dictator and democratization. But often, dictators successfully navigated the imposition of multiparty elections and remained in power. Andrea Kendall-Taylor and Erica Frantz (2014) show that since the end of the Cold War, dictatorships increasingly rely on pseudo-democratic institutions and that this accounts for part of the global increase in autocratic survival rates.

Even when some competition is allowed, dictatorial elections rarely determine either who rules or the government's policy strategy. Their prevalence, even before the end of the Cold War and despite the risks they involve, suggests that they have other important functions, however. In this section, we highlight two of these functions. First, presidential elections are costly signals of the dictator's strength, aimed at deterring elite defections from the ruling coalition (Geddes 2005; Magaloni 2006). Second, legislative and local elections create incentives that might not otherwise exist for party officeholders and cadres to

---

[10] Levitsky and Way (2010) show strong evidence that semi-competitive elections do not imply that democracy lurks around the corner.

[11] See Dunning (2004), Wright (2009), Bermeo (2011, 2016), and Dietrich and Wright (2015).

extend their patron–client and information-gathering networks to the grass-roots, which helps authoritarian regimes to survive.

Big election wins for the dictator demonstrate his capacity to run a successful mobilization campaign, which deters both elite and mass opponents from active opposition by raising the perceived probability of regime survival. If an incumbent victory appears inevitable, potential opponents are less willing to shoulder the costs of overt opposition. Wins against opposition generate the strongest signals of regime strength, but even elections without choice show that the dictatorship has the resources and organizational capacity to ensure mass voting. To be effective in deterring opposition, vote and turnout counts need to be reasonably honest (Magaloni 2006). However, dictatorships can apparently tilt the playing field by controlling the media, concentrating state resources on supporters, and harassing, threatening, jailing, or beating up opposition activists without undermining elections' usefulness in deterring elite defection. In contrast, visibly fraudulent vote counting has sometimes set off explosions of popular hostility, bringing down dictatorships (Tucker 2007; Rozenas 2012).[12]

Most dictatorships that hold executive elections also elect a legislature and/or local officials as well, usually at the same time. Although ruling parties and dictators seldom lose semi-competitive national elections, individual ruling-party candidates for the legislature or local office do sometimes lose. Moreover, competition for ruling-party nominations is often far more fierce than partisan competition. Even where a dictatorship holds choice-free elections, ambitious party militants compete with each other for party *nominations*. In the Ivory Coast under one-party rule, for example, about ten candidates competed for each party nomination. "Although electoral competition has been eliminated, in the realm of recruitment [i.e., nominations] competition still exists ... This has insured that the system remains responsive to the demands of various groups in the population" (Zolberg 1964, 272).

The real possibility of losing in either the competition for nomination or semi-competitive elections creates incentives for elected officials to deliver benefits to citizens, as Aristide Zolberg observed. During the decades when it held no national elections, the Kuomintang (KMT) regime in Taiwan "promoted electoral participation at the local level, using elections to pressure party cadres ... Chiang [Ching-kuo] openly stated that the threat of electoral punishment was necessary to force cadres to jettison 'old conceits,' internalize new attitudes, and consolidate the party's broadening social base" (Greitens 2016, 101).

---

[12] Examples include the ousters of Slobodan Milošević in Serbia and Eduard Shevardnadze in Georgia, after the announcement of election results seen as fraudulent (Kuntz and Thompson 2009). Perceptions of election fraud have also led to massive unsuccessful protests that were nevertheless costly to the ruling group, as in Iran in 2009 and Venezuela in 2013.

Party leaders' nomination decisions depend on the potential candidate's behavior in his previous office or as a party organizer, as well as loyalty and other factors. In order to hang on to their posts, officials in most dictatorships have to ensure high turnout even in elections without choice and substantial majorities for the ruling party when voters have choices. Low turnout, low vote shares, widespread absenteeism from pro-regime events, opposition demonstrations, and other manifestations of citizen anger in their districts alert central leaders to the faults of local officials and reduce their chance of renomination. In addition, any sort of electoral competition, whether with tame opposition parties or other candidates from the ruling party, gives voters the opportunity to throw out incumbents who have disappointed or exploited them.

Competition thus puts pressure on local officials and deputies to refrain from exploitation and brutality toward constituents and compete on behalf of their areas in the national scramble for schools, clinics, paved roads, and whatever else is being given out. They need to deliver some benefits and provide some local public goods in order to ensure turnout, votes for the ruling party, and participation in ruling-party rallies. The need to deliver benefits to voters gives ambitious officials and candidates incentives to convey the needs and problems of their districts to central leaders and build clientele networks to reach the grassroots. Legislative and local elections can thus improve the dictatorship's information-gathering capacity and add many more people to the group receiving benefits from the dictatorship.

Elections help dictators overcome their problem monitoring local officials as well. "[E]lections are a way of obtaining information … [T]hey provide an occasion for inspection of the party structure at the local level" (Zolberg 1964, 272). The failure of local people to turn out or vote for ruling-party candidates alerts regime leaders to officials' shirking or bad behavior and initiates investigation of local problems. By creating these incentives, local and legislative elections partially substitute for monitoring local officials, with citizens' votes serving as "fire alarms."[13] Elections thus give local officials self-interested reasons to behave as regime leaders want them to. As several scholars have noted, ruling elites have an interest in controlling predation by local officials because it contributes to popular opposition to the regime.[14]

In other words, elections help align the incentives of deputies and local officials with those of the center by giving them strong reasons to limit leakage in the transfer of benefits from the center to their regions, treat constituents

[13] McCubbins and Schwartz (1984) coined the term "fire alarm" for the use of complaints or appeals to alert principals to the misbehavior of their bureaucratic agents in situations in which continuous monitoring would be costly.

[14] Note the number of analyses of China's ruling party's use of citizen petitions and internet freedom to complain about officials as a means of monitoring local officials (e.g., Paik 2009; Lorentzen 2014). China is one of the few contemporary party-led dictatorships that holds no direct elections above the village level.

decently, and convey information about the needs and grievances of voters to central decision makers. After an election, the knowledge that they will face renomination and reelection gives legislators and local elected officials reasons to reinforce their clientele networks, compete for resources from the center for their districts, and do favors for local notables. Local officials' need to attract nominations and votes at regular intervals reduces the temptation to hide local complaints from the center, steal goods intended for distribution, abuse their authority over people in their districts, and exploit those dependent on them. In other words, even uncompetitive elections help to limit principal-agent problems between central authorities and local officials in contexts in which monitoring would be both expensive and often ineffective.

In regimes with uncompetitive elections, information about local officials is conveyed mostly by real (as opposed to reported) turnout (Magaloni 2006). In most dictatorships, low turnout means either that local officials and activists have not done their job of making sure that people go to the polls or that people are hostile enough to risk penalties for failing to vote.[15]

Elections, even if uncompetitive, thus provide regular opportunities for the generation of information useful to regime elites about how local officials have performed, whether policies work on the ground, and levels of disenchantment among citizens in different areas of the country, as a number of analysts have noted (Gandhi and Lust-Okar 2009). We think that information about lower-level officials and policy implementation has more value to leaders than the distorted information elections provide about popular opposition to the dictatorship. We do not consider elections good sources of information about citizen opinion because votes depend on which alternatives exist, whether people see ending the dictatorship as possible, and other strategic considerations. Besides, dictatorships need daily information about opposition, not information at multiyear intervals. This is the reason they invest so heavily in internal security agencies (discussed in Chapter 7).

The benefits that ordinary citizens receive because of elections are by-products of competition among politicians in dictatorships, just as in democracies. Most of this distribution flows through politicians' clientele networks, happens in person at campaign events, or involves the politically motivated allocation of local public goods, so it is tangible and visible to recipients and those close to them.

Election campaigns are a predictable time when citizens can expect to receive something, beyond whatever services and public goods they usually enjoy, in exchange for their votes. During election campaigns, many people who have no interaction with officials or party activists most of the time receive extra food

---

[15] There are a few dictatorships in which leaders seem to encourage turnout only among those whose votes are easiest to manipulate, e.g., during Mubarak's rule in Egypt (Blaydes 2011). As an example of how seriously most dictators take turnout, Cameroonian President Paul Biya has dismissed cabinet ministers to punish them for low turnout in their constituencies (Jua 2001, 39).

and entertainment in autocracies, just as they do in many democracies. For example, Egyptian calorie consumption rose during election campaigns in the Mubarak dictatorship (Blaydes 2011). Belarusian president Aliaksandr Lukashenka "fixed elections, but still spent money on his campaign as if he were part of a real contest" (Wilson 2011, 196). He staged a six-week pop music tour to entertain voters during campaign events in 2010 (Wilson 2011, 219). Salvadoran military dictator Julio Rivera "campaigned as hard as, or perhaps harder than, he would have had he been opposed" (Webre 1979, 47). Paraguayan dictator Alfredo Stroessner "stumps the country as though he were in a real race ... All his appearances are surrounded by a great deal of hoopla – fiestas, dances, barbecues, parades ... and stirring polkas praising Stroessner's deeds" (Lewis 1980, 106).

As with other institutions that engage ordinary people, elections tend to become routinized and predictable over time, even though dictators may have initially introduced them only to placate foreign donors. The ad hoc referenda held after violent seizures of power, which new dictators never lose, are seldom more than opportunistic attempts to use the appearance of popular support to give pause to opposition elites, international critics, or ambitious rivals in the inner circle. Once elections have occurred a couple of times, however, eliminating or postponing them has a much different meaning than failure to hold elections in the first place.

Because successful elections are a signal to potential elite defectors of the regime's invincibility, postponing scheduled elections signals a regime or dictator in difficulties. Postponement implies that regime leaders fear defeat. A postponed election has the same political effect as the announcement that the dictator has suffered a mild stroke: it sets off a covert struggle for power among potential successors, increases plotting, and motivates efforts to cooperate among regime opponents. Indeed, irregular elections (which include those held after a postponement)[16] are twice as likely to be followed by regime collapse as regular ones, and leaders who preside over irregular elections are more than twice as likely to face a bad post-exit fate (death, imprisonment, or exile) compared with leaders who hold regular elections. For these reasons, dictatorships rarely postpone scheduled elections, even when growth has stalled or other problems reduce their ability to control election outcomes. Only 8 percent of dictatorships that held one executive election failed to hold others. If they fear losing elections, dictators have a number of tools safer than postponement at their disposal. They can alter electoral rules, increase their control over media, and disqualify opposition candidates, usually without serious consequences.

---

[16] Unfortunately, available data do not allow us to distinguish postponed elections from other irregular ones.

Tests of the Effects of Elections

In what follows, we test some implications of the argument that dictatorships use elections to incentivize the extension of their information-gathering and distributive networks to the grassroots. We reason as follows. If elections are a costly signal of the dictator's invincibility, we would expect to see central government spending increase during election years as officials demonstrate their ability to organize and mobilize the masses. If sending a costly signal was the only purpose of elections, however, we would expect to see much higher spending during semi-competitive election years (when a costlier signal is sent) than during elections without choice. On the other hand, if an important function of elections is to incentivize local candidates to extend distribution to the grassroots, we would expect to see high spending during all elections, regardless of competition because distribution to the grassroots is costly. Our second test compares health spending in countries with dictatorships that hold either uncompetitive or semi-competitive elections with those in which no elections are held. If elections incentivize spreading benefits to the grassroots, we should see evidence that health spending reaches ordinary people. To test this expectation, the third test looks at whether elections actually affect citizen welfare. We use child mortality as an indicator of welfare.

We first compare government spending in election and nonelection years. If elections motivate additional distribution to citizens, government spending should rise in election years. Other analysts have found evidence in a number of specific dictatorships of a political-business cycle in which public spending rises before semi-competitive elections (Heath 1999; González 2002; Magaloni 2006; Pepinsky 2007).[17] To investigate whether this is a general phenomenon, we compare average spending in election years with spending in nonelection years in dictatorships with support parties.

To pinpoint the electoral mechanism, we identify the years of first-round presidential and/or legislative elections in which the incumbent party, regime leader, or a hand-picked successor was on the ballot, relying on data from the NELDA project (Hyde and Marinov 2012).[18] These elections include both uncompetitive and semi-competitive events.

---

[17] The foundational literature on political budget cycles focuses on democracies, positing that myopic voters use retrospective voting to sanction incompetent politicians. Knowing that voters do this prompts incumbents to pursue expansionary economic policy prior to elections (Nordhaus 1975). The evidence for political budget cycles in advanced industrial democracies is weak, but political budget cycles are more prevalent in new democracies (Block, Ferree, and Singh 2003; Brender and Drazen 2004; Shi and Svensson 2006). Analysts suggest that lack of transparency, high personal rents for retaining office, and a large share of uninformed voters provide stronger incentives for incumbents to pursue fiscal manipulation before elections. The same conditions characterize many dictatorships.

[18] We use *nelda20*, *nelda21*, and *nelda22*.

We restrict the analysis to regularly scheduled elections, excluding any that had been scheduled but then postponed or canceled (*nelda1* and *nelda6*). This qualification is important because the timing of both elections and spending decisions may be determined by unmodeled factors such as political instability, international shocks, or economic crises. For example, a rise in the international price of a country's main export might motivate a dictator to call elections while times are good and also encourage increased public spending. We want to exclude the possibility that dictators time elections to surf waves of popularity rather than manipulating spending at election time (Kayser 2005). The possibility of opportunistic election timing is of special concern for irregularly held elections when, by definition, the election date is not fixed ex ante, so we exclude those. In the sample period, 1961–2010, there are 174 regular election years.

To investigate whether elections influence the distribution of benefits, we examine general government spending, measured as logged per capita expenditures. We include control variables for decade, leader duration (logged), the age dependency ratio, trade (% GDP), civil and international conflict, GDP per capita (logged), population size (logged), and oil rents per capita.[19]

Standard empirical specifications in the political business cycle literature employ a lagged dependent variable model (Brender and Drazen 2004; Alt and Lassen 2006; Shi and Svensson 2006; Hyde and O'Mahoney 2010). The dependent variable is typically a change variable as a proportion of the total economy, for example, $\Delta Budget/GDP$. The main independent variable is a dummy for pre-election, election, or post-election year. We depart from this specification in three ways, while retaining the lagged dependent variable and change in spending as the dependent variable. First, we purge the dependent variable of the GDP measure in the denominator to allow for a more transparent test of the election effect. A measure of economic size and population are included as right-hand-side variables to ensure that the estimated effect of elections is conditioned on country size. Second, we estimate an error-correction model that allows for a more general test of both the long- and short-run impacts of elections. Empirical models that include only a dummy variable for elections on the right-hand side of the equation estimate the total effect of elections without separating short-term changes from long-run equilibrium relationships (De Boef and Keele 2008). Finally, because of the paucity of data on budget balance in dictatorships, we estimate the effect of elections on spending, where the dependent variable is the change in ln(*Expenditure*)

---

[19] Data on age dependency ratio, trade, GDP, and population are from the World Development Indicators (2015). Conflict data are updates to Gleditsch et al. (2002), and oil rents data are from Wimmer, Cederman, and Min (2009).

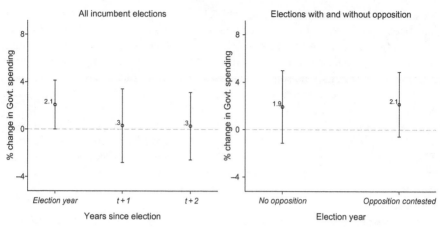

FIGURE 6.2 The electoral spending cycle in dictatorships.

measured in constant dollars, using data from the World Development Indicators (2015).[20] The specification is:

$$\Delta ln(\,Exp\,) = ln(\,Exp\,)_{t-1} + \Delta E + E_{t-1} + \Delta X + X_{t-1} + \delta_t + \epsilon_{i,t} \qquad (6.1)$$

where E is a binary indicator for election year, X is a vector of control variables, and δ_t are decade effects. We estimate this equation with a linear model that corrects for heteroskedasticity and autocorrelation in the errors.

The left panel of Figure 6.2 shows the results. The plot shows that dictatorships, on average, increase spending during election years, as expected. Expenditures move closer to the long-run equilibrium levels in the years following elections, though there is still some increased spending after elections, as would be expected if much of the extra expenditure in election years is for construction, infrastructure, and local public goods, which often have costs extending over multiple years. These findings are consistent with both the claim that dictatorial elites use spending and mobilization during election campaigns to signal invincibility and the claim that dictatorships distribute to the grassroots during elections.

Next, we compare changes in spending at the time of elections with and without opposition participation. If authoritarian elections are only a way for

---

[20] The main results for government spending are robust in specifications without control variables, with regime-case fixed effects and AR(1) errors, and with year effects, as well as alternative error estimators. We drop observations associated with the budget crisis in Zimbabwe in 2008, and the subsequent fiscal rebound the following year, because these are clear outliers in the spending data. We also drop the election in Senegal in 1968 because this a clear spending outlier. Adding these observations back into the estimating sample yields a stronger result than that reported in the right panel in Figure 6.2.

the dictatorship to demonstrate its support relative to the opposition (in order to deter elite defections) or to identify regions of opposition party strength, we would expect spending to increase before contested elections but not before uncontested ones. If, however, elections help dictatorial elites to align the incentives of local officials with their own, then we would expect to see spending increase during elections regardless of opposition participation. Because potential ruling-party candidates have to compete for nominations even when elections are uncompetitive, we argue that uncompetitive elections motivate candidate behavior and government spending similar to that of candidates who face opposition party competition.

The right panel of Figure 6.2 shows the results from a test that splits regularly scheduled elections into two groups: those in which the dictatorship allowed opposition participation and those in which no opposition contested the election.[21] The plot shows that dictatorships increase spending during both types of elections. The estimates for each type of election are roughly the same size as the estimate that pools both groups of elections together. However, the estimates for contested and uncontested executive elections are not statistically significant because there are fewer observations in each category when the sample is divided. To further explore this finding, we also tested models that separate all dictatorships with legislatures that include some opposition from those without opposition (or with no legislature). In these tests (not shown), we find that dictatorships that allow no competition at all still boost spending during election years.[22]

The evidence about government spending thus suggests that both semi-competitive and uncompetitive elections motivate increased effort by officials to reach citizens with benefits. Through this mechanism, dictatorships can use elections to monitor the behavior of local officials and buy support from citizens.

The argument that elections help to monitor the behavior of local officials implies that officials engage in less theft and abusive behavior in dictatorships that hold elections, and therefore that citizen welfare would improve. Next, we investigate this implication. We assess the effect of authoritarian elections on citizen welfare. These tests focus on the *average* effects of different election rules, not on cycles. The point of this examination is to compare the effects of semi-competitive and uncompetitive elections, relative to holding no elections, on the distribution of welfare-enhancing goods to citizens. If elections

---

[21] Opposition-contested elections, as defined here, are those that meet the following three criteria: (1) an opposition party exists to contest the election (*nelda3*), (2) more than one political party is legal (*nelda4*), and (3) there is a choice of candidates or parties on the ballot (*nelda5*). All other elections are considered uncompetitive. There are 67 uncompetitive elections and 106 opposition-contested elections in the sample (1961–2010).

[22] Replication files also report a test that looks separately at the years 1990–2010, in which uncompetitive elections remain associated with an increase in government spending.

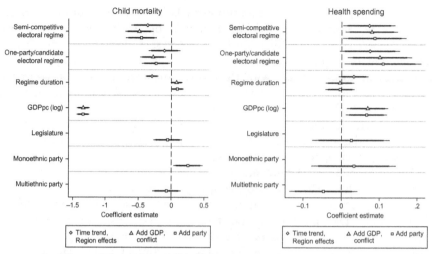

FIGURE 6.3 Dictatorial elections and health outcomes.

encourage politicians and officials to extend their patron–client distribution networks to the grassroots, as we have argued, we should see better welfare outcomes associated with elections.

This analysis relies on child mortality rates, which are a good indicator of overall popular well-being, and government spending on health care as a measure of government effort.[23] It compares dictatorships with unelected leaders with those that hold semi-competitive executive elections and those that hold one-candidate elections.[24] The left panel of Figure 6.3 shows child mortality rates, and the right panel shows central government spending on health. The top coefficient in each cluster was generated by a model that contains only controls for regime duration (logged), geographic region, and time period fixed effects, to capture world time trends in child mortality and health costs.[25] The second estimate adds GDP per capita (in constant dollars, logged) and a measure of the time since the last high-intensity conflict as controls.

---

[23] IMF data on health spending, available from 1985 to 2009, come from Clements, Gupta, and Nozaki (2011). Data on the under-five mortality rate (U5MR) come from the Institute of Health Metrics and Evaluation and span the years from 1971 to 2010.

[24] Dictatorships that hold semi-competitive executive elections nearly always also hold competitive legislative elections, whereas quite a few dictatorships with semi-competitive legislative elections do not have contested executive elections, so we use executive elections for this test. The sample used for these tests is all dictatorships: 1971–2010 for child mortality and 1985–2009 for health spending.

[25] There are eighteen region effects corresponding to the Global Burden of Disease categories from the Institute for Health Metrics and Evaluation. We do not include country effects because 84 percent of the variation in the child mortality rate is cross-sectional. However, a bivariate model with country effects yields similar results.

The third estimate adds information about legislatures and regime support parties. It includes an indicator variable for the existence of an elected legislature and indicators for ruling parties with support from just one ethnic group (*monoethnic*) and those that are supported by multiple ethnic groups (*multiethnic*). The reference category for the party variables is dictatorships without a support party. If elections in this specification improve child mortality rates, it means that elections affect welfare beyond any effect of legislative bargaining directly on welfare or on economic performance (which would affect welfare indirectly) and any advantage that dictatorships organized by parties have in the delivery of services. Recall that our argument about the effect of elections on the incentives of officials implies that more benefits should actually reach citizens if the regime holds elections. Since the vast majority of dictatorships that hold executive elections also have ruling parties, this is a hard test.

Figure 6.3 shows that child mortality rates are lower and health care spending higher in dictatorships in which executives face semi-competitive elections compared with those in which they face no elections, regardless of the specification. Even after controlling for the effects of legislatures and ruling parties, elections improve welfare, as our argument predicts.

Our interpretation of the effect of uncontested elections must be a bit more tentative because changing the specification affects results, but models that account for level of development and conflict (bottom two coefficients in each cluster) suggest that child mortality rates are also lower and health spending higher in dictatorships with uncontested elections than in those without elections. The pattern shown here is what would be expected if even uncompetitive elections create incentives for officials to attend to the welfare of ordinary people, as we have argued.

The main results with regard to legislatures and parties are that they make no independent contribution to child welfare or health spending when elections are controlled for. Indeed, ethnically exclusive dictatorial ruling parties are associated with *higher* rates of child mortality than exist in dictatorships without parties. This finding suggests that when the leadership of a dictatorial ruling party excludes some or most of a country's ethnic groups, welfare-enhancing benefits go only to included groups. We interpret the nonsignificant coefficient for multiethnic ruling party as meaning that although ruling parties distribute benefits, in the absence of elections, party cadres lack incentives to extend distribution to poorer citizens.

We find no support for the claim that dictatorial legislatures serve as fora for policy bargaining (Gandhi and Przeworski 2006, 2007; Gandhi 2008). If bargaining in legislatures contributes to economic performance, as analysts have proposed, it should lower child mortality rates, but we do not see evidence of that. We take this to indicate that in *most* authoritarian legislatures, little real policy bargaining occurs, or at least that whatever bargaining occurs has little effect on public welfare. Dictatorships do negotiate with private economic interests, of course, but primarily through informal personal contacts with business people, as documented in the many empirical studies of state–business relationships in autocracies (e.g., MacIntyre 1994; Doner and Ramsay 1997; Schneider 2004).

One of the reasons welfare-oriented policy bargaining rarely occurs in dictatorial legislatures is that potentially challenging mass-based opposition movements, of the kind discussed by Gandhi and Przeworski (2006, 2007), have seldom had enough representation in dictatorial legislatures to bargain there effectively. In less than a quarter (23 percent) of authoritarian legislatures has the opposition held more than 25 percent of seats, as would be required in order to bargain with any chance of success.[26] Moreover, several of the dictatorships that allow the largest number of opposition deputies tolerate only moderate opposition parties while excluding more popular and challenging parties (Lust-Okar 2005). Rather than bargaining with the largest opposition group, some autocrats survive by keeping the most challenging opposition divided from more easily coopted moderates who are allowed legislative seats and the private benefits that go with them. The underrepresentation of opposition in dictatorial legislatures may be the reason for our finding that distributive effort undertaken in the context of elections has more effect on popular welfare than legislatures do.

In sum, the findings offered here suggest that though dictatorial elites use elections strategically for the survival benefits they confer, elections also bring some benefits to citizens as a by-product. Post–Cold War foreign aid may thus have made some contribution to improving the lives of people living in dictatorships through incentivizing dictators to distribute more at election time, regardless of whether it has been effective in encouraging democratization.

CONCLUSION

Once elite bargaining has evolved into somewhat predictable patterns, dictatorships often face problems with the implementation of their policies, monitoring local officials to prevent theft and abuse of office, and gathering information from the grassroots. Many dictatorships use institutions that engage ordinary citizens to help solve these problems.

In dictatorships with support parties, central leaders generally assign responsibility for gathering information about local conditions and opinions, as well as implementing regime policies, to party members who serve as local officials, civil servants, or managers and employees in state-controlled firms. Leaders expect party cadres to explain policies, build support for them, and prevent ordinary people from ignoring or sabotaging central directives, while also distributing positive inducements for cooperation. They also expect officials

---

[26] Prior to 1990, this figure was 16 percent. In the subsequent two decades, this figure jumps to 38 percent.

and cadres to send information about local problems, how policies work on the ground, and signs of opposition to central authorities. Often, however, regime elites lack the capacity to monitor the behavior of party cadres and officials. As a result, they may contribute less to implementation and information gathering than regime officials had hoped. Instead, they may steal benefits earmarked for citizens, demand bribes, seize land and other assets from local residents, sabotage or distort policy implementation, falsify information about local conditions, and in other ways abuse their positions of power.

Local and legislative elections partially compensate for regime leaders' limited ability to monitor their local agents, which may be the reason nearly all dictatorships supported by parties hold elections. Low votes for regime candidates or low turnout can serve as "fire alarms" to alert leaders to especially incompetent, abusive, or corrupt local officials. The need to achieve winning votes and high turnout motivates legislators and local officials to distribute most benefits provided by central leaders to constituents rather than diverting them, to try to acquire resources from the center for their areas, and to convey information about local problems to top officials in order to secure aid. Even where no partisan competition is allowed, there is competition among potential candidates for ruling-party nominations. Nominations depend on earlier success in mobilizing citizens, which gives legislators and elected local officials reasons to care about the goodwill of constituents.

Legislative and local elections thus align the incentives of mid- and lower-level officials with the needs of top leaders. Regime leaders need reasonable levels of competence and honesty in local officials to prevent mass alienation and potential opposition mobilization. They also need information about problems and local disasters so that they can respond effectively. Elections give local politicians, job-holders, and the regime's lower-level officials reasons to develop clientele networks that reach to the grassroots to distribute resources in exchange for votes, and to bring information about local needs to the attention of central policy makers. By creating broader vested interests in regime survival, a more effective system of distribution to the grassroots, and additional information for regime insiders, elections aid regime survival.

Elections in which voters "choose" the dictator serve a different purpose, however. The dictator need not monitor himself, but nevertheless nearly as many dictatorships schedule regular executive elections as regular legislative elections. From the dictator's point of view, executive elections help deter elite defections, which are the most serious threat to both the dictator's and the regime's survival (Svolik 2012; Roessler 2016). Executive elections demonstrate the dictator's control over the resources needed to hang on to power. They show that he can mobilize very large numbers of people and demonstrate his command of a nation-wide network of political activists. They aim to show potential defectors that it would not be easy to organize enough support to replace the dictator. If campaigns are well run, potential defectors cannot tell how much popular support is genuine, but they can observe the enormous deployment of human and material resources. To achieve this mobilization, dictators distribute even larger quantities of goods than do dictatorial legislatures.

A number of previous studies have shown that dictatorships led by parties and those that have legislatures last longer than dictatorships that lack these institutions. In the current chapter we show evidence consistent with the claim that elections are the institutional mechanism that links parties and legislatures with regime durability. We show, first, that elections are associated with increased government spending, as would be expected if dictatorial governments distribute various kinds of benefits and local public goods during campaigns.

Increased distribution leading up to elections would be expected no matter what the reason they hold elections. If the only purposes of elections were to deter elite defections or to provide information about where opposition exists, we would expect to see much more public spending during semi-competitive elections than during elections without choice. Choice-free elections are a weaker signal of regime invincibility and convey little information about opposition. In order to test whether elections also help align the interests of central and local officials, our second empirical test compares the effect of elections with and without choice on public spending. We find that the increase in spending is about the same for both kinds of elections. We interpret this finding as support for the claim that all elections, even uncompetitive ones, incentivize deputies and local officials to deliver benefits to the grassroots because they entail competition for party nominations even if there is no competition in general elections.

As a further test of the argument that elections incentivize politicians to reach the grassroots with benefits, we look at whether dictatorships that hold elections spend more on health than dictatorships that do not, and at whether health outcomes actually improve. We show that dictatorships that hold semi-competitive elections spend more on health care than do dictatorships that hold no elections, and that they have lower rates of child mortality. Even uncompetitive elections are associated with higher health spending and lower rates of child mortality than exist in dictatorships that hold no elections. We interpret these findings as further support for the argument that competition for ruling-party nominations gives legislators and local officials reasons to attend to their constituencies even when there is no partisan competition. The lower rates of child mortality suggest that local officials in systems with any kind of elections are more likely to play the role regime leaders assign to them in the distribution of benefits than local officials in systems without elections. In other words, elections partially substitute for direct monitoring of local officials by central leaders. Including controls for the existence of a legislature and ruling party does not change these results, and legislatures make no independent contribution to these outcomes.

Elections for legislatures and local offices thus help protect dictatorships by providing a means of periodic monitoring to detect predatory behavior, theft, and incompetence in lower-level officials. At the same time, they give officials and deputies strong reasons to report information about local problems and discontent to central leaders, to lobby for benefits for their regions, and to distribute some of the benefits they acquire to local people. In these ways, mass institutions help the dictatorship located in the capital to extend its policies and governance to all parts of the country.

7

Double-Edged Swords

Specialized Institutions for Monitoring and Coercion

Dictatorial control rests on the threat of force. To make that threat credible to potential opponents, dictatorships need visible coercive institutions, that is, armies, internal security police, and other armed forces even if they face no threats from beyond their borders. For those dictatorships that relied on these forces to establish their rule in the first place, the credibility of the threat of further violence exists from the beginning. Even dictatorships established peacefully, however, deploy the threat of force and use some violence against opponents. The worst human rights abuses often happen during the first years of dictatorship, when the ruling group is unsure of its grip over the country and riven by internal power struggles. Violence may also be worse because new rulers lack the information needed for carefully targeted coercion (Greitens 2016). During these years, they often establish new security agencies and paramilitary forces and increase military budgets.[1] Dictatorships use these forces against people they suspect of opposition, but investment in them also increases the credibility of *threats* of violence and thus can deter further opposition.

Once the dictatorship has established a ruthless reputation and conflict within the ruling group has settled down, it usually relies less on overt coercion. Most repression is preventive, in the sense that it aims to block the dissemination of negative information about conditions in the country and members of the dictatorial elite, to discover potential plots and movements before they become organized enough to challenge the dictatorship, and to undermine and disperse groups that share critical information or opposition points of view (Dragu and Przeworski 2017). In other words, though dictatorships that have

---

[1] See Greitens (2016) for descriptions of the reorganization and creation of new security forces in Taiwan, the Philippines, and South Korea soon after the establishment of new dictatorships.

lasted a long time usually rely less on overt violence, they continue to invest in coercive institutions to deter and undermine opposition.

The decline in overt violence that usually accompanies the routinization of dictatorial rule might be caused by its high cost. Coercion uses up resources that could be spent on other things, and overreliance on it drives both elite and mass opposition underground, worsening many of the information problems that beset dictatorships.[2]

Increasing the size and political importance of the coercive institutions can also be dangerous to dictators and their closest supporters. Security services and armed forces are serious weapons that are difficult to keep under control (Svolik 2012; Dragu and Przeworski 2017). In this chapter we examine what determines who aims these weapons at whom.

We first describe the various security agencies, paramilitary forces, and army that typically guard a dictator and regime. We provide information about what the different forces guard against, how they interact with each other, and the difficulties of controlling them in an environment that lacks third-party enforcement of legal rules.

Internal security agencies are specialists in preventive repression (Dragu and Przeworski 2017). They spy on and intimidate potential dissidents, and they identify suspected opponents of the dictator inside the inner circle and the military. The main purpose of these agencies is to gather information that can be used to devise strategies for preventing overt opposition. Paramilitary forces have a narrower role. They defend the dictator and dictatorship from military coups and other armed assaults. The army defends the dictatorship from invasions, armed rebellions, and, occasionally, popular upheavals. As the tasks of the different coercive institutions make apparent, dictators use them not only to protect against different kinds of threats but also to protect against each other because the dictator cannot count on controlling them. The more powerful and effective the force, the more dangerous it could be to the dictator if it turned against him.

Dictators try to increase their own chances of survival by establishing multiple armed forces to spy on, compete with, or counterbalance each other (Quinlivan 1999; Haber 2006; Greitens 2016, 13–14, 79–80). They also try to take personal control of security agencies and promotions in the army, and to recruit paramilitary forces from especially loyal citizens. Other members of the dictatorial elite, however, resist these efforts as part of their general attempt to retain the capacity to threaten the dictator with ouster, and thus to limit his discretion.

---

[2] Since Wintrobe (1998), theories of autocracy have claimed that coercion is more costly than cooptation. Though we know of no comparative studies of relative costs, we think this claim is likely to be correct.

INTERNAL SECURITY AGENCIES

Although dictatorships may find periodic indirect monitoring (as described in Chapter 6) sufficient for controlling local officials, they invest much more in specialized institutions to gather information continuously about the loyalty and job performance of high-level officials, military officers, and other members of the elite, including those in the inner circle. These internal security agencies also spy on the opposition, but since the most serious threats to regime and dictator usually arise from individuals within the dictatorial elite, much of the surveillance focuses on them. Internal security police not only provide their bosses with information about potential challengers, but also use manipulation of information, censorship, intimidation, beating, torture, imprisonment, death threats, and murder to deter challenges. These tactics increase the costs of opposing the regime or dictator. Pervasive spying hinders opposition collective action by heightening the risk and potential cost of expressing critical opinions, thus making it harder for opponents to identify each other.

Most of the time, the internal security forces that handle day-to-day monitoring of political activity are civilian agencies, not military. They spy directly on regime officials, party leaders and cadres, civil servants, military officers, managers of state-owned firms, professors, teachers, journalists, and union leaders (e.g., Callaghy 1984, 292; Soper 1989; Micgiel 1994, 95; Schirmer 1998, 175; Tismaneanu 2003, 146; Dodd 2005, 79–83; Barany 2012, 214). In other words, they spy on anyone who might have the capacity to influence others or sabotage the implementation of regime policy, as well as on opposition leaders. They may also use large numbers of internet monitors and paid, blackmailed, or voluntary informers to report on ordinary citizens they could not otherwise observe (e.g., Lewis 1980, 150; Peterson 2002).

The East German Stasi, because they kept such extensive records, provides a window on both the costliness of coercion and how dictatorships actually deploy it. At its peak, the Stasi employed 100,000 people (Peterson 2002, 26–29). If informers are included, there was one spy for every sixty-six citizens (Koehler 1999, 9). Regime leaders put highest priority on monitoring elites. The Stasi placed informers in ministries, the Planning Commission, the army, and the Stasi itself (called the Unknown Colleagues). Agents also monitored compliance with the economic plan and performance in state-owned firms and collective farms, reporting incompetence, drunkenness, adultery, and inaccurate production reports as well as dissent (which was much less common than human frailty). In addition, the ruling party had its own separate security network of 44,000 functionaries in economic enterprises to monitor performance.

In contrast to many dictatorships, East German leaders put massive resources into monitoring ordinary citizens as well, because of the special problems caused by the existence of the very successful West German economy next door. The Stasi had internment camps in twenty-four locations. Its domestic counterintelligence sector included 4,400 agents just for inspecting mail. Every post office had Stasi officers who opened all letters and packages sent to or from noncommunist countries. Six thousand agents tapped telephones. Eighteen hundred were assigned to combat underground political movements, each of whom supervised at least thirty informers. And of course thousands of agents guarded the borders (Peterson 2002, 24–25). East Germany is an extreme case, both because of the regime's great vulnerability and because they had the resources and human capital to man such an extensive operation, but building effective security services requires significant resources everywhere.[3]

Beyond resources, it also takes time and training to build reliable internal security services. In Poland, where the communists knew that extensive coercion would be required to maintain the regime, the Soviet Union began training Polish recruits in schools supervised by the Soviet People's Commissariat for Internal Affairs (NKVD) in 1940, long before World War II ended. Once the Polish communist party had established itself in Lublin in 1943, it began sending hundreds at a time to NKVD officers' schools, even before the provisional government was formed (Micgiel 1994, 94–95; Iazhborovskaia 1997). The willingness of both the Soviets and the Poles to expend the resources required for this kind of training indicates the importance communist leaders gave to it. Resources desperately needed for the war were diverted to pay for schools large enough to accommodate thousands of East European students, while manpower and highly trained officers were diverted from the battlefield as war raged.

Of course, post-war Poland and East Germany are not typical, but they provide a sense of the cost and difficulty of creating an effective internal security service. Most dictatorships do not begin with military occupation by a more powerful dictatorship famous for its hyperdeveloped internal security agencies. In the aftermath of most seizures of power, dictatorships lack the trained and loyal practitioners an effective internal security service would require. Sheena Greitens's data on the ratio of internal security personnel to population in nine countries shows average ratios of 1:124 for North Korea (1:40 if informants are included), the most intensively policed country for which we have information, 1:5,090 for Saddam Hussein's Iraq, and 1:10,000 for Chad between 1982 and 1990 (2016, 9).

It usually takes a few years for new dictatorships to reorganize or build a loyal political police force. Even military-led dictatorships can lack effective internal security forces initially, despite their expertise in the use of coercion. In dictatorships launched by military officers, on day one each service typically controls a separate police apparatus located within its regular chain of

---

[3] East Germany was extreme but not unique. In Ceausescu's Romania, besides the other tasks of security agents, they collected handwriting samples from all residents and registered all typewriters and copy machines (Soper 1989).

command and oriented toward preventing infringements of military discipline. These agencies can be reoriented toward policing subversion among civilians, but concerns about turf and disagreements about how to handle opponents can hinder their unification and transformation into obedient instruments of the dictatorial elite. A further problem with using troops for subversion control is that many soldiers resist assignments to repress unarmed citizens (Janowitz 1977; Nordlinger 1977; Barany 2011). Soldiers often share the grievances that motivate opposition demonstrations and may balk at orders to fire partly for that reason.

Because of these problems, even military-led dictatorships typically call on the army for protection from domestic opponents only when police and paramilitary forces have failed to control opposition demonstrations or when armed insurgents challenge them. Using the military to control demonstrations can backfire. The Egyptian dictatorship begun by the Free Officers' coup in 1952, for example, used security police and paramilitary forces against demonstrators during the Arab Spring in 2011. When that failed to disperse them, the army was called out, but did not attack demonstrators. Instead, the Supreme Council of the Armed Forces, which had been a key pillar of regime support, forced the dictator to resign and took control of the country. "[E]ven had the generals been willing to shoot demonstrators, many officers and enlisted men would probably have refused to obey such an order" (Barany 2011, 32–33). Paramilitary forces are more likely than regular soldiers to shoot unarmed protesters when called upon to do so (Barany 2011; Nepstad 2015).

Other dictatorships, whether led by officers or civilians, have had similar experiences. As a number of observers have noted, autocratic regimes fall to unarmed popular opposition when generals refuse to use troops to repress demonstrators. President Ben Ali of Tunisia fled into exile when the army chief-of-staff refused to deploy troops to disperse protestors (Barany 2011, 30–31). In Georgia, then-President Eduard Shevardnadze withstood weeks of massive demonstrations, but resigned at the end of the day when "one by one the heads of police departments and army units declared" their unwillingness to continue defending him (Wheatley 2005, 185). In the last months of Duvalierist Haiti, Tonton Macoutes and the police beat, arrested, and murdered rampaging protesters, but top Duvalierist army officers refused orders to shoot them (Abbott 1988, 306). Even when officers' interests link them firmly to the regime, as they did in the Haitian and Egyptian examples, they resist using troops to repress demonstrators if they fear soldiers would refuse to fire or would hand their guns to protestors (Pion-Berlin and Trinkunas 2010; Dragu and Lupu 2017).[4]

---

[4] There are obvious exceptions to this statement, especially during civil wars and violent ethnic mobilization, when soldiers drawn mostly from some ethnic or regional groups fight insurgents from other groups. See Roessler (2016) for examples.

The discomfort many officers and soldiers feel about using violence against unarmed fellow citizens partly explains the military's unwillingness to put down the protests that overthrew these and several other dictatorships (Haddad 1973, 195; Woodward 1990, 164; Kuntz and Thompson 2009; Barany 2011). As a result of these attitudes, military-led regimes often create civilian security services to deal with internal opposition, just as most party-led dictatorships do (Plate and Darvi 1981).[5] Some also sponsor informal armed civilian forces (e.g., death squads) to further deter "subversion."

Party-based seizure groups that achieve power via authoritarianization or popular uprising may also initially lack loyal security services. On assuming dictatorial powers, they must decide what to do with the preexisting military and police forces, which may reflect interests and ethnic groups opposed to those that dominate the ruling party. Unreliable police forces reduce the new elite's ability to induce cooperation from the population, and the military tends to incubate coup attempts rather than keeping the dictatorship safe. Many party-led regimes create new party-controlled internal security services after authoritarianization.

Parties that have led insurgencies, in contrast to other party-based dictatorships, usually have cadres specialized in internal security before seizing power. Since successful insurgency requires the maintenance of organized networks for recruiting manpower, extracting resources, training soldiers, and disciplining dissidents and "shirkers," insurgent groups often have the monitoring and coercive capacity needed to spy on opponents and those who occupy influential positions while ensuring citizens' cooperation with the seizure group's project. Parties that have fought lengthy civil wars are likely to have the organization and personnel to take over and/or replace preexisting state coercive institutions rapidly and thoroughly. As a result, pre-seizure security organs created by insurgents can be carried over into the new regime.

To sum up this section, most dictatorships not brought to power by insurgency initially lack their own loyal and effective internal security agencies. Since police forces carried over from the ousted government tend to have inadequate resources, loyalty to the new rulers, and commitment to the new task, dictatorships often establish new security forces staffed by loyalists. It takes resources and time to build a dependable internal security force because of the need for trained and committed personnel to staff it.

The creation or strengthening of internal security services can increase the information available to the inner circle, not only about potential opponents, but also about each other. This is what makes them potentially dangerous to members of the inner circle as well as their enemies.

---

[5] Janowitz (1977) finds that men employed in various internal security and national police services outnumber those in the army in a sample of military-led dictatorships.

The Dangers of Personalized Control of Internal Security

Societal opposition may first motivate the establishment of new internal security agencies. Members of the seizure group usually support the creation of a strong security apparatus to protect the regime from opposition threats. These institutions, however, bring real risks for the dictatorial inner circle if the dictator comes to control them personally. A dictator who commands the security apparatus and has access to the information it collects can eavesdrop on the private conversations of his closest collaborators, making possible preemptive strikes against anyone suspected of disloyalty or too much ambition. Meanwhile, the dictator's plans for humiliating, discrediting, arresting, or executing his erstwhile colleagues remain secret until he acts.

Reports from the security services help the dictator identify which members of the inner circle might challenge him, and hence which he might want to exclude preemptively, worsening the inner circle's difficulty in enforcing limits on the dictator. The dictator's advantage comes not only from his access to the information collected, but also from his ability to order security officers to arrest his colleagues. If the dictator can, in effect, choose members of the inner circle by excluding anyone he wants, then he has become a free agent with immense resources and murderous powers.

The dictator's information advantage may also allow him to hide some transgressions, as Svolik (2012) argues. We do not see the dictator's ability to hide overstepping his delegated powers as a major cause of the inner circle's inability to hold him accountable, however, since transgressions often involve appointments, dismissals, arrests, and arbitrary policy choices, all of which are highly visible. Instead, we see the inner circle's main difficulty as arising from the riskiness of trying to punish overreaching dictators. The dictator's control of security forces can make talking about ousting the dictator so dangerous that party executive committees with the formal power to replace dictators never discuss doing so and plots are never developed. If members of the inner circle cannot oust the dictator for overstepping agreed-on limits, they cannot enforce constraints on him even when they observe violations.

If both the dictator and his lieutenants understand that plots are unlikely to succeed, the dictator will concentrate additional resources and power in his hands, and his lieutenants will acquiesce. If the likelihood of ouster is very low, lieutenants are better off as marginal members of the dictator's coalition than as ex-members.

With so much at stake, members of the inner circle who understand the situation they face should try to prevent the dictator from establishing personal control over the security apparatus in order to safeguard their ability to limit his discretion. Usually a unified seizure group can in fact prevent the dictator from taking over internal security in the same way that they can prevent other power grabs, though specific circumstances can sometimes give dictators unexpected opportunities.

In regimes led by more professionalized military forces, juntas are usually able to prevent the personalization of internal security. Among the South American military regimes in Argentina, Uruguay, Brazil, Ecuador, Peru, and Chile during the 1960s to 1980s, for example, only Pinochet in Chile usurped personal control of security forces (Remmer 1991).

Pinochet's control seems to have been an unforeseen consequence of a consensual junta decision taken to solve a different problem. In the months immediately after the 1973 Chilean coup, the junta gave provincial military commanders responsibility for internal security, including the arrest, trial, and punishment of "subversives," in their regions. Each commander handled these responsibilities according to his own views about the legal norms in force, which led to wide variation in the treatment of the accused. The Chilean military, with no authoritarian experience during the four decades before the coup, had virtually no past involvement in subversion control, and some officers found the new role repugnant. Pinochet and his allies favored a harsh and violent anti-subversion policy, but some of the provincial commanders refused to ignore the democratic legal norms still formally in force despite pressure from Pinochet and other military hard-liners. These disagreements caused conflict and disunity among high-ranking officers (Policzer 2009).

To maintain the unity and discipline of the officer corps in the face of deep disagreements over how to treat opponents, junta leaders decided to centralize subversion control in an agency outside the regular chain of command of the armed forces. In other words, junta leaders created a new security agency outside the military chain of command in order to remove subversion control from the hands of legalistic officers and reduce disagreements that were under-cutting unity in the army (Policzer 2009).

This decision inadvertently gave Pinochet the opportunity to appoint the new agency's top leadership, and thus to control it (Policzer 2009). It resolved the problem of conflict within the officer corps but gave Pinochet the capacity to use the security agency to spy on and coerce officers as well as other citizens, changing the balance of power within what had started out as a relatively equal military junta. Thus, it seems that the Chilean military's lack of recent authoritarian experience made it more vulnerable to the personalization of dictatorial power than other professionalized armed forces in the region, most of which had more recent experience governing.

Where a dictator gains personal control of the security apparatus, he has taken a giant step toward the personalization of rule, even in countries with a united military or disciplined ruling party. In such settings, control of the security apparatus may not be enough to personalize the dictatorship fully, but it moves in the direction of power concentration, as in Chile.

In contrast to the South American military dictators who came from rela-tively professionalized military forces, dictators who were creating a new officer corps as they seized state power, such as Anastasio Somoza García in Nicaragua, Mobutu Sese Seko in the former Zaire, and several other early

African military dictators, faced few impediments to personal control over security forces. Top officers in these armies often owed their recruitment and promotions directly to the dictator, making them unlikely to contest his appointments to security agencies or constrain his decisions in any other realm.

Dictators seek personal control over internal security in order to protect themselves from ouster, but the personalization of internal security is associated with greater regime longevity as well as more stable dictator tenure. Our data indicate that regimes led by dictators who exercise personal control over security forces last on average seven years longer than similar regimes in which they do not.[6] We interpret this increase in *regime* longevity as a result of reductions in plotting and intra-elite conflict when the dictator controls security forces, because other members of the inner circle understand that plots are unlikely to succeed. Intra-elite conflict is one of the main causes of authoritarian breakdown (see Chapter 8).

To sum up this section, dictatorships need internal security services to spy on potential opponents and deter overt opposition. Security agencies can also threaten members of the ruling elite, however. If the dictator secures personal control over internal security forces, then he can also spy on and monitor other members of the dictatorial inner circle. Control over internal security provides the dictator with a major information advantage relative to others in the dictatorial elite, which reduces the likelihood that plots can be kept secret and thus diminishes their chance of success. Control over the security service also means that the dictator can order agents to arrest, interrogate, torture, and execute his inner-circle colleagues. The possibility of such punishments obviously changes the distribution of power within the inner circle, rendering constraints on the dictator's discretion unlikely if not impossible.

If the dictator gains the advantage conveyed by direct control over the security apparatus, he will want to hang on to it, and other members of the inner circle would face great risks if they tried to remove it from his control. Between 1946 and 2010, only 3 percent of dictators who gained control of the security apparatus lost it later.

THE ARMY: BULWARK OF THE REGIME OR INCUBATOR OF PLOTS?

The army serves as the dictatorship's defense against foreign invasion, insurgency, and popular uprisings that the police and security troops have failed to suppress. Dictatorships need to maintain armies to defend them against armed challenges and make the threat of violent repression credible, but officers'

---

[6] Regimes without this feature last fourteen years, on average, while those with it endure for twenty-one years. This pattern holds in standard duration models of regime failure.

training, access to weapons, and command of armed men mean that *they* can more easily overthrow the dictator than can others.

Some analysts see the uniformed military as the key component of the opposition-control apparatus in dictatorships (Svolik 2012; Debs 2016). We find that view problematic. Although officers have played this role in some Latin American military regimes, dictators have not usually used military officers to spy on, intimidate, intern, torture, and murder suspected opponents. Dictators sometimes call on the military to repress particularly threatening demonstrations, but not for routine subversion or crowd control.

Instead, the officer corps often nurtures challenges and plots, as the figures in previous chapters on the frequency of military coups show. There are many reasons for plots. Officers commissioned before the seizure of power may have received their promotions because of loyalty to the leaders ousted by the new regime and may want to reverse the seizure of power. Officers may come from ethnic groups or political factions not represented in the dictatorial elite and resent disadvantages for their group. They may be angered by slow promotions, low pay, or poor living conditions. They may simply be ambitious to rule. Consequently, dictators have more often felt the need to protect themselves *from* potentially disloyal officers than been certain enough of officers' devotion and reliability to use them in subversion control. Philippine dictator Ferdinand Marcos, for example, told reporters that what he feared most was overthrow by the military. He imagined being assassinated during a coup, with US complicity, like South Vietnamese dictator Ngo Dinh Diem (Greitens 2016, 126).

This is the reason internal security police spy on officers, and it is the reason that some dictatorships spend substantial resources to indoctrinate soldiers and impose commissars with the power to countermand officers' orders in military units (Fainsod 1967, 468–81; Bullard 1985, 65–83; Greitens 2016, 89–90, 97–99). A few dictators have even stored ammunition in areas inaccessible to the army. The Duvaliers of Haiti kept the entire national arsenal, even heavy weaponry, in the basement of the National Palace. They put up with explosions that required rebuilding three times rather than allow the military access to weapons (Crassweller 1971, 317–18).

Since the means of overthrowing the dictator are always at hand for officers (unless weapons are locked up), their critical opinions or divergent ethnic loyalties can be dangerous to dictators even if they were allies at the time of the seizure of power (Roessler 2016). Crafting strategies to maintain military acquiescence is a challenge all dictatorships face. We described some of the strategies used in military-led regimes in Chapter 5. Here we consider some less nuanced strategies used by civilian as well as military dictatorships.

Counterbalancing

Many dictators (63 percent) try to meet the challenge of a possibly untrust-worthy military by creating presidential guards or other kinds of paramilitary forces outside the regular military chain of command. The high frequency with which dictators establish new paramilitary forces indicates how little most of them trust regular officers to defend their rule. Dictatorships have created three main kinds of paramilitary force: armed civilian forces to help the regular military fight insurgents (for example, Orden in El Salvador); party militias, which are typically armed youth adjuncts of the ruling party; and paramilitary forces recruited from groups thought to be especially loyal to the dictator himself and expected to defend him from coups led by regular army officers. We refer to the third kind as *loyalist* paramilitary forces to distinguish them from the others. Dictators expect loyalist paramilitary forces to be more reliable than the regular military because they recruit them from partisans, co-ethnics or both, while highly ranked regular officers would often have been recruited and promoted before the dictatorship began and thus represent a broad range of ethnicities, regions, religions, and partisan leanings.

Paramilitary loyalty is reinforced if the new force is closely identified with the dictator because of shared ethnicity or partisanship and would thus likely be disbanded if the dictator fell. If that happened, its officers would lose their special privileges and face possible prison or exile. In other words, loyalist paramilitary officers stand or fall with the dictator (Snyder 1998; Escribà-Folch 2013). In contrast, senior officers in the regular military are more likely to turn their backs on the dictator during periods of crisis because they typically have fewer ties to the ruler and a more developed "corporate" identity linked to defending the state, rather than the particular leader. Senior officers in the regular military often survive successive dictators in the same regime with their ranks intact, and they may even survive regime collapse, especially if they cause it. The fates of regular military officers are not routinely linked to the dictator's fate.

Dictators establish loyalist paramilitary forces to change the assessments of regular army officers about the likely risk of failure for coup attempts. To enhance the deterrent power of paramilitary forces, the dictator may buy them better arms and training than the regular army. He may schedule ostentatious parades of uniformed paramilitary forces and their weapons. Loyalist paramilitary units are often stationed in or near the dictator's residence as a specialized and highly visible defender of the dictator and dictatorship.

We see the coup deterrence value of loyalist paramilitary forces as arising from their staffing by officers and men from groups identified with the dictator who expect to share his fate if he is overthrown. An alternative explanation for why the establishment of paramilitary forces reduces the likelihood of coups is that the existence of multiple independent armed forces in the dictatorship raises the collective-action costs of committing to and executing coups (Quinlivan 1999; Böhmelt and Pilster 2015). In this view, coups do not succeed unless officers from both the regular military and the paramilitary go along with them.[7] This argument simply applies the well-known logic of collective action: the more independent actors are needed to accomplish a collective goal, the greater the difficulty of doing so. As obstacles to cooperation increase, coups should decrease (Singh 2014).

Dictatorships sometimes also create party militias to help defend themselves. On average, party militias cost less and receive much less training than presidential guards and other forces stationed near the dictator's residence. In a few well-known instances, party militias were well funded and grew into very well-armed and important elite political players, as during the Banda dictatorship in Malawi and Qaddafi's rule in Libya. In Malawi, the militia reported directly "to the president on the mood in the countryside and on all significant new arrivals in every village in the country" (Decalo 1998, 86). In these cases, militias effectively armor the dictator. Most of the time, however, militias have a less central role. They engage large numbers of young men, provide them with light weapons and rudimentary training, and assign them tasks such as keeping order and rooting out subversion among students or ordinary citizens. Members of militias are expected to inform on their neighbors, patrol problem areas, help to mobilize others for regime projects, and train as auxiliary national defense forces in case of invasion or rebellion.

Regime insiders create party militias to coopt the part of the population (young men) most likely to lead popular opposition by giving them a stake in regime persistence. Militias are supposed to help with internal security while delivering benefits to those who join them – at low budgetary cost, since they usually receive no salaries. The benefits to militia members include the power to order others around, recognition from political leaders, camaraderie, and informal opportunities to steal, extort, and demand sex from those they police.

Militia members have a lot of discretion over who they stop, search, and demand fines or payments from, as well as how much force to use, which naturally leads to abuses. They often become undisciplined and venal, making use of the powers granted them to pursue their own ends. In Congo/Zaire, for example, Disciplinary Brigades set up unauthorized barricades to "stop and harass people indiscriminately, demand 'tips,' and illegally detain people" (Callaghy 1984, 293). Like death squads, these forces may commit many human rights abuses without making the dictatorship safer because regime leaders cannot control their behavior. In practice, popular militias have often caused opposition to dictatorships because of arbitrary acts of violence, theft, and intimidation, and they have eventually been disbanded or integrated into the regular military as a means of imposing discipline in a number of cases.

---

[7] Because counterbalancing creates an additional armed actor within the regime, it opens up the possibility that these actors will take different sides during periods of unrest even if one does not automatically side with the dictator (Morency-Laflamme 2017).

Controlling Military Leadership

Many dictators also try to control their military forces through direct interference with promotions. The source of officers' autonomy from the dictator, if it exists, is the professional norms that determine promotions, recruitment, and retirement. Meritocratic recruitment and promotion based on competence and seniority mean that career success in the military does not depend on political loyalty. As long as recruitment to the officer corps is open to talent and promotions depend on performance and years of service, ethnic and partisan groups different from the dictator's will be represented in the higher ranks of the officer corps as will a range of opinion. If, however, the dictator can override professional norms to recruit, promote, and retire individual officers on the basis of loyalty or ethnicity, the officer corps cannot maintain its autonomy because the dictator can reserve high ranks for loyalists.

Nearly all dictatorships (and many democracies) use loyalty as one criterion for highest-level promotions, but in some, the existing officer corps is all but destroyed by purges, forced retirements, and promotions aimed at ending military autonomy. At the extreme, insurgents may replace the whole military they have fought against with their own officers and troops when they take power. The decimation of the officer corps was almost as severe after the communist takeovers in Eastern Europe. Many officers were imprisoned or murdered in order to keep communist party rule safe from potential military intervention.

Some dictators see the promotion of co-ethnics as the best strategy for achieving interest congruence between officers and themselves. Reserving the most sensitive military posts for clan or even family members, as in Syria under the Assad family, a number of monarchies, and Iraq under Saddam Hussein, takes this strategy to an extreme. Using ethnicity or partisanship as the main criterion for promotion increases the value to co-partisan/co-ethnic officers of the dictatorship continuing to rule. As with limiting the dictatorial inner circle to co-ethnics, discussed above, this strategy aims to reduce factionalism, and thus decrease the likelihood of rogue coups, while increasing interest congruence between soldiers and political leaders (Roessler 2016). The politicization of promotions boosts the power of loyal officers while marginalizing or retiring those thought less reliable. For officers disadvantaged by partisan promotions, however, this strategy makes opposition more attractive.[8]

The extreme examples of dictatorial interference in the military are possible when the armed forces backing the dictator (e.g., the Soviet occupation army in Eastern Europe or victorious insurgent forces) can defeat the regular army he wants to subjugate. A dictator who lacks his own military force, however,

---

[8] See Roessler (2011, 2016) for an analysis of how excluding ethnic rivals from the inner circle to lower coup risk can increase the chance of civil war.

would face the immediate threat of a coup if he tried wholesale interference with promotions and retirements. Promotions are central to the career interests, day-to-day well-being, and future prospects of officers. One of the attractions of careers in the military is the clear, predictable career path and the opportunity for upward mobility it provides to young men who lack political or social connections. Political or ethnic favoritism in promotions threatens career expectations and is immediately visible to other officers. It is a relatively easy grievance to organize around because it affects not only personal welfare but also military professionalism and *esprit de corps*, which even officers who are not personally disadvantaged may feel strongly about.

Officers passed over for promotion, forced into retirement, or dismissed have led quite a few coups, and soldiers loyal to jailed former commanders sometimes free them as the first stage of a coup. Dismissed and jailed former high-ranking officers have led a number of insurgencies as well (Roessler 2016). So, dictators have to make careful strategic calculations before trying to take control of the officer corps through recruitment, promotions, and dismissals.

The establishment of a countervailing paramilitary force increases the feasibility of interfering with promotions because it can reduce the odds of a successful coup, though the creation of paramilitary forces itself carries some risk. The diversion of scarce resources to pay and arm them reduces the benefits that can be allocated to the regular military, and descriptions of why coups occurred sometimes also mention officers' complaints about the better weapons and nice uniforms of paramilitary troops (Nordlinger 1977).

The implications of creating a new presidential guard or other paramilitary force, however, may be less initially obvious to regular officers than interference with promotions. These new forces are usually announced with patriotic fanfare, and they may at first appear to add new units to the regular forces. Thus, they can seem to strengthen the military rather than challenging its monopoly of force. Because the consequences of creating new paramilitary forces are less obvious, dictators may establish them before they try to interfere with promotions. Once a well-funded paramilitary unit guards the presidential palace, prospects for successful coups decline, and officers may plot fewer attempts because they fear violent defeat by the new armed force. The establishment of paramilitary forces may thus embolden dictators to interfere with promotions in the regular army.

THE RELATIONSHIP BETWEEN COUNTERBALANCING AND INTERFERENCE

One implication of this discussion is that dictators who counterbalance the regular army by creating loyalist paramilitaries will then be more likely to interfere in the military's promotion decisions. We evaluate whether the successful pursuit of one strategy for reducing the potential threat from the military – counterbalancing – paves the way for the successful pursuit of another – interfering with promotions. As with other power grabs by dictators, we expect the success of one to increase the likelihood of the next one in the kind of spiraling consolidation of personal dictatorial control described in Chapter 4.

Our argument about the linked fates of dictator and paramilitary forces recruited from his group also implies that *loyalist* paramilitary units should deter coups more effectively than paramilitary forces created for other purposes, such as to keep youth loyal or to battle insurgency alongside the military. If loyalist paramilitaries more effectively deter coups, they would have a larger effect on dictators' propensity to manipulate military promotions than would other kinds of paramilitary. In contrast, claims that paramilitary forces reduce the likelihood of coups by increasing the number of independent armed forces that must agree to oust the dictator imply that any kind of paramilitary force would have the same effect, both on the incidence of coups and on interference with promotions. Our data on different types of paramilitary forces allow us to test these two logics: (1) the *linked fate* story, which implies that loyalist paramilitaries should increase the likelihood of interference with promotions but that other types of paramilitary force should not and (2) the *collective action* logic, which implies that all kinds of paramilitary should increase the likelihood of interfering with promotions.

To classify paramilitary forces, coders first noted the creation or existence of armed forces that were both outside the regular military chain of command and not part of the regular police or internal security service. Once such a force had been identified, it was coded according to the following rules:

- Coded 2 if paramilitary forces are created to fight on the government's side during civil wars or insurgencies (e.g., anti-insurgent forces in El Salvador or Thailand) or to carry out other tasks the military or security service wants accomplished.
- Coded 1 if a party militia or other irregular armed force organized by the regime support party has been created.
- Coded 0 if the regime leader creates a paramilitary force, a president's guard, or new security forces apparently loyal to himself.
  - Use this code if a military or paramilitary force has been recruited primarily from the regime leader's tribe, home region, or clan; if they report to him; or if they are newly garrisoned in the presidential palace.

The same code was then used for every subsequent country-year until the paramilitary force was disbanded or integrated into the regular military or until the regime ended.

Some dictators created more than one loyalist paramilitary force. In these cases, the country-year was coded as "0" after the first was created and continued to be "0" in subsequent years until all loyalist paramilitaries were disbanded or the dictatorship lost power. For country-years in which more than one *kind* of paramilitary force existed, the lowest applicable code was used.

To test our arguments, we examine two related forms of meddling in the military's leadership: purges (defined as arrests, executions, or murders) of senior officers and dictatorial control of promotions. Our argument implies that these kinds of interference should be more likely to occur when the dictator has already established a loyalist paramilitary force.

We coded a purge when one or more military or security service officers were jailed or executed without reasonably fair trials or was murdered. Coders were instructed to rely on country specialists and/or journalists for judgments about whether arrests for plotting or treason trials were government responses to real events. They were told not to code a purge if the evidence indicated that a person tried for treason really did try to overthrow the government by violent means and was given a reasonably fair trial.

Dictatorial promotion strategies were coded as follows:

- Coded 2 if country specialists do not report that the regime leader promotes officers loyal to himself or from his ethnic, tribal, regional, or religious group or that he forces officers not from his group into retirement for political reasons
- Coded 1 if country specialists report promotions of top officers loyal to the regime leader or from his group, but not widespread use of loyalty as a criterion for promotion or retirement.
- Coded 0 if country specialists report promotions of large numbers of officers loyal to the regime leader or from his group, or large numbers of forced retirements.

The same historical event might, in some cases, serve as the basis for coding both purges and promotion practices. For example, the communists in Hungary both arrested (purged) many senior officers when they took over and began interfering with promotions at the same time. For this reason, we test separate models for each of these forms of interference with military leadership. Importantly, however, the creation of paramilitary forces is not only conceptually distinct from interference in the regular military, but also coded in our data as a distinct phenomenon in the historical record.

The data on military purges and promotion practices are constructed such that once we find evidence that the dictator pursues either of these strategies for the first time, the variable is coded the same way for all subsequent years while he remains in power unless a change in strategy is reported in the country specialist literature.[9] This coding procedure assumes that a dictator who can

---

[9] For example, immediately after the Communist victory in China, Mao controlled some top promotions, but the revolutionary army included many officers with views very different from Mao's, and military leadership was very decentralized. The first years after the seizure of power are coded as "1." In 1954, however, under Soviet influence, Peng Dehuai was appointed defense

interfere with promotions in one year could probably do so again but may not be observed doing so because he has already put the officers he wants in place. The dictator's control over the military tends to persist over time because the officers he promoted retain their posts or are further promoted, and they in turn promote their allies.

To test whether loyalist paramilitaries increase the likelihood of interfering with military leadership, we restrict the analysis to years in which the dictatorship does *not interfere* with military promotions, and test whether dictators with loyalist paramilitaries in those years are more likely to interfere with promotions in the regular military the *following year*. This design means we are testing whether dictators with loyalist paramilitaries initiate interference in the military more quickly than dictators who lack them, given that the dictator has *not yet interfered* in these ways.

In the full data set, loyalist paramilitaries are more common (35 percent) than party militias (18 percent) and irregular forces created to fight alongside the regular military (9 percent). However, in the samples we employ that restrict the analysis to years prior to military interference, the incidence of different types of paramilitaries is more evenly distributed. Prior to observing promotion interference (921 observations), loyalist paramilitaries (16 percent) are less common than party militias (19 percent) but still more common than anti-rebel paramilitaries (10 percent). Prior to observing the first military purge (2,555 observations), loyalist paramilitaries (27 percent) are the most common, with party militias (20 percent) and anti-rebel paramilitaries (9 percent) less prevalent.[10]

We begin the analysis by comparing the baseline probabilities in Figure 7.1.[11] The plots in the top two panels of the figure show the probabilities of dictatorial interference with promotions and military purges, both with and without an existing paramilitary force of *any* kind. Just under 5 percent (0.046) of dictators who lack a paramilitary force initiate interference with promotions, while just under 8 percent (0.077) of those supported by paramilitary forces of one kind or another do so. Dictators unsupported by a paramilitary force begin a purge

---

minister and began intensive professionalization of the armed forces, which included limits on Mao's interference (Whitson 1973, 98–100). From 1955 until 1959, when Mao succeeded in purging Peng Dehai from the regime's inner circle, Chinese promotions are coded as "2" because Mao had little influence on them.

[10] The data are constructed so no observations were coded with more than one type of paramilitary. Therefore, colinearity issues do not arise in the analysis that includes all three types of paramilitaries in the same specification.

[11] The analysis examines pooled leader-year observations when the dictator did not interfere the previous year. There are 164 leaders in 74 countries (921 observations) in the analysis of promotions; this excludes leaders who interfered in military promotions in their first year in power. The purge analysis examines 340 leaders in 115 countries (2,555 observations), again excluding leaders who purge the military in their first year in power. It is more common for leaders to interfere in promotions than to purge the military during their first year.

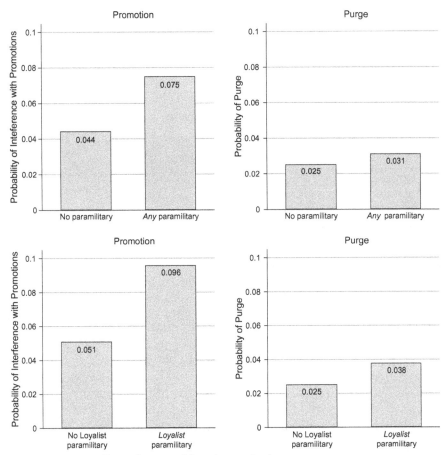

FIGURE 7.1 Paramilitary forces and interference in the army.

of officers in 2.5 percent of observed years, while those supported by one initiate a purge 3.1 percent of the time. These percentages may seem low, but recall that all country-years in which dictators had previously interfered with promotions or purged officers have been excluded from the data set. So, these are estimates for the beginning of dictatorial efforts to control military leadership in countries in which the dictator has previously not interfered.

The lower two panels compare dictators who lack *loyalist* paramilitaries with those who have them.[12] Just over 5 percent of dictators unsupported by loyalist paramilitary forces begin interference in the military's promotion practices, while almost 10 percent of dictators who can count on the support of a

---

[12] The group that lacks loyalist paramilitary forces includes dictatorial country-years in which party militias and/or anti-rebel irregular forces exist plus country-years that lack any kind of paramilitary.

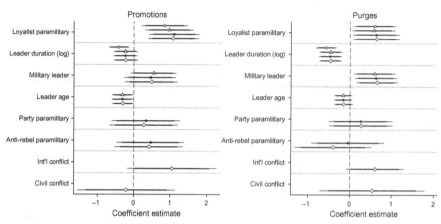

FIGURE 7.2 Loyalist paramilitary forces and interference.

loyalist paramilitary force do so. The relative increase from the baseline probability of 5.3 percent is more than 80 percent. For purges of officers, we find that 2.5 percent of dictators unsupported by loyalist paramilitary forces initiate a purge of senior officers, while 3.8 percent who can depend on loyalist paramilitary support do so. The relative increase for purges is 50 percent.

Next we test a series of logistic regression models that control for the length of time the dictator has been in power.[13] The first specification, shown by squares in Figure 7.2, includes only the indicator variable for the existence of a loyalist paramilitary force and the natural log of leader time in power. The next set of specifications, shown as triangles, adds two variables that pertain to individual dictators: their age and whether they were military officers before becoming regime leaders. Next, we add indicators for other types of paramilitary forces (party militias and anti-rebel irregular forces). The final specification, shown as diamonds, adds indicators for civil and international conflict.

The left panel of Figure 7.2 shows the results for initiation of interference with promotions in the regular military, while the right panel shows results for first military purges. In all tests, the coefficient for loyalist paramilitary is positive and significant, indicating that these specific paramilitary forces are associated with a higher likelihood of interfering with leadership in the military.[14] Models with a full set of covariates (depicted by diamonds) indicate

---

[13] This design mimics standard hazard models; we control for log duration in the reported analysis and show in replication files that the results remain when using duration time polynomials instead.

[14] Replication files show that this result is robust to including indicators for how the regime seized power and structural covariates (GDP per capita, population, oil rents, and growth). Models with leader-specific random effects yield similarly sized coefficient estimates but larger estimates of the variance in the purge model.

that loyalist paramilitary forces are associated with a 5.7 percent increase in the probability of beginning to interfere in military promotions and a 1.7 percent increase in the likelihood of starting a military purge, which is roughly similar to the increases depicted in the lower two panels in Figure 7.1.

The models in Figure 7.2 also suggest that dictators are more likely to interfere in military leadership earlier in their tenures, when they are younger, and when they came to the dictatorship from careers in the military. Finally, participation in an international conflict increases interference in military leadership, but the estimates are significant only at the 0.10 percent level.[15]

Importantly for our argument, the estimates for other kinds of paramilitary forces are not statistically significant, suggesting that these forces do not encourage the dictator to grab more power from the regular military. In the replication files, we test similar models for party militias and anti-insurgent irregular forces separately and again find no consistent association between them and initiation of interference in regular military promotions or purges.

These findings provide initial evidence that loyalist paramilitaries help dictators to consolidate power over the regular military by interfering with their promotion procedures and purging senior officers of doubtful loyalty. We find no evidence linking paramilitary forces of other kinds, namely, party militias and anti-insurgent irregulars, to interference with the regular military. This suggests that counterbalancing is not simply a numbers game in which dictators need only increase the number of security veto players to increase plotters' collective action problems in order to protect themselves. Rather, we suggest that the informal personal ties between the dictator and the loyalist paramilitary he creates by recruiting from co-ethnics, co-partisans, or his home region allow him to interfere with impunity in the internal workings of the regular military.[16] When regular army officers know that loyalist paramilitary forces will defend the dictator to the bitter end because their own futures are tied to his fate, they are less likely to attempt coups to stop the dictator's manipulation of promotions or purges of senior officers. Regular officers' reluctance to risk punishment for failed coups emboldens dictators to interfere more.

CONCLUSION

Coercive institutions in dictatorships maintain the credibility of the dictator's threat to use force against challengers and opponents. Most of what such institutions do is preventive rather than active repression. They deter overt opposition and monitor elites and ordinary citizens in order to interrupt plots and opposition movements before they have even been organized.

Internal security services focus much of their effort on high-ranking and mid-level elites. They gather information about party officials, military officers,

---

[15] We caution against interpreting the estimate for international conflict because identification relies on a very few "positive" cases in each model.

[16] This set of findings is consistent with Morency-Laflamme's (2017) analysis of Benin and Togo.

high-level civil servants, and administrators, in addition to union leaders, teachers, journalists, opposition leaders, and anyone else able to undermine policy implementation or plot the dictator's ouster. Security agencies combine spying with the authority to arrest, intimidate, interrogate, and execute people thought to represent a threat to the regime or dictator. Some security services also employ informers to spy on ordinary people, but this level of surveillance requires more financial resources than many dictatorships have. The internet has increased the feasibility of monitoring ordinary citizens and interfering with their access to information and ability to express opposition, however.

The coercive institutions of dictatorships are weapons that can be used by the dictator to undermine or even murder other members of the dictatorial elite if he can gain full control over them. Other members of the elite, however, have strong incentives to resist the personalization of control over security services and the dictator's efforts to undermine the autonomy of the army.

If the dictator has secured personal control of the internal security apparatus, he has a major advantage in the power struggle with other members of the inner circle. Control of internal security tilts the distribution of two crucial resources, information and capacity for violence, in the dictator's favor and thus reduces the likelihood that other elites could oust him or constrain his behavior via credible threats to oust. The dictator's control of internal security amounts to a major step in the direction of the personalization of rule, and other members of the inner circle can rarely reverse it within a dictator's lifetime.

Armies are the last defense of dictatorships threatened by rebellion or uprising, but since military coups are the most frequent means of ousting them, dictators often fear their armies. Consequently, many dictatorships create paramilitary forces to defend against coups and counterbalance the regular army. We term paramilitary forces recruited from ethnic, partisan, or regional groups closely tied to the dictator "loyalist" to distinguish them from other irregular armed forces such as party militias and anti-insurgent forces.

As a further safeguard against the army, dictators also want to manipulate recruitment, promotions, and retirements to favor loyal officers, and they may want to purge, arrest, and execute officers whose loyalty they suspect. The main impediment to interference with military leadership is the dictator's fear of coups, which officers may risk in order to safeguard the army's autonomy and their own careers and futures. Because the establishment of a loyalist paramilitary force increases the risk that coups will fail, dictators supported by them can interfere with military leadership with greater impunity.

These strategies for keeping armed supporters in check work some of the time, but officers can at times fight back, and other members of the dictatorial elite may support them. The establishment of paramilitary forces and the politicization of promotions have been mentioned as causes for a number of coups (as discussed in Chapter 3), and purged officers have also gone on to lead insurgencies in some instances (Roessler 2016). Such a backlash can lead to authoritarian breakdown, a subject to which we now turn.

PART IV

DICTATORIAL SURVIVAL AND BREAKDOWN

8

Why Dictatorships Fall

The Egyptian monarchy fell to a coup led by Colonel Gamal Abdel Nasser and the Free Officers in 1952 (Haddad 1973, 7–23). The dictatorship established by Nasser lasted until 2012, when popular protests forced its final attenuated incarnation to allow a fair election. Massive, largely nonviolent demonstrations forced the resignation of the regime's fourth dictator, Hosni Mubarak, in 2011, but the officer corps, a pillar of the regime since 1952, remained in control of the country until their candidate lost the 2012 election. This election ended Egypt's second modern authoritarian regime. The new democratically elected regime lasted only until another military coup ended it in 2013.

Egypt's experience illustrates that dictatorships can fall in a variety of ways, ranging from coups carried out by a handful of officers to election losses and popular uprisings. In some instances, the end of a dictatorship leads to democratization; in others, a new autocratic leadership group takes over, as in 1952 Egypt, bringing with it new rules for making decisions, a new elite group, and a different distribution of benefits and suffering. This chapter investigates how and why dictatorships end, as well as why democracy sometimes follows, but often does not.

We begin with some basic information about *how* dictatorships end. Next, we describe the decision calculus facing regime insiders as they decide whether to desert a dictatorship, followed by a discussion of how economic and other kinds of crisis can alter their assessment of the costs of opposition. We then analyze how characteristics of the dictatorship itself contribute to destabilizing conflict within the inner circle. In the sections that follow, we investigate how specific pre-seizure-of-power features of the group that established the dictatorship influence the way the dictatorial elite responds to challenges and the opposition they cause. We explain why some kinds of dictatorship survive crises better than others and, finally, why some tend to exit peacefully through fair, contested elections when faced with strong opposition, while others grip power with tooth and claw until violently cast out.

HOW DICTATORSHIPS END

Potential opposition leaders exist at all times in all dictatorships. They may come from groups outside the regime's distributive network, but they often come from groups currently or formerly allied with the dictator. Because ties to the dictatorship often entail resource and network advantages, it is easier for those linked to it to challenge the dictator and regime than it is for those without such resources (Svolik 2012; Roessler 2016). Overthrows led by current or former regime allies are thus common.

Citizens living under dictatorship, whether regime insiders or not, must decide whether to challenge it and, if so, the method for taking action. Potential opposition leaders assess their options carefully, taking into account whether they have the support and resources they need to mount a particular type of challenge successfully, as well as the risk and potential cost of failure.

These strategic choices depend on the costs and difficulties of creating and maintaining different kinds of opposition in varying circumstances. Some methods of ending dictatorships, such as election campaigns, require much more overt opposition support than others, such as coups. In 1952 Egypt, many people felt angry about British control of the Suez Canal, but citizen anger was not aimed at ousting the king. Officers chose a coup as their method of overthrow because they had a comparative advantage in the deployment of force, but also because a coup had a reasonable chance of success at a time when organizing sustained popular opposition would probably have been impossible. Political and economic circumstances also influence when potential opposition leaders can attract enough support to succeed. The Free Officers chose a time when many Egyptians felt their government had failed to defend their interests, and when the government itself was in chaos. This timing reduced the chance that citizens would defend the king and that the government would respond to the military challenge quickly or coherently.

Potential opposition leaders' choices about how to try to end dictatorships cause regime breakdowns to unfold in the patterns that we label coups, popular uprisings, opposition election victories, and so on. Each of these labels identifies not only the form an attempt to overthrow a dictatorship takes but implicitly the kind and approximate number of people involved in the effort. "Coup" labels an ouster of political leaders carried out by military defectors from the regime. Coups require the voluntary cooperation of only a few officers because lower-level officers and soldiers usually obey orders. They typically take only a day or two, and usually no more than a few people are killed during them. They are thus relatively easy for officers to organize. "Popular uprisings" require the voluntary cooperation of many more people, usually civilians; they can last from a few days to many months; and they often result in quite a few deaths

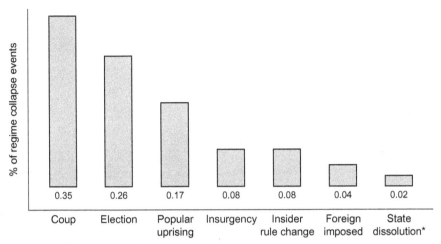

FIGURE 8.1 How autocratic regimes end.
*State dissolution includes cases in which a previously independent state was subsumed into another one, cases in which a state broke up into constituent parts, and cases in which a dictatorship ended but was not immediately followed by a government that controlled a substantial part of the state's territory.

and injuries even though protesters are generally unarmed. "Insurgencies" also require the cooperation of substantial numbers of people, but involve confrontation between armed opposition and the military forces defending the dictatorship. Consequently, many more are likely to be killed. Insurgencies can last from a few days to many years, and during that time, insurgent leaders must find ways to arm, train, and feed their troops. So, this strategy requires a much more substantial commitment from participants than popular uprisings. Finally, a successful opposition election campaign requires cooperation from even more people than uprisings or insurgencies, usually near 50 percent of the adult population, but participation is relatively costless compared with other methods of ousting dictatorships.

Figure 8.1 shows how dictatorships ended between 1946 and 2010. It reveals that more dictatorships fell to coups than to other kinds of challenge. The second most common means of ending dictatorships is elections won by someone not supported by the dictatorship.[1] Overthrow by popular uprising occurred less often before 1990, but has become much more frequent since the

---

[1] Regime-ending elections include both semi-competitive elections that the dictatorial ruling party expected to win but did not and fair elections that dictatorships that had agreed to step down organized as a means of determining who would succeed them. The latter are usually organized by military dictatorships.

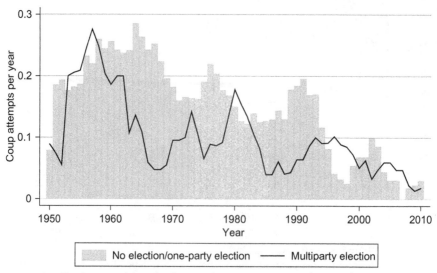

FIGURE 8.2 Semi-competitive elections and coup attempts in dictatorships.

end of the Cold War. Insurgencies toppled some dictatorships, as did foreign invasions. Some ended when regime insiders changed the basic rules governing leadership choice, e.g., adopted universal suffrage, transforming oligarchy into democracy.

Coups are the most common method of ending dictatorships for the same reason that they are the most common means of initiating them: coups require the cooperation of the fewest individuals, and soldiers have weapons. Though coups are easier to coordinate than other forms of regime ouster, however, they entail risks. About half of coups fail (Singh 2014). Failed coups can lead to dismissal from the army, imprisonment, and execution for treason, so the cost of failure for the top officers involved can be high.

The high cost of failure and the irreducible element of luck in whether coups succeed lessen the appeal of plotting where alternative mechanisms for ending dictatorships exist. Coup attempts have declined since the end of the Cold War, when more dictatorships began to allow semi-competitive elections in which multiple parties can compete (Kendall-Taylor and Frantz 2014). Figure 8.2 shows the relationship between semi-competitive elections in dictatorships and the frequency of coup attempts from 1946 to 2010. The vertical bars show the yearly rate of coup attempts in dictatorships that either hold no elections or hold elections that offer voters no choice. The solid line shows the attempted coup rate in dictatorships that hold semi-competitive elections. As the graph demonstrates, coup attempts tend to be more common in dictatorships that do not allow the opposition to compete in elections – as expected if potential opposition leaders chose methods for trying to end dictatorships strategically.[2] Where the opposition can participate in elections, however unlikely they are to win, regime opponents are less likely to take the risk of a coup attempt.

In sum, potential opposition leaders try to end dictatorships using the means of doing so with the best chance of success – given their resources and support networks – and the lowest potential cost for failure. They seldom indulge in quixotic acts. They also choose times to act when they expect substantial support from others for regime change. We discuss the dynamics that underlie potential opposition leaders' decisions to take action against the dictatorial elite in the section that follows.

INDIVIDUAL SUPPORT AND OPPOSITION

Dictatorships provide substantial benefits to regime insiders and some citizens, as described in Chapter 6, but they also survive because most of the time those who do not receive benefits avoid the costs of opposition. Opposition increases when the benefits that individuals usually receive have declined, when the risk of opposition has fallen, or both. In order to build a foundation for analyzing the effects of specific events and institutions on the survival of dictatorship, this section develops an abstract description of individuals' decision calculus as they decide whether to oppose the dictatorship.

The Interests of Regime Insiders

Ordinary citizens can play a large role in ending dictatorships, but they rarely do so without leadership, and the individuals who lead them often spent earlier stages of their careers as supporters of the dictatorship. This is so partly because the dictatorship is often the only game in town for the politically ambitious and partly because participation in the dictatorship is the best way to gain access to the resources and build the clientele networks that facilitate opposition mobilization later. When members of the inner circle defect, they can often take with them the clientele networks originally built within the ruling group using state resources (Garrido 2011).

Members of the inner circle will defect to the opposition if:

---

[2] The attempted coup rate is the average number of attempted coups per year. In regimes lacking semi-competitive elections, the attempted coup rate is 14.0 percent; in those holding semi-competitive elections, the attempted coup rate is 9.6 percent. During the pre-1990 period, the attempted coup rate is 50 percent higher in regimes lacking semi-competitive elections than in regimes with semi-competitive contests. But the gap narrows during the two decades from 1990 to 2010: the coup rate is only 25 percent higher during this period.

$$p\left[qO_j + (1-q)\sim O_j\right] + (1-p)\left[sO_l + (1-s)\sim O_l\right] < t(1-p)\left[rO_k + (1-r)\sim O_k\right] - pC$$

$$(8.1)$$

where:

> p is the probability the status quo regime will survive
>
> q is the probability of maintaining/acquiring office in the status quo regime
>
> r is the probability of achieving office in the new regime (for a partisan of the new)
>
> s is the probability that a partisan of the old regime achieves/retains office in the new regime
>
> $q > s$
>
> t is the probability of the new regime turning out as anticipated[3]
>
> O_j is the benefit of office to a partisan of the status quo in the status quo regime
>
> O_k is the benefit of office in a new regime to a partisan of the new regime
>
> O_l is the benefit of office in a new regime to a partisan of the old regime
>
> $O_j > O_l$
>
> C is the cost of opposing the status quo regime.

The term qO_j captures the idea that the better the posts individuals have or expect, the more they would have to lose by defecting, but also that no one in a dictatorship can be sure of occupying the same post or receiving the same benefits tomorrow that they receive today. Dictatorships lack enforceable contracts to ensure that promises of future rewards will be kept or that legal provisions that have governed past events will govern future ones. Potential defectors must assess their future prospects based on incomplete but well-informed insider information.

If, however, a potential defector has been excluded from the inner circle or has failed to receive a hoped-for post and does not expect it in the future, then qO_j becomes zero, substantially reducing the cost of defection. A member of the elite's failure to receive a hoped-for office can trigger defection – as happened when leaders of the Mexican *Partido Revolucionario Institucional* (PRI) nom-inated someone else as the party's presidential candidate, and Cuauhtémoc

---

[3] We assume that if the new regime turns out different from what those who invested to bring about regime change had hoped (e.g., if a popular uprising results in a new dictatorship rather than democracy), then those who hoped for a different outcome receive zero. We do not assume a benefit from the fall of the status quo regime for individuals excluded from the new ruling group because the new regime could turn out worse than the status quo regime (e.g., Qaddafi's dictatorship was worse than the monarchy it replaced for most Libyans, and Qaddafi's regime may have been better for most Libyans than the failed state that followed its overthrow).

Cárdenas left the party in order to organize a new opposition party to challenge the PRI dictatorship. Loss of current positions of power can also result in defection. After the Iraqi coup of 1958, Brigadier-General 'Abd al-Karim Qassem became commander-in-chief of the armed forces, prime minister, and defense minister in the new dictatorship. His closest collaborator, Colonel 'Abd al-Salam Aref, became deputy prime minister, interior minister, and deputy commander-in-chief of the armed forces, but when disagreements arose, Qassem excluded Aref from the inner circle by naming him ambassador to Germany. Rather than accepting the sinecure, Aref defected and returned to Iraq to challenge Qassem's leadership. Although he was arrested and served time in prison, a few years later Aref led the coup that overthrew Qassem (Dann 1969, 20–32, 37–41, 77–89, 363–72).

Cárdenas and Aref are examples of members of dictatorial elites who defected after events that caused a reassessment of their likely future in the dictatorship. Most members of the PRI remained loyal in 1987, however, as did many Iraqi officers during Qassem's rule. The dictators' supporters defect only if they think their chances of achieving their ambitions by joining the opposition outweigh the future benefits of loyalty to the current ruling group. The term $(1-q)\sim O_j$ captures the idea that loyal members of the dictatorial elite continue to receive benefits (such as the German ambassadorship) as long as the regime survives, even if they lack high-level posts.

Insiders also decide to defect when events lead them to believe that the regime may fall, lowering their assessment of p, the perceived chance of regime survival. If the regime is going to collapse, those who jump ship earlier have better prospects for achieving respected positions in the opposition than those who cling longer to the old order. Because no one knows whether and when the regime will fall, however, one insider may defect while others see defending the dictatorship as the more sensible strategy.

In some situations, members of the status quo ruling group may continue to occupy valued posts after regime change. If democracy replaces the dictatorship, for example, the former ruling party often becomes a viable party in the new regime, and some of its members may be elected to Congress or continue to occupy high-level bureaucratic posts. Military officers also often retain their posts after democratic transitions, even when commanding officers are forced to retire or prosecuted. The term $(1-p)sO_l$ captures the possibility of continued benefits for members of the old status quo ruling group after regime change. If individuals expect continued benefits from remaining members of the old ruling party or clique even after regime change, they have no reason to defect.

The terms on the right-hand side of the inequality are analogous to those on the left, but refer to expected benefits under a different regime. The main difference between left and right is that the right-hand term includes C, the cost of opposition, and t, the probability that the new regime really turns out the way its supporters claim or hope it will. The cost term is included because opposition to dictators is invariably costly, and that cost must be borne regardless of whether the opposition ultimately succeeds. The cost is likely to be greater if the old regime survives, captured by the term p, which would be low if the regime is expected to collapse and very high in stable autocracies.

The probability that the new regime will function as anticipated, t, is included to reflect the uncertainty that exists about what will happen after regime change. In order to attract citizen support, those who lead opposition parties, uprisings, or insurgencies must promise democratization regardless of what they intend or what is likely. The ubiquity of such promises suggests that opposition leaders understand this. The outcome of successful ousters is uncertain, however, for both elites and citizens, as they cannot be sure that they will receive promised benefits from the change. In fact, they cannot be certain that the new regime will be more democratic, or better in any other way, than the old one (Bueno de Mesquita et al. 2003). Slightly more than half of authoritarian breakdowns since World War II were followed by new dictatorships, not democratization (Geddes, Wright, and Frantz 2014).

The Interests of Others

Lower-level regime insiders face a similar decision calculus. Ordinary citizens' decision-making differs from that of regime insiders in that they have little expectation of achieving office in the current regime or a future one. So their decisions about joining the overt opposition depend on whether they are receiving benefits from the current dictatorship, their assessment of the probability that it will persist, the benefits they expect from an alternative to the status quo, and the cost of opposition.

Potential opposition leaders unaffiliated with the dictatorship share a similar decision calculus with ordinary citizens, except that they have a good chance of securing office under the future regime. Their calculation would therefore include terms like those on the right-hand side of Equation 8.1.

If citizens receive a stream of benefits under the status quo (e.g., a salary or advantages associated with a clientele network linked to regime leaders), they are unlikely to participate in a movement to unseat the dictator. Mass actions to remove dictators most often occur when economic misfortune or policy failure prevents regime insiders from delivering benefits, economic growth, and everyday services to citizens (Bratton and van de Walle 1997).

A dictatorship's reputation for zero tolerance of opposition and for draconian punishments deters the expression of opposition by raising C. Effective security services, pervasive networks of informers, and intrusive mass-level institutions for social control raise the likely costs of opposition. Citizens are more likely to join the opposition, however, if large numbers of others have joined, both because large numbers increase the likelihood that the regime will fall and because the presence of large numbers indicates a lower risk of suffering punishment for joining (Kuran 1989, 1991; Lohmann 1994). Unless the cost of opposition is near zero, however, as in secret-ballot elections, most will not participate because they will receive any benefits of regime change whether they participated or not.

Perceptions about Regime Survival

Dictatorships rarely end unless many citizens oppose them, but they often fail to end despite widespread citizen opposition, especially when people keep their opposition private, as they do most of the time (Kuran 1989). As Adam Przeworski (1986) explained long ago, in stable dictatorships most people seem to support the regime, but after the dictatorship falls, almost everyone seems to have wanted regime change. This kind of process is called a tipping phenomenon.

Perceptions about the *likelihood* of dictatorial collapse follow the same tipping logic. Before the dictatorship faces serious challenges, individuals inside and outside the dictatorial elite expect it to survive. They adapt their behavior to do the best they can within the current political system and, even if they hate the dictatorship, see little point in shouldering the costs of overt opposition. Once challenges begin to reduce perceptions of dictatorial invincibility, however, assessments can cascade downward until nearly everyone believes the regime will fall.

Understanding that a minor challenge can precipitate a dramatic downward rush in assessments of regime strength, some members of the dictatorial elite may defect at this point in order to establish reputations with the opposition in anticipation of regime change, but most will remain loyal. In this way, some politicians who spend their early careers as loyal servants of the dictator can become stalwarts of democratic politics during transitions – joining those who defected after loss of office.

Some citizens may also then make their opposition public when the first challenge emerges, but most will play it safe. As soon as some people begin to express opposition, however, others recalibrate the likelihood of dictatorial survival, leading more citizens to express opposition, and so on. As citizens update their estimates of the prospects for regime survival, more and more become comfortable expressing their discontent in election campaigns or demonstrations. If the dictatorship can crush or defuse early demonstrations, perceptions about likely survival may increase again. If not, however, they can drop sharply. Eventually, those who sincerely support the dictatorship begin to see costs associated with such support and keep quiet about it, contributing to the perception that the regime is done for.

In this way, perceptions about future regime survival affect the willingness of members of the dictatorial elite to defect and of citizens to express overt opposition by changing their calculus of p, the probability of regime survival.

THE EFFECT OF CRISIS ON DECISIONS TO OPPOSE
THE DICTATORSHIP

Many observers believe that economic crisis contributes to authoritarian break-down. Here, we focus first on the mechanism through which externally induced economic problems might threaten regime survival. As an example of an external crisis, consider a fall in the international price of a country's most important export. Typically, such a decline would reduce the growth rate, affecting the benefits available to citizens, and reduce government revenues. Reduced revenues could result in downward pressure on public employment, wages in the public sector, spending on schools and health care, state invest-ment, and all the benefits that dictatorships provide for their supporters. After the international price of oil dropped in 2013, for example, Venezuela's reduced ability to pay for imports led to empty shelves in many grocery stores. These included the centerpiece of the Chávez/Maduro regime's most popular program for channeling benefits to supporters, the state stores that sell food at subsidized prices in poor neighborhoods. So, not only was the benefit stream provided by the dictatorship for all citizens reduced by the price shock, but the ruling elite even lost some of its ability to deliver special advantages to its most loyal supporters. These problems have worsened over time.

What happened in Venezuela is an extreme example of what happens after price shocks and other economic crises. For those regime beneficiaries who occupy posts in government, such challenges reduce the expected value of future benefits from office, O_j, as wages fall. The likelihood of being appointed to a new and/or better post or retaining the one held, q, also declines because of budget pressures to reduce public employment, as do expectations about future benefits from the regime in case one fails to achieve or retain a particular job, $\sim O_j$. For ordinary citizens, such crises reduce the expected benefits from the current government, including expectations about future economic growth.

These reductions increase the attractiveness of joining the opposition, for both regime insiders and ordinary citizens. If individuals see that many others have become visible regime opponents, as often happens during economic crises, their assessment of the probability of regime survival, p, also falls. Through these two mechanisms, overt opposition can grow and the likelihood of regime survival decline.

Dictatorial policy makers can mitigate or exacerbate the effects of exogenous crises by their actions, just as democratic governments can. They make politic-ally motivated choices not only about policy responses but also about which parts of the population will bear the largest cost of the downturn. Members of the dictatorial inner circle try to distribute the costs of the crisis so that they fall most heavily on those with the least capacity to destabilize the regime, usually the less organized and economically weaker parts of the population. The Chávez/Maduro dictatorship, for example, closed many subsidized grocery stores, but not those in politically volatile Caracas.

ECONOMIC CRISIS AND BREAKDOWN

Despite the belief that economic crisis destabilizes dictatorships and the plausibility of the scenario described, some careful statistical studies have shown little effect (e.g., Przeworski et al. 2000). We suggest that the contradictory results found in large-N studies are caused by differences in the capacity of dictatorships to respond to economic crisis by redistributing the costs in politically effective ways. In other words, we think that economic crisis is more destabilizing for some kinds of dictatorships than others, leading to weak or contradictory results when all dictatorships are lumped together.

Regime elites, we suggest, can decrease popular opposition by building the kinds of organizational infrastructure that can deliver help after economic crises or natural disasters, and can prevent regime insiders from stealing aid meant for disaster victims. The party-based networks of officials and supporters built to incorporate more citizens into the dictatorship's support base and facilitate the collection of information about events and attitudes at the grassroots, described in Chapter 6, can also be used to deliver disaster aid or redistribute the costs of economic crisis. We believe that the extensive patron–client networks developed in party-led dictatorships help regime elites to continue distributing to those most essential for their survival while shifting the burden of the crisis to other, politically weaker parts of the population. During economic crises, ruling parties with wide-ranging distributive networks can help prevent benefits from the status quo regime from dropping too far among those citizens most capable of overthrowing the dictatorship.

All dictatorial support parties try to coopt citizens, but we believe that those that had established extensive patron–client networks before the seizure of power have an advantage over parties created after seizures of power. Their advantage arises from the necessity of developing relationships between central party leadership, local party leaders, and people living in different areas in order to survive while out of power and, often, subject to repression. We expect these relationships to have been especially strong where the party needed to exchange protection or other benefits for manpower and resources in order to maintain an insurgency or where it needed to exchange goods and services for votes in competitive or semi-competitive elections. Because of their more developed and extensive patron–client networks, we expect such support parties to contribute to regime durability during crises.

In contrast, dictatorships that have failed to build such penetrating party networks may lack the means to respond effectively when natural disaster or economic crisis strikes. Even a manageable natural disaster or economic challenge can become calamitous for the dictatorship if it fails to respond effectively.

In the next section we test whether institutions associated with extensive patron–client networks insulate dictatorships from the destabilizing effects of economic crisis.

Empirical Approach

To investigate how economic crisis affects regime stability, we create a binary variable that flags observations if the country has experienced negative growth during the previous two years, which we call *crisis*. If the lagged two-year moving average of economic growth (per capita) is less than −2 percent, *crisis* takes the value of 1, and zero otherwise. We create a similar indicator for good economic times, which we call *boom*; it is coded 1 if growth (per capita) is greater than 5 percent.[4] Separating out the two extremes of economic growth allows for a more transparent test of the proposition that economic *crisis* undermines authoritarian rule. If we simply examined the effect of economic growth as a continuous variable, we would not be able to assess the potentially destabilizing influence of unusually poor growth easily, or the potentially stabilizing effects of especially good economic times.

As in earlier sections, we use an exogenous indicator of political institutions that encompass citizens in well-organized networks, *inherited party*, which identifies regimes led by a political party that was organized either to lead an insurgency or to participate in elections before the authoritarian seizure of power. This variable does not vary over time within particular regimes since it measures a pre-seizure characteristic of the party that later became the dictatorial ruling party.

To estimate the effect of economic crisis on regime breakdown, we test a linear probability model with country fixed effects and time period effects, while controlling for duration dependence with a cubic polynomial. This approach allows us to model all country-specific characteristics, such as geography, colonial history, and religion, without dropping dictatorships that remain in existence throughout the time period covered by the data, such as the Communist Party regime in China or the monarchy in Saudi Arabia.

We use a minimum number of control variables because many factors that influence regime stability, such as protest and civil war, are post-treatment phenomena; that is, economic crisis may *cause* protest or insurgency. Even international war can result from a dictator's initiation of conflict to divert citizens from economic distress. Therefore, we include only three potential confounders: prior experience of democracy, whether the dictator was a rebel leader before the seizure of power, and whether he was a member of the military. These variables ensure that the *inherited party* variable is not simply picking up the destabilizing effect of earlier democratic experience or the stabilizing influence of revolutionary party organization. First, we test the following specification:

---

[4] Crises occur in roughly 17 percent of observations, while booms occur in 19 percent.

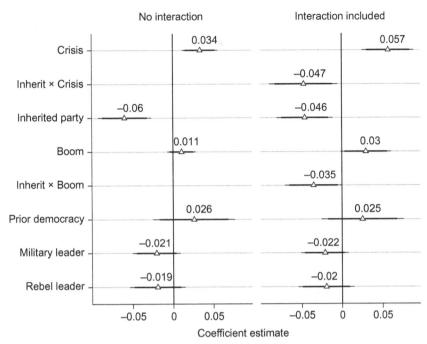

FIGURE 8.3 Economic crisis, party networks, and authoritarian breakdown.

$$Pr(Y_t = 1 | Y_{t-1} = 0) = \alpha_0 + \beta_1{}^* Inherit_{it} + \beta_2{}^* Crisis + \beta_3{}^* Boom$$
$$+ \beta_4{}^* Rebel\ leader + \beta_5{}^* Military\ leader + \beta_6{}^* Prior\ Democracy + \delta_i + \eta_t + \varepsilon$$

$$(8.2)$$

where δ_i are country effects and η_t are five-year time period effects. Then we include an interaction between *crisis* and *inherited party* as well as one between *boom* and *inherited party*. This allows us to test whether the effect of crisis varies depending on whether an inherited support party leads the dictatorship.

Figure 8.3 reports the results. When no interaction is included in the specification (left side), the estimates for *crisis* are positive and significant, indicating that economic crises are associated with authoritarian breakdown. Further, the estimate for *inherited party* is negative and significant, showing again that such parties contribute to regime durability. This result suggests that the patron–client networks established in long-lasting parties, the ability to cope with succession (also a feature of inherited parties), or both contribute to regime resilience. This model does not show whether such parties specifically help dictatorships weather economic crises, however.

The second model (right side) does that. Including an interaction term allows us to examine the effects of patron–client networks that reach ordinary citizens on the likelihood of breakdown *during* or soon after economic crisis. The estimate for the effect of the interaction between *crisis* and *inherited party* is negative and statistically significant. This means that economic crises are less likely to destabilize dictatorships led by parties that have developed extensive patron–client networks.[5] The positive estimate for *crisis* alone means that economic downturns increase the likelihood of collapse in dictatorships that *lack* extensive party networks. In short, the data analysis confirms the argument that a well-organized ruling party can help dictatorships survive economic crises.

POWER CONCENTRATION AND REGIME SURVIVAL

External crises are not the only challenges dictatorships face. Conflict within the inner circle can threaten regime survival even without other challenges. As Guillermo O'Donnell and Philippe C. Schmitter (1986) noted decades ago, the collapse of authoritarian regimes can begin with factionalism and disagreements among the dictatorship's most powerful decision makers. Insider conflict can motivate the dictator to demote or exclude members of the inner circle, potentially weakening it; alternatively, losers in factional struggles may defect from the regime in order to lead opposition to it. If elite conflict becomes public, it can also change citizens' perceptions of the likelihood of regime survival, p, increasing their willingness to undertake overt opposition. Intra-elite struggles can thus make the regime seem weak to outside opponents, emboldening latent opposition to mobilize against it, as well as directly causing elite defections.

Elite conflict often involves challenges to the incumbent dictator. In Chapters 4 and 5 we showed that early leadership conflict can result in either power sharing between the dictator and his closest allies or the concentration of power in one man's hands. Chapter 5 focused on the special difficulty of enforcing power-sharing bargains among members of armed seizure groups. Now we investigate how those earlier outcomes affect longer-run regime resilience and the ways dictatorships break down.

We focus on how the concentration of power can reduce subsequent conflict within the dictatorial inner circle. In order to concentrate power, dictators engage in strategies that end up reducing internal differences. They purge members of the inner circle most inclined or most able to challenge them, while frightening the rest into quiescence. Over time, they develop ways to control the futures, lives, and welfare of other members of the dictatorial elite. Spy agencies, as noted in Chapter 7, often report the contacts and conversations of members of the inner circle to them, making possible preemptive strikes against anyone suspected of critical thoughts, let alone deeds. When dictators control appointments to top offices and the political police report directly to them, open

---

[5] The estimate for the linear combination of *crisis* plus the interaction is 0.010 and not statistically different from zero.

disagreement and criticism of the dictator disappear from the corridors of power. Plotting becomes riskier. The dictator's ability to use rewards, privations, and violence against his closest allies prevents most inner-circle conflict during his lifetime.

The strategies that dictators with concentrated powers use to keep themselves safer can undermine prospects for regime survival after the dictator dies, however. Typically, personalist dictators exile, jail, or execute the country's most able politicians, administrators, and officers in order to reduce the likelihood that they will eventually lead opposition. Such dictators value loyalty more than competence when promoting officers or making administrative appointments, which undermines the military as a fighting force and the bureaucracy as a reservoir of technical skills, further reducing the likelihood of challenges. The dictator's worry about survival often also leads to the rapid rotation of officials through offices and locations and of military officers through commands, which reduces their ability to build loyal political networks of their own that might serve as the core of a plot or opposition movement, but also undermines their ability to develop experience and expertise. These strategies reduce the competence and organizational resources of potential successors.

The dictator's strategic use of corruption can also damage prospects for regime survival after his death. Corruption tends to be higher in more personalized dictatorships than in those in which power is less concentrated (Chang and Golden 2010). The dictator's personal corruption arises not only because he needs resources to buy political support but also from his knowledge that he and his family are likely to lose their in-country assets and wind up in exile (at best) if he loses power. So he needs a substantial insurance fund held safely outside the country.

The dictator's lieutenants engage in corruption for the same reason; in case the regime falls or *they* fall out of the dictator's favor, they will need funds to support their families in exile. The supporters of personalist dictators are vulnerable to loss of office, arrest, exile, and murder if the dictator becomes suspicious about their loyalty. So they need insurance funds. And if the dictator rotates supporters rapidly through offices, they have incentives to amass these funds quickly, while they can. Few supporters of personalist dictators can continue political careers post-dictatorship, another reason to get it while they can (Bratton and van de Walle 1997).

Facilitating lieutenants' corruption can be part of the strategy of power concentration. Dictators who allow rampant corruption often use their security police to collect information about it so that officials who displease them for any reason can be humiliated, deprived of office, and jailed when their corruption is "discovered." Even though nearly all officials engage in corruption and everyone knows that everyone does it, corruption scandals erupt frequently in personalized dictatorships, as the dictator uses this strategy to keep his lieutenants on their toes, off-balance, and insecure.

The strategies dictators with concentrated powers use to maintain control reduce destabilizing inner-circle conflicts during their lifetimes, but also increase the difficulties anyone who follows them in office will face. If the dictator dies or is assassinated, his disarticulated supporters, accustomed to competing against each other for his favor, have difficulty overcoming the collective action problem of regime maintenance. The dictator's hollowing-out of regime institutions leaves them incapable of shaping bargains between the dictator's successor and other regime insiders. As a result, like the initial bargaining period following the seizure of power, uncertainty is pervasive and the risk of regime collapse is high.

These features of personalized dictatorship lead us to expect that, all else equal, regime breakdown would be less likely during the lifetimes of dictators with concentrated power, but would become more likely after their deaths. The overall effect of personalism on regime survival, however, depends on how long an otherwise similar dictatorship would have been expected to survive under more collegial leadership. If we would expect a regime to survive only a few years, then increasing its resilience during the dictator's lifetime would, on average, increase its duration. If, on the other hand, a dictatorship has the characteristics that would lead us to expect survival for many decades, then the increased vulnerability to breakdown after the first dictator's death associated with personalism would likely reduce its expected duration.

The two regime characteristics with well-established effects on the duration of dictatorships are dominant-party rule, which tends to increase it, and military rule, which tends to decrease it. Party-led dictatorships can enforce norms about the selection of leaders better than other dictatorships can, and thus are more capable of managing succession without crisis. Yet party constraints on dictators are precisely the things a dictator intent on concentrating power in his own hands wants to change. We therefore expect the personalization of rule to increase the likelihood of the dictator retaining office until he dies, but to reduce *regime* longevity in dictatorships organized by parties.

In contrast, military-led dictatorships tend to replace dictators frequently via sometimes-violent coups. The dispersal of arms within the dictatorial elite in military-led regimes encourages recurring conflict within the inner circle. This instability can in turn prompt officers to return to the barracks if they believe conflict threatens the military's unity (Geddes 1999). In military-led regimes, we therefore expect personalization to extend not only the dictator's survival but also the regime's because the average collegial military regime has a shorter lifespan than the average dictator.

To test these ideas, we examine the direct effect of the personalization of power on dictatorial resilience and how personalism interacts with exogenous characteristics of the seizure group that tend to be carried over into the dictatorship.

Data and Measurement

To carry out this investigation, we use the time-varying measure of personalism introduced in Chapter 4. As a reminder, it is a composite measure of personalism from an item response theory (IRT) two-parameter logistic model (2PL), rescaled on the [0,1] interval, where higher levels of personalism approach 1 and lower levels of personalism approach 0. The items used to derive the latent estimate capture both personalization of the supporting political party (*rubber stamp, party executive committee, appointments*, and *new party*) and the leader's consolidation of power over the military and security forces (*security apparatus, paramilitary, promotions*, and *purges*). This time-varying indicator measures differences in power concentration between regimes, between leaders in the same regime, and over time during any individual leader's tenure in power. It thus allows us to investigate how personalism influences regime stability in different contexts.

Because our indicator of personalism "measures" post-seizure behavior, we cannot rule out the possibility that dictators pursue these strategies after considering their prospects of survival, which we cannot observe. Indeed, we believe that this is exactly what they do. However, our goal here is not to show that personalism causes regime survival but rather to examine whether the concentration of personal power in the leader's hands correlates with regime longevity and whether exogenous traits – such as military rule or dictatorial leadership organized by a political party – shape this relationship.

To review the measurement of the exogenous seizure group characteristics we focus on in this section:

- A dictatorship with an inherited support party (*inherit*) is one in which the ruling party was originally organized during an earlier regime either to participate in (democratic or autocratic) elections or to lead an armed insurgency. While this measure only uses information about the seizure group prior to gaining power, it nonetheless identifies most of the same country-years as the older regime-level indicator, dominant party, proposed by Geddes (1999, 2003) and updated by Geddes, Wright, and Frantz (2014).[6] The older regime-type coding tried to distinguish dictatorships in which the ruling party was strong enough to constrain the dictator from those in which it was not. The latter were labeled personalist. Thus, the cases with *inherited parties*, though measured before the seizure of power, are party-led dictatorships in which the level of personalism tends to be relatively low. This may increase the difficulty of showing how personalism affects the survival prospects of such regimes. We note, however, that

---

[6] Eighty-four percent of regimes coded as dominant party by Geddes, Wright, and Frantz have an inherited support party, and 68 percent of regimes (but 80 percent of observations) with inherited parties are coded as dominant party.

though dictators have greater difficulty concentrating power when an inherited party organizes the regime elite (as shown in Chapter 4), some dictators – e.g., Stalin, Mao, and Kim Il-sung – have nevertheless succeeded in doing so.

• We define a military-led regime (*military-led*) as one in which the first dictator was an active-duty or recently retired member of the military of the regime that governed immediately before the seizure of power.[7] Dictators whose military titles were earned in the insurgency that brought them to power are coded as insurgents, not military, and therefore the regimes they lead are not considered military-led. This operationalization, again, uses only information from before the seizure of power and thus does not contain information about the behavior of the regime or its leader once in power. *Military-led* simply identifies dictatorships initiated by military seizure groups.

Military-led does not distinguish between more and less personalized military-led regimes, as did the older regime-type coding. All of the regimes coded by Geddes, Wright, and Frantz (2014) as "military" have a first military leader, but only a little more than half (56 percent) of dictatorships with a first military leader were coded as "military" in the older data. The coding rules for that data set limited the term "military" to regimes in which the officer corps could constrain the dictator's discretion.[8] Other dictatorships led by officers were coded as "personalist." In the data we use now, personalism can be measured as a separate time-varying characteristic measured yearly.

By using measures of military-led and inherited party that rely only on pre-seizure characteristics of the first leader and the seizure group, we can examine how the post-seizure behaviors that we identify to measure personalism influence regime survival in different contexts. We have constructed two ways of defining the autocratic context (*military-led* and *inherited party*) that are exogenous to regime survival. That is, dictatorial leaders' strategies for avoiding regime collapse cannot have influenced the formation of a political party organized before the seizure of power. Nor can it have affected whether military officers first seized power.

Because we define *military-led* regimes and *inherited-party* regimes in this way, we can use them as stand-ins for "political institutions" in the Northian sense of constraints or norms that shape political behavior and thus structure

---

[7] If the first leader of the regime is not a member of the military but a subsequent leader comes from the military, we do not consider this regime military-led because choosing a subsequent leader of a certain type may be a by-product of attempts to enhance regime longevity. In the main estimating sample of the 270 regimes in 117 countries, 38 percent of regimes have an inherited party and half are military-led.

[8] See Geddes, Frantz, and Wright (2014) for a discussion of different meanings of the term "military rule" and the conceptual underpinnings of different ways of coding military-led dictatorships.

equilibrium outcomes (North 1990). These institutional features thus circumvent the Rikerian objection to institutional analysis (Pepinsky 2014) because dictatorships cannot change these characteristics after seizing power.[9]

Empirical Approach

We examine the effects of personalism and exogenous characteristics of the seizure group on autocratic breakdown using two types of estimators. First, we test a logistic regression model with control variables, including decade dummies to capture trends in autocratic survival across time and regime duration polynomials to model time dependence in the data. The duration polynomials allow the logistic regression to mimic standard survival approaches, such as the Cox proportional hazard model (Beck and Katz 1995; Carter and Signorino 2010). For this estimator, we model heterogeneity across regimes using regime-level random effects. Second, we estimate a linear probability model with country and year fixed effects. This estimator allows us to incorporate fixed unit effects without dropping countries that do not experience regime change in the period from 1946 to 2010. With each estimator we cluster the standard errors by regime.

We control for confounders thought to affect regime breakdown: log GDP per capita, log oil rents per capita, conflict (civil and interstate), and prior democracy.[10] Further, we include a variable that indicates whether the regime originated in revolution, from Levitsky and Way (2013), who argue that post-revolutionary regimes are especially durable. Including this variable is important because we want to know whether our findings hold even after we account for the revolutionary origins of some of the most durable autocracies of the twentieth century.[11] In other words, we want to make sure that the effect we show for inherited parties is not entirely due to revolutionary parties.

Finally, each specification includes binary indicators for *military-led* regime and *inherited party* regime. These are not mutually exclusive categories because some military-led dictatorships seized power with the aid of inherited political parties. After estimating a specification without interaction terms, we report estimates from separate specifications, one of which includes an interaction between *military-led* and *personalism* and the other an interaction between *inherited party* and *personalism*. We use these interactions to show that the

---

[9] There may, however, be unobserved factors that cause selection into military-led or inherited party regimes that also cause regime (in)stability. We rule out unobserved country-specific sources of spurious correlation by employing country fixed effects estimators.

[10] We also tested models with two potential post-treatment variables, economic growth and anti-government protest, with similar results.

[11] We drop this variable with the fixed effects estimator since only ten countries have periods of rule under both a revolutionary regime and a nonrevolutionary regime. Results including this variable, however, remain consistent.

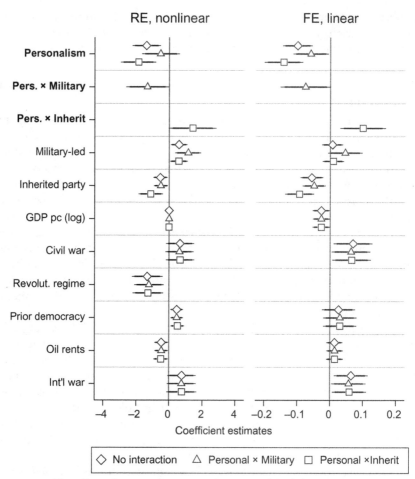

FIGURE 8.4 The effect of personalism on authoritarian breakdown.
FE, fixed effects. RE, random effects.

effects of the concentration of power in a dictator's hands differ depending on whether his initial support base was rooted in the military or in an inherited party.

Results

Figure 8.4 shows the results. Estimates from the first specification (top line in each cluster) in the left panel do not include either interaction term and thus simply estimate the average effect of personalism across all dictatorships in the sample. The coefficient for personalism is negative and statistically significant, suggesting that more personalism on average is associated with a lower probability of regime breakdown. The estimate for *inherited party* is also negative and significant, indicating that inherited parties prolong dictatorships, all else equal.[12] That for *military-led* regime is positive and significant, consistent with prior research showing that military regimes tend to be fragile (Geddes 2003). Like previous studies, our results link specific autocratic institutions to greater durability (Geddes 1999; Gandhi 2008; Magaloni 2008). Unlike previous studies, however, we are able to rule out the possibility of reverse causation. That is, the possible tendency of more durable dictatorships to adopt party institutions (Pepinsky 2014) could not cause the relationship because the measures we use to capture institutions pre-date the existence of the dictatorship.

The next two models (identified by triangles and squares) include interaction terms, which estimate the effect of increases in personalism in military-led dictatorships (triangles) and in those led by inherited parties (squares). These estimates show statistically significant effects in opposite directions. The estimate for the effect of increases in personalism in military-led regimes (the linear combination of *military* × *personalism* plus *personalism*) is negative and significant. In contrast, the estimate for the effect of increases in personalism in party-led regimes (the linear combination of *inherit* × *personalism* plus *personalism*), while negative, is not statistically significant.

The negative estimate for personalism in military-led dictatorships means that as leaders in these regimes concentrate more power in their own hands, the regimes they lead become less vulnerable to overthrow. This result makes sense because for military dictators, power concentration involves building up non-military security forces such as internal security police, who usually spy on officers as well as civilians, and paramilitary forces recruited from regions and ethnic groups especially likely to be loyal to the dictator.[13] These forces loyal to the dictator reduce the ability of officers in the regular military to oust the dictator and thus also to force him to consult with them. Power concentration also often includes a gradual change in the dictator's support base from primarily military to greater reliance on organized civilian, ethnic, or even family networks. A dictator who succeeds in replacing some of his initial military support with civilians has reduced the proportion of members of the inner circle who control the arms and men needed to replace him at relatively low cost. He may at the same time replace officers from multiple regions and ethnic groups with co-ethnics, co-regionalists, or family members, thus further reinforcing the likelihood of future loyalty.

The positive coefficient for *military-led* by itself in the model that includes the interaction indicates that more collegial military regimes (those with the

---

[12] Recall that the specification includes regime-case random effects as well as a control for revolutionary regimes. The result for *inherited parties* remains after dropping revolutionary regimes from the estimating sample.

[13] Remember that control of security forces and the creation of loyal paramilitary forces are two of the indicators that go into the measure of *personalism*.

lowest concentration of power in the leader's hands and lowest *personalism* scores) tend to be short-lived. This result reinforces earlier findings about collegial military rule and statements above about the fragility of dictatorships in which armed force is widely dispersed within the ruling group. In more collegial military-led dictatorships, security services often remain within the military chain of command, and paramilitary forces are not usually created unless the military wants help fighting insurgencies. Thus in collegial military-led dictatorships, the dictator may personally control no armed forces to defend him if other officers decide to remove him.

In contrast to the findings about personalization in military-led regimes, the results show that power concentration in dictatorships led by inherited parties makes them more vulnerable to breakdown. The coefficient for *inherited party* by itself indicates that party-led regimes with relatively collegial inner circles are more durable than other kinds of dictatorship. The coefficient for the interaction between *inherited party* and *personalism* means that the personalization of party-based rule decreases its durability. This reflects the difficulty of maintaining personalized rule after the death of the individual who has concentrated vast powers in his own hands even in party-based regimes.

The control variable estimates are stable across specifications and in the expected directions: oil-rich autocracies and revolutionary regimes are more stable, while dictatorships in countries with a prior history of democracy and those experiencing conflict are more likely to collapse.

Next, we turn to the estimates from the specifications with fixed effects, shown on the right side. Recall that this estimation approach accounts for all unobserved country-specific factors – such as religion, state strength, colonial legacy, ethnic fractionalization in society as well as in the military at the time of independence, history of democratic experience, geographic region, terrain, and climate – that might influence the propensity for either a group led by officers or an inherited party to seize power. The first specification (top estimate in each cluster) excludes interaction terms. The estimate for *personalism* in this model is negative and statistically significant, indicating that even when we look only at variation over time within countries, concentrating power in the hands of the dictator increases regime longevity on average.

The estimate for *military-led* regimes is positive but very close to zero and not statistically significant. Because the group of military-led regimes includes about equal numbers in which the dictator concentrates power (what Weeks [2014] calls "strongman" regimes) that last much longer than other military-led regimes and those in which he does not (what she calls "juntas"), the near-zero estimate for *military-led* in a fixed effects specification should not be surprising.

The estimate for *inherited party* is still negative and statistically significant, providing strong evidence that dictatorships led by inherited parties are more durable, on average, than those that lack such parties. Remember that we have coded this regime characteristic based only on pre-seizure information, and thus it is not contaminated by the strategic maneuvers of regime elites trying to retain power after they have seized it.[14] Further, because we have estimated the effect of this feature of dictatorships in a fixed effects model, we can rule out the possibility that relatively time-invariant factors specific to individual countries – such as the historical legacy of strong states (Slater 2010) or aspects of political economy that shape dictators' or elites' political preferences (Pepinsky 2014) – explain the finding.

In the second fixed effects specification (middle estimate in each cluster), we include the interaction between *personalism* and *military-led* regimes. The estimate for *military-led* regimes alone is positive and statistically significant (though only at the 0.10 level). The positive estimate suggests that military-led regimes in which the dictator has not concentrated power in his own hands are roughly 5 percent more likely to collapse in a given year than collegial, civilian-led dictatorships.

The estimate for *personalism* alone is negative and statistically different from zero. This suggests that personalism stabilizes authoritarian rule in dictatorships initially led by civilians (when *inherited party* is controlled for). The civilian-led dictatorships that lack inherited parties include monarchies, some post-Soviet dictatorships in which the dictator juggles multiple, often short-lived parties, the Sukarno regime in Indonesia, two brief Ecuadoran dictatorships led by Velasco Ibarra, and a few others. These regimes tend to be highly personalized.

The estimate for the interaction between *personalism* and *military-led* regimes is strongly negative and significant, confirming the earlier result that the regime-prolonging effects of personalism are greatest in military-led regimes.

Finally, the last model reported on the right side includes the interaction between *personalism* and *inherited party*. The estimate for this term is positive and statistically significant, meaning that personal concentration of power makes dictatorships led by inherited parties *less* resilient. The estimate for *personalism* alone is negative and significant, indicating that power concentration strongly stabilizes regimes that lack an inherited party. The estimate for *inherited party* alone is negative and significant, indicating that regimes led by inherited parties with relatively collegial leadership are the most durable. Combined, these results confirm the pattern identified by Geddes (1999), in which what she labeled "military regimes" (roughly equivalent to less personalized military-led regimes here) are least resilient; "dominant-party regimes" (equivalent to less personalized regimes led by inherited parties here) survived longest; and "personalist regimes" (a combination of personalized military-led and personalized civilian-led) occupied the middle ground.

---

[14] In addition, there are no "hybrid regimes" in this analysis (Pepinsky 2014, 641). We have simply used a concrete, observable feature of the pre-seizure history of the regime support party to operationalize what we believe is a theoretically important concept.

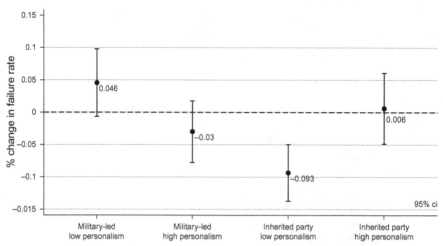

FIGURE 8.5 The effects of personalism in dictatorships with different leadership configurations.

Figure 8.5 summarizes the findings for personalism in dictatorships with different leadership configurations, using the estimates reported in the two fixed effects models in Figure 8.4. Military-led regimes with the lowest personalism score are almost 5 percent more likely to fail in a given year than civilian regimes. Military-led regimes with the highest personalism scores, however, are *less* likely to fail than civilian regimes. Turning to regimes with inherited parties, we see the opposite pattern. Those with low personalism scores are 9 percent less likely to collapse than regimes without inherited ruling parties, while regimes with inherited parties but high personalism are no more or less likely to fail than regimes without inherited support parties. This figure illustrates the very different effects that concentration of power in the dictator's hands has on regime survival, depending on other inner-circle characteristics: it enhances regime survival in military-led dictatorships but decreases it in dictatorships led by inherited parties.

This pattern of results reflects the consequences for regime durability of the modes of bargaining and handling intra-elite conflict in dictatorships led by different kinds of groups. Regimes based on collegial military rule tend to break down easily, both because the dispersal of armed force encourages intraregime conflict and because officers sometimes choose to return to the barracks if internal conflict threatens military unity (Geddes 1999). The personalization of military-led regimes reduces intra-elite conflict by concentrating power in one man's hands and thus tends to prolong regime survival during that man's lifetime. If military seizure groups cared only about regime survival, more officers would consent to the personalization of rule. They also care about the integrity of the military as a fighting force, however, and their own standing within the regime, both of which pull them toward maintaining greater collegiality.

In contrast, the personalization of party-based dictatorships increases their vulnerability to breakdown. As we show later, personalization undermines the ruling party's ability to cope with succession. Many of the strategies dictators use to concentrate power in their own hands reduce prospects for regime survival after their deaths.

Overall, these findings suggest that personalism erodes the institutional framework – regardless of whether the framework is provided by inherited parties or military institutions – through which elites bargain over power with the dictator. How personalism influences regime survival differs in these two contexts because, in the absence of personalized power, the dispersal of arms and norms of obedience inherent in military institutions tend to shorten regime duration, while cohesive party institutions stabilize and lengthen dictatorships by improving the elite's ability to handle leadership succession.

LEADERSHIP CHANGES AND REGIME BREAKDOWN

In the full sample of cases, nearly half (47.5 percent) of all leader exits coincide with regime collapse, which suggests that leadership transitions pose serious challenges for autocratic stability.[15] Here, we investigate how the personalization of power affects the likelihood of regime survival in the immediate aftermath of a dictator death or ouster.

Because of the threat to regime survival caused by elite disunity, whenever some members of the inner circle organize to remove a dictator, they risk not only their lives and livelihoods if they fail, but also the survival of the regime regardless of whether they fail. Those whose posts and benefits depend on the threatened dictator may mobilize against the challengers, especially if they expect to be purged along with the dictator – as in many cases they do. Even if the dictator is successfully removed, a deep split within the regime elite makes the new dominant faction vulnerable to power grabs by other insiders ambitious to concentrate resources in their own hands, as well as to external opposition.

The Dominican Republic's experience after Rafael Trujillo's assassination illustrates what tends to happen. Trujillo's right-hand man, the puppet civilian president Joaquín Balaguer, succeeded Trujillo smoothly, but a three-sided power struggle began immediately among what had been the main beneficiaries and supporters of the Trujillo regime: the military, Trujillo's initial base of support, which saw itself as his natural heir; Trujillo's extended family, which had gained control of most of the Dominican economy under Trujillo and

---

[15] We restrict our analysis to regime leaders who held power on January 1 and thus exclude most leaders who held power for less than a year.

wanted one of their own to lead the regime to safeguard their interests; and Balaguer, who led the ruling party and controlled government administration. These three groups failed to achieve a power-sharing agreement, and no one group could dominate the others, leaving the dictatorship vulnerable to outside opposition. A minority faction of the military that favored democratization seized power and ended the dictatorship less than a year after Trujillo's death (Wiarda 1975, 263; Hartlyn 1998, 96).

The difficulties the Trujillo inner circle faced in trying to reconsolidate the regime under a new leader are not unusual in personalized dictatorships. Figure 8.6 shows how increased personalism affects the probability that the dictator's removal from office coincides with regime collapse. The analysis looks at the 465 dictator exits in the data set. We report the results of four specifications. The first simply controls for how long the regime and the dictator have lasted up to the time of the leader's exit. The second adds calendar time to control for world trends; and the third adds a battery of control variables shown in other research to affect dictatorial resilience: GDP per capita, oil rents, protest, civil conflict, inherited party, military-led, and revolutionary party. The last specification excludes monarchies to check the suspicion that monarchies, which tend to be long-lived and personalistic, might be driving results. Depending on the specification, the estimate for the effect of personalism shows that increasing the personalism index from its lowest to highest value increases the probability that dictator exit coincides with regime collapse by more than 50 percent. In short, replacing the dictator, whether because of death or ouster, without destabilizing the regime becomes substantially less likely as the dictator concentrates personal power in his hands.

Two different processes contribute to the result in Figure 8.6. First, as in the post-Trujillo example, regime elites in personalist dictatorships have difficulty cooperating to maintain the regime after the dictator is gone. This difficulty arises from the dictator's strategy of negotiating separately with different support factions and the weakness of institutions within which bargaining and policy choice formally occur. Second, personalist dictators' strategies for securing their own safety result in fewer ousters by regime insiders and consequently more by regime outsiders, who generally seek to end the regime as well as ousting the dictator. In the next section we focus on a smaller sample of cases that excludes those in which the opposition intended to overthrow both the dictator and the regime: natural deaths of dictators.

Death of the Dictator and Regime Survival

Unlike other kinds of leadership change, a dictator's natural death in office is an exogenous challenge to the regime he led. Regime weakness or inner-circle conflict does not cause it, and thus cannot explain why dictatorships are vulnerable in the wake of it. Some dictatorships can better handle a leader's death than others, however. In the next section, we test the argument that personalized dictatorships have greater difficulties surviving succession than

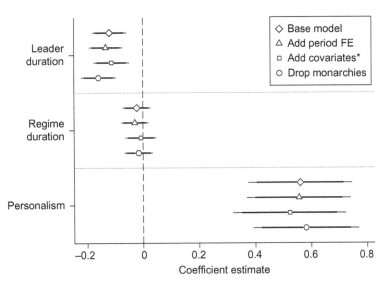

FIGURE 8.6 Probability that dictator exit coincides with regime collapse.
Note: *Added covariates: growth, GDP pc, oil rents, protest, civil conflict, inherited party, military-led, revolutionary regime

those with more collegial leadership by investigating what happens after the natural death of a dictator. We show that concentration of power in the dictator's hands undermines the dictatorial elite's capacity to retain its hold on power after the dictator's natural death.

To evaluate the effect of power concentration on the capacity of dictatorships to handle succession after a leader's death, we examine the relationship between *personalism*, measured as its average level during the three years prior to the first dictator's death, and the square root of the number of years the regime survived after it.[16] The data include all forty regimes in which the first dictator died a natural death in office. The left panel of Figure 8.7 plots these two variables against each other to reveal a strong negative relationship: regimes in which the first dictator had concentrated more power collapse much sooner after his death than regimes in which the first leader accumulated less personal power. The right panel shows the same relationship after conditioning on a number of other factors: calendar time, regime duration up to the time of

---

[16] The post-death regime duration variable is skewed, so we use the square root of duration in this analysis. Tests for normality indicate that the square root transformation results in a less skewed distribution than the untransformed number of years or the log. For regimes with leader death before the regime's third anniversary, we take the average level of personalism during the tenure of the leader. The right panel of Figure 8.7 is an added-variable plot from a kernel regression.

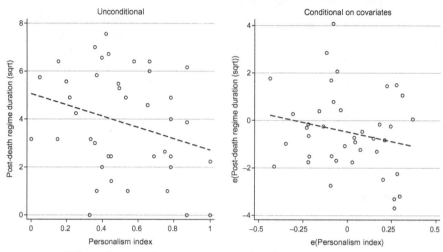

FIGURE 8.7 Effect of personalism on capacity to handle succession.

the first leader's death, whether the first dictator came from the military, and the average oil rents accruing to the regime during the first leader's time in power.

Next, we extend the analysis to all 61 dictators whose tenure ended in natural death. This group includes the 40 first regime leaders in the prior analysis as well as 21 subsequent leaders who died natural deaths. We examine how personalism during the time just before the dictator's death influences later regime stability in a standard empirical model of regime failure. This analysis differs from prior analyses in that we look only at the 52 regimes in which at least one dictator died naturally while in office, and we examine only how long regimes last *after* leaders' deaths.

Since we examine only regimes in which a dictator left office as a result of natural death, we need not worry that the death reflects strategic efforts to constrain or oust the leader in order to preserve or destabilize the regime. The design excludes cases such as the reshuffling coup that ousted the senile Tunisian leader in 1987 or the rebellion that forced out the cancer-ridden leader of Zaire in 1997. In cases like these, we do not observe natural death in office precisely because actors who saw a leader nearing death removed him in order to preserve the regime in Tunisia and to end it in Zaire. By examining regime duration post–natural death, our design looks only at the cases in which the level of personalism (during the years just before the death) is plausibly exogenous since new leaders cannot alter what happened in the past (Jones and Olken 2005).

Mimicking a survival model, we test a binary cross-section time series model with regime failure as the dependent variable and log regime duration to account for duration dependence (*duration after leader death*). The explanatory

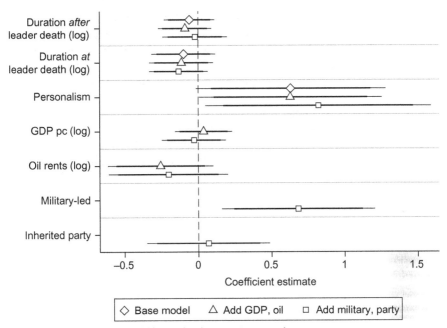

FIGURE 8.8 Personalism and post-death regime survival.

variable of interest is the average level of personalism in the regime during the three years before the dictator's natural death, as above. The covariates in the base model include decade dummies and the log number of years the regime had been in power at the time of the leader's death (*duration at leader death*). Decade dummies account for global temporal patterns in the rise and fall of dictatorships, while *duration at leader death* accounts for the possibility that regimes that have existed for a long time before the dictator dies may be more resilient than young ones.

The top estimates in each cluster in Figure 8.8, depicted as diamonds, show the results from this test: personalism during the time just before a dictator's death increases the likelihood of regime collapse afterward. Next, we add two structural covariates to the model, GDP per capita and oil rents. The result for *personalism* remains. Last, we add two measures of exogenous institutions discussed throughout this chapter, indicators for *military-led* and rule based on an *inherited party*.[17] Again, the result for *personalism* persists. Military-led regimes are more vulnerable to breakdown in this sample as in other analyses.

[17] Results in the replication files show that the estimated effect of personalism varies (i.e., there is a nonproportional hazard): as regimes survive longer after the natural death of a leader, the marginal effect of his pre-death level of personalism declines. Thus, personalism has the strongest effect soon after the natural death of a dictator, as intuition would suggest. If readers want to

The findings in Figures 8.7 and 8.8 are consistent with the claim that personalism is destabilizing during successions. Importantly, the measure of personalism used in these tests is exogenous to the behavior of dictators who follow after the death of a previous leader. Instead of capturing the potentially strategic behavior of post-death leaders, the personalism variable used here is constructed using only information about the dead leader's behavior while in office. It is thus a proxy for the institutional environment bequeathed to new dictators after the natural death of their predecessors.

Up to this point, we have investigated some of the causes of dictatorial collapse. We turn now to what happens after dictatorships fall.

THE DICTATOR'S FUTURE AND THE LIKELIHOOD OF DEMOCRATIZATION

What happens after a dictatorship falls depends to a considerable extent on how the dictator and his closest allies respond to angry citizens, embittered officers, and demanding foreigners when they face regime-threatening challenges. In this section, we investigate one of the factors that determines those responses: the expectations of dictators and their closest supporters about what will happen to them and their families if the regime falls, that is, the right-hand side of Equation 8.1. The costs of losing power vary across dictatorships and across individuals within dictatorial elites. These differences affect the willingness of dictators and other members of the dictatorial elite to negotiate peaceful transitions when regime survival appears doubtful. The willingness to negotiate in turn affects how dictatorships end and what kind of political system follows them.

Negotiation to end a dictatorship empowers parts of the opposition committed to democratization and aims to devise a peaceful means of choosing the specific individuals to whom power will be transferred. For these reasons, negotiated regime transitions tend to end in competitive elections and to result in democracy. By contrast, the dictator's refusal to negotiate increases the likelihood that regime opponents will resort to force to unseat him. Forced ousters, in turn, reduce prospects for democratization (Geddes, Wright, and Frantz 2014).

The Costs of Losing Power

For dictators who have concentrated great power in their hands, losing office can be personally disastrous. Earlier research using regime-type data shows that dictators who concentrate more power in their hands while they rule face a higher probability than other ex-dictators of exile, imprisonment, execution,

interpret this substantively, the pattern suggests that dictatorial elites may be able to consolidate against the destabilizing effect of past personalism over time, if they can survive the first year or two.

and assassination after ouster, even if democratization follows their overthrow (Geddes, Wright, and Frantz 2014). In the abstract terms of Equation 8.1, the personalization of power causes the dictator's expectations about future benefits under a different regime to drop very low. Because of their greater chance of a bad fate after stepping down, dictators who have amassed great personal power tend to resist negotiations with the opposition that might lead to peaceful transition and instead cling to power until violently overthrown (Geddes, Wright, and Frantz 2014).

Characteristics of the seizure group also affect the costs of losing office for the dictator and his close allies. We turn now to an examination of these costs and how personalism interacts with these traits to influence the chance of democratization.

Costs of Losing Power in Military-Led Dictatorships

The cost of returning to the barracks for most military officers is low if the regime democratizes. They simply continue their chosen careers. Sometimes the dictator himself and a handful of other top officers are forced into exile or prosecuted for human rights abuses, but such punishments have rarely extended to the rest of the officer corps after a peaceful transition to democracy. Violent overthrow can lead to much higher costs for officers if insurgents, foreign invaders, or a rebellious faction of the military defeats them, especially if the violent overthrow results in a new dictatorship. After violent overthrows, top officers of the ousted dictatorship are often jailed or exiled and sometimes executed; insurgents may replace the entire officer corps. Ghana's multiple experiences with military rule fit this pattern. Ghana has experienced three negotiated democratizations after military interventions; the most serious punishment imposed on outgoing officers after democratization was the forced retirement of a few at the top. In contrast, after Ghana's one experience with the violent ouster of a military regime, the mutiny led by Flight Lieutenant J. J. Rawlings in 1979, a number of officers were executed (Singh 2014). Recent events in the Middle East show the same pattern. After the 2012 democratization in Egypt, the old dictator was arrested for corruption and a few top officers were forced to retire. The rest of the military remained intact and, indeed, able to seize power again a year later. In Libya, however, where the old dictator was violently defeated by a combination of insurgency and foreign intervention, the dictator was killed and his army disbanded.

Officers who have served in military governments should thus prefer democratization if they fear regime breakdown, since their prospects for punishment are higher in a future dictatorship than in democracy (Geddes, Wright, and Frantz 2014; Debs 2016). If they prefer democracy for these reasons (or others), they should negotiate their extrication when p, the likelihood of regime survival, has fallen. The incentives facing the military *dictator*, however, can differ from those facing other officers. The dictator faces a higher risk of punishment than do others, so he may try to cling to power when other officers want to negotiate extrication.

As a result of these differences in interests, collegial military-led regimes, in which other officers can constrain the dictator's choices or remove him if he makes choices they oppose, are more likely to negotiate a return to the barracks. When the dictator resists a return to the barracks, other officers can force him from office. The replacement of a military dictator by a faction intent on democratization has occurred many times since 1946. Hard-line Argentine General Galtieri's replacement by the moderate General Bignone in 1982 is one example. After their humiliating defeat in the Malvinas/Falklands conflict and massive protests against military rule, the military junta replaced Galtieri with Bignone, oversaw competitive elections in 1983, and rushed a transition to civilian government. Other officers also forced Colombian General Rojas Pinilla to resign after a popular uprising, so that his replacement could oversee elections and a transition to democracy (Martz 1962, 249–53).

In these examples and many others, a military faction responded to wide-spread popular opposition to military rule by ousting the dictator clinging to power, and then organized a transition to democracy via competitive elections. These are cases in which other officers imposed their own interests on military dictators who were trying to avoid the potential costs of losing office – and did so through means visible to observers.

In contrast, military-led regimes in which the dictator has concentrated great power in his own hands and can therefore act to further his individual interests often refuse to negotiate. Further, when they do negotiate, they may later renege on power-sharing agreements. Examples include Colonel Mobutu Sese Seko in Zaire/Congo, who agreed to power sharing with the opposition in 1992, but retained control of the army and ruling party, which enabled him to break his promises and reconsolidate his position as dictator (Schatzberg 1997, 70). Similarly, ex-Sargent Gnassingbé Eyadéma in Togo "surrendered power" in 1991 to the interim prime minister who had been selected by a national conference,[18] but was able to use the military to wrestle control back into his own hands by the end of the year (Press 1991). Dictators who have concentrated great power in their hands tend to resist losing office to the bitter end. Insurgents forced Mobutu from office five years after he broke his promises about power sharing. Eyadéma remained in power until he died of natural causes more than ten years after breaking his agreement with the opposition. He was succeeded by his son, who still rules as this is written.

In other words, in military-led dictatorships in which one officer has concentrated immense discretion in his hands, other officers have lost the ability to pursue their own interests in a peaceful return to the barracks if regime survival is threatened. In more collegial military regimes, however, the interests of

---

[18] "Togo's President Agrees to Yield Power to a Rival," *New York Times*, August 28, 1991.

officers other than the dictator tend to prevail, which increases the likelihood of a negotiated transition and democratization.

Earlier research confirms that collegial military regimes are more likely to be followed by democracy than are regimes led by officers who have concentrated greater power in their hands (Geddes, Wright, and Frantz 2014). This relationship could be spurious, however. If more professionalized military institutions can better obstruct the personalization of rule, and richer countries tend to have more professionalized military institutions, then wealth may be the underlying reason for the correlation between collegial military rule and democratization. To rule out this possibility, we conduct more rigorous tests of this relationship below (see Figure 8.9).

The Costs of Losing Power in Party-Led Dictatorships

The minimum cost of ending dictatorship for members of a party-based dictatorial inner circle is that they must compete with other parties for the benefits associated with rule rather than having a monopoly. If they lose elections, they lose automatic access to state resources for personal consumption or use in election campaigns, and they lose opportunities for corruption and business advantages associated with their political connections. Party cadres may also lose their government jobs. So the losses can be substantial, but loss of office does not usually lead to jail or execution except sometimes for top leaders.

As with military regimes, former members of the dictatorial government are better off under a subsequent democracy than under a new dictatorship (Geddes, Wright, and Frantz 2014). Members of the inner circle may therefore want to increase the chance of a peaceful, nonviolent regime change by negotiating with the opposition and agreeing to reforms that increase the fairness of elections, but dictators, who face the possibility of jail or assassination if they step down, often refuse to negotiate. In contrast to the many coups that have ushered in democratic transitions when military dictators opposed compromise, however, civilian members of the elite surrounding a dictator who refuses to negotiate have more difficulty ousting him in order to oversee a peaceful transition. As a result, democratization is less likely to follow party-led dictatorships than those led by military officers.

The dictator's concentration of power in party-led dictatorships further reduces the likelihood of democratization. Officials of personalized party-led dictatorships face less difficult futures than do top leaders but are more likely to be politically marginalized and deprived of economic assets after democratization than are officials from dictatorships with more collegial decision-making. As Michael Bratton and Nicolas van de Walle note:

Recruited and sustained with material inducements, lacking an independent political base, and thoroughly compromised in the regime's corruption, they are dependent on survival of the incumbent. Insiders have typically risen through ranks of political service and, apart from top leaders who may have invested in private capital holdings, derive livelihood principally from state or party offices. Because they face the prospect of losing all visible means of support in a political transition, they have little option but to cling to the regime, to sink or swim with it. (1997, 86)

This difference in future prospects between officials of regimes in which the dictator has concentrated great power and those in which a party organization maintains a degree of power dispersal arises from the dictator's control of appointments in the former. The personalistic dictator's exile, imprisonment, or execution of the most able and popular politicians in the ruling party, while at the same time making appointments based on loyalty alone, reduces the likelihood that the party will be able to transform itself into a successful competitor if democracy succeeds the dictatorship.

These considerations mean that party-led dictatorships are less likely to negotiate transitions than collegial military-led dictatorships, especially if power is concentrated in the hands of the dictator.

Costs of Losing Power for Monarchs

Twelve monarchs have lost dictatorial control since 1946, three of them in Nepal.[19] Coups ended seven of the monarchies, popular uprisings three, and insurgency one. Seven authoritarian monarchies remain in countries with more than a million inhabitants, all but one in the Middle East or North Africa. In only one instance was a transition to constitutional monarchy and competitive elections negotiated: in Nepal in 1991. In this instance, the constitutional monarchy survived until a later king usurped unconstitutional powers in 2002. The Nepali monarchy was abolished a few years later after a popular uprising. Of the monarchs ousted by coup, popular uprising, or insurgency, one was murdered along with his family during the coup, one died in prison afterward along with several family members, and the others were exiled. Much of their property was confiscated. None survived as constitutional monarchs in democracies.

In short, since 1946 monarchs ousted by force have not enjoyed a peaceful, economically secure retirement in their own countries, and other members of their families have also faced punishments and exile. Since these numbers are small, conclusions have to be tentative, but these experiences suggest that monarchs and their families have a lot to lose if they are forcibly ousted. It might seem that a ruling family's best strategy in the face of opposition or demands for democracy would be to pursue gradual democratization (that is, steps toward constitutional monarchy as practiced in Europe), which might safeguard their lives and quite a bit of their status and property.

---

[19] This number does not include a few monarchs who briefly held formal power but never actually ruled, such as King Michael of Romania during Soviet occupation.

The majority of the monarchies ousted by coup, however, appeared to be following exactly that strategy. They held regular semi-competitive parliamentary elections. Elites controlled these parliaments, as occurred before full democratization in Europe, and monarchs controlled substantial areas of policy. These regimes might have gradually become fully constitutionalized and democratic over time as some European monarchies did, but they were overthrown before that could happen. These experiences suggest that the strategy that worked for a number of European monarchies may not be available to contemporary monarchs.

In contrast to much of Europe when parliamentary supremacy was being imposed on monarchies, nearly all countries that achieved independence after World War II (which includes most contemporary authoritarian monarchies) created standing armies more or less immediately. Coups carried out by small, recently created armies occurred within ten years of independence in a quarter of countries that gained independence after World War II, including a number of monarchies. Once a country has a professional army (that is, one not raised by tribal levies or maintained by regional aristocrats) and an officer corps open to the middle class, monarchs apparently become susceptible to dissatisfied officers just as other rulers are. This may have reduced the feasibility of incremental democratization strategies for monarchs. It should perhaps not be surprising, then, that most contemporary monarchies have opted to rely on repression and cooptation through distribution rather than steps toward democratization when faced with opposition demands.

To sum up our argument about prospects for democratization, the costs of losing power for dictators and their closest collaborators influence their willingness to negotiate stepping down once the dictatorship's prospects look dim. When dictators negotiate an exit, authoritarian breakdown usually results in democratization. When the dictatorial elite circles the wagons, however, and fights until the end, the fall of one dictatorship is likely to coincide with the beginning of a new one. In the next section, we test some of the implications of this argument. We investigate, first, the effect of the personalization of dictatorial rule on prospects for both democratization and a peaceful transition. Second, we show that the effect of personalization on the likelihood of democratization varies depending on whether dictatorial elites come from the military or a ruling party.[20]

THE EFFECT OF PERSONALIZATION ON PROSPECTS FOR DEMOCRACY

Figure 8.9 shows how the personalization of power influences the chance of democratization and a peaceful transition. For these tests, we estimate kernel regression models, including common covariates of democratization: GDP per

---

[20] We cannot test claims about monarchies because their number is too small.

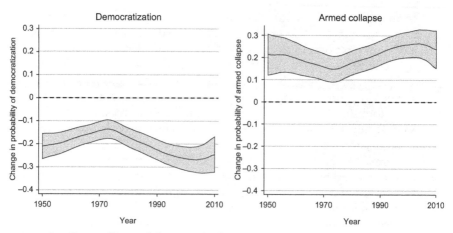

FIGURE 8.9 Personalism and democratization.

capita, regime duration, a Cold War dummy, civil conflict, prior democracy, and regime institutions (military-led, inherited party, personalism). The left panel shows that personalism lowers the chances of democratization during the entire sample period, conditional on old regime breakdown.[21] The estimates on the vertical axis correspond to the difference in the probability of democratic transition (given old regime collapse) between dictatorships with collegial leadership (0 on the personalism index) and those in which the dictator has concentrated power (1 on the personalism index). While not shown, the control variables yield intuitive results as well. Wealthier dictatorships, military-led regimes, and those that were preceded by democracy are more likely to democratize. New autocracies were more likely to replace dictatorships that collapsed during the Cold War than those that have broken down more recently. The substantive effect of personalism is larger than that of any covariates except the Cold War.[22] These results suggest that concentration of power in dictators' hands impedes democratization in the wake of authoritarian breakdown.

One of the mechanisms through which we believe personalism affects the likelihood of democratization is that dictators who have concentrated power in their hands resist negotiating peaceful transitions, which results in more of those that eventually do fall being ousted by force. In the right panel of Figure 8.9, we show the results of an investigation of this claim. The dependent variable in the right panel is forcible regime overthrow (conditional on the occurrence of regime collapse). Personalism increases the likelihood that the

[21] The plot depicts the nonlinear fit for the point-wise derivatives for *personalism*, over time.
[22] The standardized coefficient from a linear model is also larger than that of any other variable except time period. Adding *personalism* to a logit model increases the area under the curve from 0.809 to 0.835.

dictatorship ends in violence. Paralleling the results for democratic transition in the left panel, model results also suggest that dictatorships in wealthier countries, military-led autocracies, and those with a prior history of democracy are less likely to end violently (and thus more likely to have negotiated transitions). Dictatorships that collapsed before 1990 were more likely than those that have ended since then to hang on until forced out by armed opponents.

In sum, personalist dictators tend to resist negotiating transitions, possibly because they face high risks of post-exit punishments. Their lieutenants also have more to lose from regime breakdown than do high-ranking supporters in more collegial dictatorships. And of course, it is more dangerous for members of a personalist dictator's inner circle to try to oust the dictator or negotiate with the opposition behind the dictator's back. These differences in the costs of regime breakdown to high officials of personalized dictatorships help explain why personalist rulers fight to hold on to power even when the fight looks fairly hopeless – as in Syria after 2011 – and why, in turn, their opponents often use violence to try to force them out. Recall that contemporary Syria scores almost as high on our measure of personalism (shown in Figure 4.3) as North Korea.

Personalism in Military-Led Regimes

Past research has shown that military regimes are more likely than other dictatorships to end with democratization (Geddes 2003; Debs 2016; Kim and Kroeger 2017). In this section, we investigate the effect of personalism within this subset of dictatorships by adding an interaction term between *personalism* and *military-led rule* to a model of democratic transition.[23] We report the results from a series of linear models with controls for duration dependence in Figure 8.10. First, we test a specification that includes only an indicator variable for *military-led* regimes, the measure of *personalism*, and an interaction between the two. Next, we test a specification with country and time period fixed effects, and finally a specification with an assortment of control variables: economic growth, GDP per capita, conflict, oil rents, prior democracy, and revolutionary regime, as coded by Levitsky and Way.

In all specifications the estimate for *military-led* regimes is positive and significant, indicating that collegial – or less personalized – military regimes are more likely to democratize than similarly collegial civilian-led dictatorships. This finding confirms earlier research (see especially Kim and Kroeger 2017). The estimate for the interaction term between *military-led* and *personalism* is, as expected, negative and significant: as power becomes more concentrated in a military dictator's hands, democratization becomes less likely. Highly

---

[23] Recall that *military-led* is measured before the seizure of power and is thus exogenous to the dictator's behavior once in office.

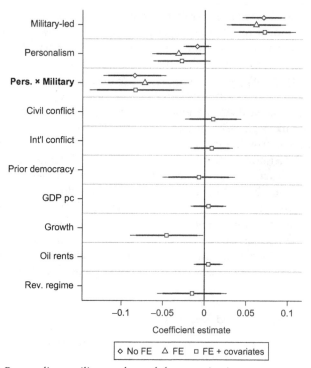

FIGURE 8.10 Personalism, military rule, and democratization.

personalized military-led regimes are thus no more likely to democratize than civilian dictatorships.

To conclude this section, on average, military-led dictatorships are more likely than those led by civilians or monarchs to negotiate exits from power and thus more likely to end in democratization. When a military dictator has concentrated great power in his hands, however, other officers cannot impose their preferences on the dictator. Consequently, he tends to resist negotiation with the opposition and, if he is ultimately ousted, to be overthrown by force by a group that establishes a new dictatorship.

CONCLUSION

Most dictatorial regimes end when coups replace them, incumbents agree to fairer elections and lose, a popular uprising forces incumbents to resign, or an insurgency defeats them in battle. Each of these events means that important political actors not only oppose the dictatorship but consider it worthwhile to take potentially dangerous and costly public action against it. Latent opposition is widespread in many dictatorships, but most of the time opponents have strong reasons not to plot or engage in public expressions of discontent. In this chapter, we investigated some of the factors that can transform latent opposition into overt political activity and some characteristics of the dictatorial elite that increase its vulnerability to ouster.

The chapter began with a schematized description of the incentives facing dictatorial elites and others as they contemplate opposition. The schematization shows the interplay among the benefits individuals receive from the dictatorship, their expectations about future benefits under a different regime, their perceptions about the likelihood that the current regime will fall, and the cost of overt opposition. This abstract version of the situation facing political actors in dictatorships helps situate different real-world events and crises in relation both to each other and to the likelihood of regime change. The remainder of the chapter describes how various events and regime characteristics can change the decision calculus of individuals and thus the likelihood of authoritarian breakdown and what follows it.

Events such as economic crises and natural disasters typically reduce benefits for both citizens and elites. All else equal, a decrease in benefits would increase public opposition and the likelihood of regime collapse. The dictatorial elite may, however, be able to distribute the costs of crisis to shield the individuals most able to threaten regime survival, and may also deliver help effectively. When dictatorships can do these things, they tend to survive. They have greater ability to respond to crises effectively if leaders have previously built patron–client networks that reach ordinary people. An effective response is also more likely if sufficient discipline has been enforced within the ruling group to prevent the theft of relief supplies and other benefits meant for people afflicted by the crisis.

Our analysis shows that dictatorships led by parties that began as insurgent or electoral organizations in the political systems that pre-dated their seizure of dictatorial power survive longer than dictatorships in which regime elites created parties after achieving power or remained unstructured by a party. Importantly, dictatorships led by inherited parties are less affected by economic crises than other authoritarian governments. We interpret this finding as meaning that patron–client networks that encompass a substantial part of the citizenry help to perpetuate dictatorships, not only by including more people in routine distribution during normal times, but also by maintaining the organizational resources needed to manage crises.

Not all challenges to dictatorial survival arise in the external world. Conflict within the inner circle of dictatorships can also precipitate regime breakdown. Our investigation shows that power concentration in the dictator's hands increases the durability of military-led dictatorships, which otherwise tend to be relatively short. In collegial military regimes, wide dispersal of arms results in frequent inner-circle conflicts over leadership, which can destabilize the regime. The concentration of power in the dictator's hands limits the ability of other officers to overthrow him, and thus increases regime stability during the dictator's lifetime, as well as leader security.

Civilian-led regimes experience less leadership conflict on average. The ouster of a dictator by a civilian ruling group requires coordinated action by most of the inner circle (Svolik 2012), which is harder to organize than a coup. This is one reason civilian-led regimes tend to survive longer. More collegial dictatorships led by inherited parties tend to be even more stable. They rely on the ruling party's executive committee for high-level decision-making, so policy choices tend to have wide backing from the inner circle, reducing conflict. Members of the inner circle also have a lot of experience bargaining with, and a lot of knowledge about, one another. These characteristics and experiences contribute to orderly successions and thus, on average, to highly durable dictatorships.

In contrast to the orderly successions characteristic of relatively collegial dictatorships led by inherited parties, the death of a dictator who has concentrated great power in his hands often leads to regime crisis. Dictatorships are less likely to fall in the aftermath of the dictator's natural death than after a coup or other violence ouster, but much more likely to fall than during periods of stable leadership (Kendall-Taylor and Frantz 2016). Besides the conflict over who will succeed the old dictator, succession usually results in a period of uncertainty and struggle over what norms will govern elite bargaining under the new dictator. The high stakes and extreme dangers involved in choosing the next dictator increase the likelihood of intra-elite conflict, and thus the chance of both regime collapse and the purge of parts of the ruling group even if the regime survives.

Besides affecting how long dictatorships survive, the concentration of power in one man's hands also affects the likelihood of a peaceful, negotiated transition, once survival appears unlikely. Dictatorships with more collegial decision-making tend to negotiate their extrication from power when they doubt their ability to hang on to it, but personalized dictatorships often fight to the bitter end. Two factors contribute to this difference. First, dictators who have concentrated great power in their hands have more reason to fear jail, execution, or assassination after ouster than do more consultative dictators, regardless of whether they are officers or civilians. Second, dictators with more power concentrated in their hands can exclude from the inner circle, arrest, or kill allies who want to negotiate with the opposition, and in this way retain a monopoly over decisions about how to respond to challenging situations. In more collegial regimes, in contrast, dictators have to bargain with other members of the inner circle over whether and how to negotiate. Dictators' top supporters generally have less to worry about post-exit than dictators themselves (Albertus and Menaldo 2014), so they tend to favor negotiation when they fear regime collapse.

In regimes led by a military junta rather than a strongman, a dictator who refuses to negotiate when the rest of the junta favors it is likely to be ousted and replaced by another officer who favors a return to the barracks. The ouster of a hard-line dictator by a faction that favors negotiated transition has happened many times near the end of military-led regimes.

Members of ousted dictatorial elites are usually better off under democracy than in hostile new dictatorships. Consequently, when they negotiate stepping down, they rarely resist democratization.

These differences among members of dictatorial elites in the costs and risks of transition result in a tendency for junta-led dictatorships to negotiate peaceful transitions to democracy via fair elections to choose new civilian rulers. Civilian-led dictatorships with collegial leadership are less likely to exit peacefully via elections than junta-led regimes, but more likely to do so than civilian regimes in which the dictator has concentrated great power in his hands. Where a transition occurs peacefully via negotiation and elections, the immediate outcome is usually democracy. Where, however, the dictator retains his steely grip until forceful overthrow, democracy is less likely to follow. Ouster by coup, insurgency, or foreign invasion leads to control by the leaders of the group that led the armed overthrow. Such leaders nearly always promise democratization, but deliver on their promises only some of the time.

9

Conclusion and Policy Implications

Between his accession to full power in 1979 and the US invasion of Iraq in 2003, Saddam Hussein concentrated immense discretion over policy, personnel, and life itself in his own hands, undermining the Iraqi military's professionalism and ability to fight in the process, and the capacity of the Ba'th Party to run a government. His drive to concentrate power began immediately. Less than two weeks after replacing the previous dictator, Saddam announced the discovery of a plot involving top regime officials; a special party court met, judged twenty-two guilty, and sentenced them to execution. Those executed included five members of the dictatorship's sixteen-man inner circle, the Revolutionary Command Council (RCC). Saddam and other remaining members of the RCC carried out the executions in person. Up to 500 other party members were executed along with numerous military officers (Amnesty International 1980, 331, 336; Farouk-Sluglett and Sluglett 1987, 209–10; Tripp 2007, 214). Needless to say, when the dictator can murder other members of the inner circle, they have little ability to constrain his decision-making or enforce power sharing.

Before taking the top post, Saddam had already gained control of the regime's extensive internal security forces and overseen earlier purges of the military and party. Nevertheless, at each subsequent crisis, Saddam purged more people in order to further narrow decision-making circles and concentrate ever more control in his hands. After terrible losses during the Iran-Iraq War in the early 1980s, Saddam reshuffled the RCC, the Ba'th Party Regional Command (the party's executive committee), and the cabinet to eliminate everyone except his relatives, closest allies, and protégés. He appointed close relatives, including sons, sons-in-law, and several half-brothers, to key security and ministerial posts (Brooker 1997, 119; Tripp 2007, 228, 244).

As soon as the war ended in 1989, Saddam again turned his attention to reducing potential threats from the officer corps – which he had had to rebuild to prevent defeat by Iran – through retirements, demotions, "accidents," and arrests (Tripp 2007, 240–45). In 1995, the *Economist* explained why the army was unlikely to oust Saddam: "the army is demoralized, barely a serious fighting force; its senior officers have been switched, fired, executed or so tarred with Mr. Hussein's brush that they have no future outside his orbit."[1] Even relatives had become unsafe by the mid-1990s, when two sons-in-law (high-ranking officers holding very powerful posts) were murdered along with many members of their families.

In short, Iraq under Saddam Hussein was an extreme example of what we have labeled personalist dictatorship. Our analysis in Chapter 8 of how personalized dictatorial rule influences the likelihood of democratization implies that if foreigners intervene militarily to remove a personalist dictator like Saddam Hussein or Moammar Qaddafi of Libya, the intervention is unlikely to result in democracy. Not only do new dictatorships often follow the violent ouster of personalist regimes, but civil war and state disintegration follow these kinds of authoritarian breakdown more often than other kinds (Geddes, Wright, and Frantz 2014).

If the goal is democratization, our analysis suggests that violent foreign intervention to overthrow dictators similar to Saddam Hussein has only a modest chance of success. In the remainder of this conclusion, we summarize our findings chapter by chapter and then discuss the policy implications (in boxes) that follow from our results. Though no one can know for certain what consequences a policy choice will have since many factors contribute to final outcomes, the evidence we provide in this study enables a probabilistic prediction. We think that the academic and policy communities should seek to develop "evidence-based" policy guidelines modeled on those that inform many decisions in medicine, and we see our study as a step toward doing that.

Chapter 2 focuses on the initiation of dictatorship and the situation that faces new autocrats immediately after the seizure of power. Most post-1946 dictatorial seizures of power replace other dictatorships, but about 30 percent replace democracies. The vast majority occur when many citizens are fed up with the incumbent, whether democratic or not. Those who overthrow governments often promise democracy and other desirable goals such as growth and an end to corruption, but they rarely deliver.

Military factions or political parties initiate most dictatorships. The former usually seize power via coups. The latter most often either authoritarianize a democratic government they already lead or seize control via armed rebellion. During the whole post–World War II period, foreigners installed as many dictatorships as did homegrown insurgencies, but foreign imposition of dictatorship has become less frequent during recent decades. Since the end of the

---

[1] "Saddam Sacks a Henchman," *Economist*, July 22, 1995, 46.

Cold War, authoritarianization has grown more common, while military coups and foreign interventions have decreased.

Those who oust governments rarely have detailed plans about what they will do once they have control. This is especially true for forcible seizures of power such as coups and insurgencies. The need for secrecy before coups prevents wide consultation about policy during the plotting stage, and the lack of government experience of most coup and insurgent leaders limits their ability to foresee the decisions they will face once in office.

Consequently, most dictatorial seizures of power are followed by a period of chaos, uncertainty, and conflict within the ruling group. They argue over what to do, who will lead, and how much power the new dictator will have relative to others in the dictatorial elite. This situation makes it hard for foreign policy makers to figure out a best response. Even participants may not be able to predict how the new dictatorship will shape up and what policies it will follow.

Because poor incumbent performance partly motivates dictatorial seizures of power, and plotters strategically time them to coincide with widespread popular disenchantment, the new elite has to grapple immediately with the serious problems that undermined the old regime. New dictatorial elites often take power during economic crises, and their first order of business may be the urgent search for foreign aid. The policy implications that flow from Chapter 2 are outlined in the box below.

The difficulties and uncertainty new dictatorships face mean that international actors can exercise more influence immediately after a seizure of power than later, after the seizure group consolidates its control. Early on, strategies are unsettled, but later, vested interests will have developed. In cases where the leadership position remains contested after the seizure, foreign policy makers may be able to disadvantage hard-line or extreme factions by promising a more positive future relationship should the moderate faction secure control.

International actors may even persuade members of the seizure group to hand power to a neutral political actor instead of holding onto it. This kind of strategy seems to have guided recent international responses to some coups. During the last two decades, members of the international community have been quick to pressure some coup makers to return power to civilians, and some of these interventions have persuaded the military to give up direct power. In Honduras in 2009 and Mali in 2012, for example, officers turned power over to civilian interim governments after becoming convinced that aid and international recognition would be withheld until they did so.

Members of the international community have been slower and less united in condemning the authoritarianization of democratic politics led

by elected leaders such as Recep Tayyip Erdogan of Turkey. After a
failed coup attempt in 2016, Erdogan ordered the arrest of about 50,000
people, including much of the opposition. The following year, a
constitutional revision granted Erdogan quasi-dictatorial powers.[2] It is
harder to achieve international consensus about such democratic
breakdowns because regime transition often occurs incrementally.
Knowing that the authoritarianization of previously democratic
governments has been one of the more common means of initiating
dictatorship (responsible for 16 percent of new dictatorships since World
War II), and has become more common since the end of the Cold War,
might help policy makers agree to withhold aid after explicit
authoritarianizing actions such as Erdogan's.

Military officers initiate most dictatorships. In Chapter 3 we investigate the
conditions associated with coups that install new dictatorships. We find, contrary to several popular theories, no relationship between coups and widespread popular opposition to incumbents, mass political mobilization, or
inequality. Instead, our findings suggest that officers pursue their own interests
when deciding whether to intervene in politics. We find that soldiers are less
likely to seize control when they come from the same groups and share interests
and ideas with political leaders. We confirm other research showing that coups
are more likely in poor countries and that they were more frequent during the
Cold War than since it ended.

Our findings raise questions about the wisdom of using military aid to
support one side or another in the political conflicts of other countries.
Resources meant to shore up incumbents may instead contribute to the
fulfillment of officers' unlawful political ambitions. US military and other
forms of aid played a large role in the buildup of deadly and extensive
security services in numerous Cold War allies, while the Soviet Union
and China contributed to similar buildups among their allies.
Competition between the United States and the Soviet Union also
motivated US support for coups that ousted leftists and Soviet support
for coups against conservatives. In that context, coups were frequent,
and military dictators ruled many countries.

　　During recent decades, most coups have faced international
disapproval and sanctions, though the al-Sisi coup in Egypt is a

---

[2] "Turkey Is Sliding into Dictatorship," *Economist*, April 15, 2017.

conspicuous exception. The sharp decline in the incidence of coups since the end of the Cold War suggests the responsiveness of officers to international pressure. Our findings, along with those of others, imply that the decisive withdrawal of foreign support after coups can reverse military seizures of power. We believe that other potential military interventions have been deterred by knowledge of the hostility of international aid givers toward coups and that this is one of the reasons for the substantial decrease in coups since 1990 (Marinov and Goemans 2014).

During the consolidation stage that follows the initiation of a new dictatorship, members of the new dictatorial elite bargain and fight over how to distribute power among themselves. Struggles among members of the dictatorial elite during the first months and years of the dictatorship determine the degree to which the dictator can concentrate control in his own hands – as opposed to sharing power within a collegial inner circle.

Chapter 4 begins the explanation of why some dictators can concentrate so much power in their hands while others cannot. After the seizure of power, the ruling group must choose one member as leader if they have not already done so. All members of the dictatorial elite want to maintain the dictatorship, but at the same time, they want to increase their own power and access to resources relative to others in the inner circle. The day he is chosen, the dictator has little more power than his colleagues, but that can soon change because dictatorships lack third-party enforcement of bargains and contracts. Once the man who is delegated leadership powers has the additional resources that control of the state gives him, other members of the dictatorial elite may find it difficult to enforce limitations on the dictator's discretion agreed to earlier.

The lack of binding third-party enforcement in dictatorships means that the only way the rest of the elite can constrain the dictator and enforce consultation during decision-making is by credibly threatening to oust him if he fails to share power (Magaloni 2008; Svolik 2012). A unified and disciplined elite can bargain effectively with the dictator because their unity reduces collective action problems, and thus they can make credible threats to oust if the dictator usurps more power than was delegated to him. A factionalized, divided, or undisciplined seizure group, however, cannot create the kind of inner circle that can bargain effectively with the dictator. Instead, the dictator can bargain with each faction separately. Factions compete for the dictator's favor, driving down the price he has to pay for support. Factions also increase the collective action problems involved in trying to replace a dictator, which reduces the credibility of threats to oust.

Bargaining between the dictator and a factionalized inner circle can result in narrowing of the dictatorship's support base and the concentration of great power and discretion in the dictator's hands, which we label personalism. If the dictator does not need the support of everyone who joined in the effort to overthrow the old regime in order to hang on to power, he can exclude some members of his initial support coalition and keep their share of spoils or distribute them to remaining supporters. This is the reason we often see some of the supporters of a seizure of power jettisoned from the dictatorship's support coalition within the first year or two. Those thrown over the side tend to be those most likely to disagree with the dictator over policy or to challenge his right to rule.

Because dictators often exclude some members of the initial inner circle and narrow their initial support coalition, international observers should not view the inclusion of moderates or pro-democracy figures in the first authoritarian cabinet or command council as guarantees of moderation. Dictators strategically include such figures precisely in order to reassure foreign lenders, investors, and aid givers while also allaying the fears of influential domestic actors, but these individuals may be the first to go once the dictatorship seems a little safer.

Unity and discipline tend to be higher in seizure groups whose organization long pre-dates the establishment of dictatorships. At the moment of seizure, the military that takes power in a coup could be united and highly disciplined or factionalized by ethnicity or competing partisan loyalties. Long-established military forces tend to be less factionalized than recently created ones. The party that seizes power could be a highly disciplined "organizational weapon" or a loose coalition of parties and groups put together to compete in the last fair election before authoritarianization. These group characteristics develop before the seizure of power. In social science terminology, they are exogenous to the dictatorship. Consequently, these seizure-group characteristics can help to explain things that happen later during dictatorships because they could not have been caused by decisions made by the post-seizure dictatorial elite.

The empirical section of Chapter 4 shows that factionalism within the seizure group before the establishment of the dictatorship is associated with greater concentration of power in the dictator's hands post-seizure. We find that ruling parties formed before the dictatorship to lead insurgencies or compete in elections inhibit the later personalization of dictatorship and that dictators from more undisciplined militaries are more likely to concentrate power in their own hands than other military dictators. Dictators who have taken initial steps toward personalization during the first three years of rule tend to concentrate further power in their hands over time.

The personalization of dictatorship has dire consequences for people living under it, as well as their neighbors. As a number of studies have shown, the personalization of dictatorial rule is associated with worse governance, more erratic and aggressive international behavior, and enhanced prospects for violence during and after regime overthrow (Frantz and Ezrow 2011; Weeks 2012). The concentration of power leads to erratic decision-making and international adventurism, which results from the absence of consultation within the regime leadership and the unwillingness of the dictator's terrified assistants to give him accurate information either about other countries' likely responses or about their own country's capacities.

Personalist dictators replace subordinates at will, often isolating themselves from information and advice that might have dissuaded them from engaging in risky and ultimately costly acts of international belligerence. Saddam Hussein, for example, consulted only his son-in-law (a general) before the final decision to invade Kuwait. The army chief of staff, whom Saddam had consulted earlier, had told him that an invasion would lead to war with the United States, which Iraq would lose. So, Saddam dismissed him (Ashton 2008, 266–69).

Given the consequences of personalist rule, we think members of the international community concerned with development and peace should do what they can to inhibit its emergence. An obvious implication is that policy makers should take an especially discouraging stance toward military dictators ranked low before the seizure of power because the choice of a low-ranking officer to become dictator indicates a factionalized military seizure group. Even if we believe that some circumstances legitimate support for military coups, we should avoid supporting post-coup dictatorships led by junior officers (such as Captain Moammar Qaddafi or Liberia's Sergeant Samuel Doe), who have the potential to become some of the most violent and erratic dictators.

The findings in Chapter 4 also imply that incremental authoritarianizations led by parties organized during the president's election campaign, like the ones that backed Hugo Chávez in Venezuela or Alberto Fujimori in Peru, are likely to turn out worse than authoritarianizations led by longer-established parties. Policy makers should be especially quick to respond to actions such as arrests of opposition leaders when carried out in authoritarianizing democracies led by recently created parties unable to constrain their leaders.

Chapter 5 highlights the effects of a second characteristic of the seizure group that pre-dates the dictatorship and shapes bargaining between the dictator and his supporters: the dispersal of arms across members of the group. In this chapter, we focus on dictatorships brought to power by armed groups. Most armed groups achieve power in coups, but some lead insurgencies or are imposed by foreigners. In armed seizure groups, many individual commanders could potentially oust the dictator. If the group is also unified and disciplined, then the relative ease of ousting the dictator gives them strong bargaining power, and they can establish a power-sharing agreement with the dictator. Governments with this form are sometimes labeled juntas. If, however, the dictator's armed supporters are divided into factions, then superior officers may not be able to make credible promises to support the dictator if he shares because they may not be able to commit subordinates in other factions to refrain from rogue coups.

In this situation, power-sharing bargains are not credible and therefore cannot secure the dictator's position, so he has no incentive to share with other officers. Instead, he must try to find different strategies for increasing his security. Among those strategies, we suggest that the creation of a civilian support party can counterbalance the dictator's unstable military support base. We argue that this strategy may be safer than creating counterbalancing paramilitary forces (though many dictators do this too) because officers see civilians as less threatening to their prerogatives and monopoly of force than armed groups. The creation of a civilian support base helps defend the dictator from coups because officers try to avoid confrontations between troops and crowds of civilians, and parties are good at mobilizing crowds into the streets when dictators need shows of support.

Our empirical investigation supports this argument. Dictators create civilian support parties to counterbalance and marginalize their original factionalized, armed support base. Post-seizure party creation helps dictatorships that seized power by force survive longer. Dictatorships that lack support parties face a 10 percent chance of breakdown each year, while similar dictatorships in which a party was created post-seizure have less than a 5 percent chance of break-down per year.

"Civilianization" is the term used to describe the replacement of a military ruling council by a mostly civilian party-led ruling body under the same dicta-tor. The dictator may formally retire from the military as well. Such systems are usually augmented by controlled elections for a tame legislature and some form of election to legitimate the dictator. Dictators who have civilianized their regimes usually claim to be democratizing, and observers may be confused about whether these are steps toward democracy. Our findings show that, on the contrary, civilianization substantially prolongs the survival of dictatorships.

The main policy implication of Chapter 5 is thus clear: members of the international community should not view the civilianization of military-led regimes as an indication of impending democracy. As long as the dictator himself remains in control, they should not reduce any costs they have imposed on the dictatorship. Post-seizure party creation, and civilianization more generally, are dictatorial strategies for concentrating more power in the dictator's hands at the expense of wider consultation within the officer corps, while prolonging dictatorship.

A large majority of armed seizure groups are composed of military officers, meaning that officers lead the bulk of dictatorships discussed in Chapter 5. Several studies have shown that dictatorships led by somewhat collegial groups of officers (juntas) end sooner than other kinds of dictatorship. Not only are they relatively short-lived, but they are more likely to negotiate a peaceful return to the barracks via fair, competitive elections than are other kinds of dictatorship. In short, junta-led military regimes are more likely to democratize after shorter periods of rule than personalized military-led dictatorships or civilian-led dictatorships. For international policy makers concerned about democratization, it is thus better to encourage a return to the barracks rather than multiparty elections in which the dictator competes. Many dictators have found ways to win multiparty elections.

In order to extend their control beyond the apex of the political system, dictatorial elites must find ways to monitor lower-level officials and gather information about all parts of the country. These are difficult problems in dictatorships. Local officials may oppose the new dictatorship, or they may simply be motivated by self-interest. They may sabotage official policies, abuse the people who depend on them for services, and steal from both ordinary people and the government. Accurate information gathering poses problems even if the dictatorship replaces all officials with individuals who support it because the future careers of officials may depend on things going well in their districts. Officials may fear bringing the dictator bad news. In Chapter 6, we consider some of the institutions dictatorships use to monitor officials and gather information.

The common institutions that link citizens to political leaders in information-gathering, mobilizational, and distributive networks are ruling parties, elections, and legislatures. These institutions incentivize the extension of patron–client networks from the center to ordinary citizens and the trans-mission of information from the grassroots to the center.

Dictatorial ruling parties link central elites to large numbers of public employees and local officials via a patron–client network that distributes jobs and other advantages and opportunities in return for loyalty and effort on behalf of the party. These secondary elites administer central and local govern-ments and distribute whatever benefits citizens receive from the center. To survive, the dictatorship needs local officials to refrain from sabotaging policies and stealing from those they govern. One element in the dictatorship's strategy for maintaining good behavior among its officials is to limit employment to those thought to be loyal because party officials have vetted them. Ruling parties control access to government jobs in nearly all dictatorships organized by parties.

In most dictatorships, however, it is easy to join the ruling party. Even where the party requires ideological knowledge and a period of probation to demonstrate commitment before membership is granted (like the communist parties or the Iraqi Ba'th), most observers report that opportunists outnumber those committed to party ideals. Apparent ideological commitment or party loyalty has failed to restrain self-interested behavior by officials.

So, top leaders in dictatorships need ways to monitor officials. Some dictatorships, such as the communist regime in East Germany, have used very extensive secret police networks for this, but most dictatorships lack the resources necessary for such individualized surveillance. We argue in Chapter 6 that elections for legislative assemblies and local government create incentives that induce officials and elected representatives to behave better than they otherwise would. We believe that this substitute for direct monitoring is sufficiently valuable to dictatorial leaders to make elections worth their expense and risk.

Dictatorial ruling parties rarely lose elections, but individual candidates for legislative and local office lose more often. When officials know that they will have to run in semi-competitive elections before too long and that they could lose, they have reasons to extend their patron–client networks all the way to the grassroots, distribute as much as they can to the people who will vote, restrain their own and others' predation on the powerless, and convey information about local needs and problems to the center in the hope of getting help. Even where popular elections are uncompetitive, officials and deputies have to compete for party nominations. Elective offices come with many benefits, so competition is stiff. In this way, elections and nominations take the place of direct monitoring by central party officials. They give local officials strong reasons to behave as the center wants them to, and they supply the punishment for not behaving that way in the form of loss of valuable offices and the salaries and perquisites that go with them.

We see executive elections as having a function different from legislative and local elections. The main purpose of executive elections is to demonstrate to potential rivals within the inner circle of the dictatorship that the dictator and his faction have the resources and organization to be unbeatable, and in this way to deter elite defections (Magaloni 2006). Other elites would not be deterred by fraud. Instead, the ruling faction demonstrates its resource advantage by staging an expensive, nationwide campaign; distributing things of value to many citizens; and often manipulating the economy to give the impression of prosperity. Overwhelming votes for the incumbent show that opposition challenges have little hope of success.

The loyalty, monitoring, and information that elections foster must be paid for. In Chapter 6, we show that government spending in dictatorships rises in election years. A side benefit of regular elections is that some spending reaches ordinary people that might not have done so in the absence of officials' concern about winning future nominations and elections. We show that infant mortality is lower on average in dictatorships that hold regular elections, even when elections allow no choice.

A policy implication of Chapter 6 is that conditioning aid or loans on semi-competitive elections may help improve popular welfare by incentivizing local officials to work to make benefits and services intended for ordinary citizens available to them. Although the introduction of semi-competitive elections while the dictator remains in control may have little effect on near-term prospects for democratization, such elections do seem to give dictators reasons to extend welfare-enhancing services to more people.

In contrast to Chapter 6's focus on democratic-looking institutions for indirect monitoring and information gathering, Chapter 7 examines the coercive institutions that dictatorships use directly and openly for information collection, deterring overt opposition, and protecting themselves from overthrow. New dictatorships often create or revamp internal security forces to increase their capacity to ferret out plots, intimidate opponents, and impose extrajudicial punishments on those suspected of opposition. They also often raise military pay and promote officers to deter potential opposition in the army.

Internal security forces focus most of their attention on powerful people because they are most likely to be able to oust the dictator. They thus spy on high party officials, military officers, high-level bureaucrats, elected officials, union leaders, teachers, professors, journalists, and others with potential for mobilizing opposition, persuading others, and spreading discontent. Where the dictator has managed to take personal control of internal security, he can use it to spy on members of the dictatorial inner circle and to arrest or kill anyone he sees as a potential challenger. We find that about two-thirds of dictators have personal control over internal security.

In addition to security police, dictatorships also need armies to protect them against armed attacks from insurgents and external enemies. Usually, dictatorships inherit the armies of their predecessors, so they cannot count on their unconditional loyalty. If past recruitment has been open to talent and promotions based on seniority and merit, then the officer corps will include men from the various ethnic, regional, religious, and partisan groups that exist in the country. This diversity of backgrounds and underlying interests helps explain why armies so often incubate plots, even when the dictator is himself an officer. If the army retains professional norms, including standard promotion rules, it retains some autonomy from the dictator, and the dictator has reason to fear it. The army is the political actor most likely to be able to credibly threaten the dictator with ouster if he violates sharing agreements.

In response to fear of the army, dictators establish loyalist paramilitary forces recruited from groups especially close to them to counterbalance the regular army and defend them from coups. Paramilitary forces can thus undermine the army's ability to constrain the dictator. Dictators also interfere with military promotions and purge distrusted officers to render the military less dangerous, but this kind of interference can itself motivate coups by officers trying to defend professional autonomy or their own career interests. So dictators have to calculate their strategy toward the military with care. We show that dictators with paramilitary forces to defend them from coup attempts are more likely to interfere with promotions and purge officers.

> Our analysis suggests that international actors should avoid providing kinds of aid that can be used to build up internal security police. Engorged security police enhance the dictator's concentration of powers and unrestrained policy discretion. Foreign policy makers should probably avoid providing support for political police in dictatorships in general, but that should be especially true if the internal security police report directly to the dictator, and thus enhance his capacity for arbitrary and violent action.

Chapter 8 investigates the breakdown of dictatorships. Exogenous shocks such as international economic crises, natural disasters, and the death of the dictator can challenge the survival of dictatorships. However, regimes established by seizure groups with some traits (for example, those organized by inherited parties) are more resilient in the face of crises than others. These exogenous traits interact with institutions and strategies chosen after the seizure of power to enhance or limit the dictatorship's vulnerability to breakdown. In this chapter, we show the consequences for regime survival of some of the decisions made earlier to enhance the power of particular actors relative to others in the dictatorial elite (and described in Chapters 4–7).

The chapter focuses first on describing how dictatorships break down. Coups, elections, and popular uprisings are the most common ways of ending dictatorships. Coups still oust more dictatorships than other methods, though their incidence has fallen since the end of the Cold War. Almost as many dictatorships end in contested elections as in coups. Unarmed popular uprisings have become a more frequent means of deposing dictatorships since the end of the Cold War.

Most of Chapter 8 investigates the reasons for the breakdown of dictatorships. Popular hardship can motivate citizens to take the risk of demanding regime change, but some dictatorial elites respond more effectively to crisis than others. We show that economic crisis increases the chance of regime failure in dictatorships not organized by inherited parties, but *not* in those led by parties originally organized to compete in elections or lead insurgencies. We interpret these findings as evidence that the distributive networks developed by parties that had to work to attract followers during their formative stages help dictatorships survive economic hardships. Dense, preexisting networks reaching into the grassroots increase the ability of the dictatorial elite to respond effectively to crises. Party networks can organize a safety net or redistribute costs to protect the citizens most capable of threatening the dictatorship.

We also explain how the leadership configuration arrived at through the bargaining described in Chapters 4 and 5 affects both the likelihood of regime breakdown and whether democratization results from it. We investigate the consequences of the concentration of power in the dictator's hands on the durability of autocracies and what kind of regime tends to follow them.

Concentration of powers interacts with exogenous seizure-group characteristics, resulting in different outcomes, depending on other traits of the leadership. We show that the personalization of power in military-led regimes tends to increase their durability because it reduces leadership conflict, which otherwise tends to be high. Seizure groups organized by inherited parties, however, are weakened by the personalization of rule because it increases their vulnerability to succession crises.

Leadership succession is an inherent weakness of dictatorship. Otherwise invincible ruling groups may disintegrate during succession struggles. These struggles are a time of uncertainty and intense bargaining even in regimes with well-institutionalized succession rules, but they are fraught with fear and real potential for individual and regime disaster in those that lack such institutions. Dictatorships in which the leader has amassed great personal power rarely have binding succession institutions, because such leaders put a high priority on eliminating them. Instead, personalist dictators may refuse even to identify a successor, though some groom sons or other close relatives to succeed.

We show that succession is more challenging for dictatorships in which the dictator has concentrated power than in those with more consultative decision-making. The likelihood that the dictator's exit, whether by natural death or ouster, coincides with immediate regime collapse increases by roughly 50 percent as the personalism score varies from its lowest to highest value. As a further examination of the effect of personalization on the dictatorship's capacity to deal with succession, we look at what happened after the deaths of all dictators who died of natural causes while still in power. Regimes in which the dictator had amassed substantial personal power (measured during the three years before his death) are less likely to survive after he dies than regimes with a more collegial leadership.

Since the timing of natural death is not controlled by the dictator or members of the inner circle, our finding can be interpreted as showing a causal link between personalism and regime durability: personalization *before* the dictator's death decreases the ability of successors to reconsolidate the regime under new leadership. Dictatorships led by inherited parties with collegial leadership handle succession relatively well, while even inherited parties have difficulty with succession when the dictator has concentrated great power in his hands.

Personalism also influences *how* dictatorships break down, and what is likely to follow their collapse. We find that concentration of power in the dictator's hands reduces the likelihood of nonviolent regime change. We have shown elsewhere that coerced or violent transitions increase the likelihood that a dictatorship is replaced by a new dictatorship rather than a democracy (Geddes, Wright, and Frantz 2014).

What happens after a dictatorship falls depends to a considerable extent on how the dictator and his closest allies respond to the challenges they face from angry citizens, embittered officers, and foreigners pressing for change before the regime falls. We investigate one of the factors that determines those responses: the expectations of dictators and their closest supporters about what will happen to them and their families after they leave power.

We observe that military dictators are sometimes prosecuted for human rights violations and sometimes forced into exile, but other officers can usually continue their military careers untarnished after returning to the barracks. Consequently, collegial military-led dictatorships tend to negotiate in response to challenges because most officers do not fear returning to the barracks, and they have the weapons and control over men needed to replace dictators who resist negotiation. Negotiated transitions tend to lead to democratization.

In personalized military-led dictatorships, however, the dictator himself makes decisions about whether to negotiate, ignoring the interests of other officers. Other officers have less capacity to oust a military dictator with concentrated power because of his control over the security police and, often, loyal paramilitary forces as well. Since the dictator faces a higher probability of punishment post-exit, he tends to refuse to negotiate and to hang on until forced out. Consequently, personalist military-led regimes are less likely to democratize.

Personalization of civilian-led regimes also lowers prospects for democratization. Personalist dictators purposely undermine national institutions such as the military, government administration, and the ruling party that might serve as springboards for opposition challenges. A by-product of these strategies is that the individuals who might otherwise have led a movement for democratization may no longer live in the country (or at all), and the institutions that often incubate new opposition organizations may have been destroyed. Further, the dictator's marginalization, exile, imprisonment, or execution of the most able and popular politicians in the ruling party reduces the likelihood that the party will be able to transform itself into a successful competitor if democracy succeeds the dictatorship. As a result, other members of the dictatorial elite have reason to remain loyal to the dictator as he refuses to negotiate a peaceful transition and instead clings to power with tooth and claw until the bitter, violent end.

For all these reasons, democracy is less likely to follow personalist rule than other kinds of dictatorship. We find that concentration of power in one man's hands reduces dictators' willingness to negotiate peaceful exits. Personalist dictators often hang on until forced out by violence. Violent regime breakdown, in turn, stacks the deck against subsequent democracy, regardless of whether foreign invaders, domestic insurgents, or army officers led the overthrow.

We and other researchers have amassed many different kinds of evidence that personalist dictators wreak havoc in their own countries, threaten neighbors, and set the stage for a renewal of dictatorship after they fall. In short, dictatorship causes more damage when one man can deploy vast, arbitrary powers of life and death. The principal policy recommendation implied by this research is that international policy makers should avoid contributing to the personalization of dictatorial rule, even if current security interests suggest supporting such dictators against neighboring autocrats.

The almost uncritical support of "our" dictators ended with the Cold War, but decisions about which dictators to provide with loans and aid still depend heavily on strategic interests. We do not suggest that strategic interests be ignored, but rather that policy makers should also take into account the extent of concentration of power in the dictator's hands because dictators with unlimited policy discretion can switch sides easily and unpredictably, using the very weapons provided by their allies to turn against them later.

While aid and loans are positive forms of intervention that can be used to shape the behavior of leaders in other countries, sanctions and military intervention try to change behavior by imposing costs. We suggest that decisions about economic and military intervention to destabilize dictatorships should be informed by realistic assessments of whether the intervention is likely to succeed and what will happen if the dictator falls. Escribà Folch and Wright's (2015) finding that economic sanctions destabilize personalist dictators only in countries that lack substantial oil exports implies that sanctions aimed at bringing down dictatorships should be used only against personalists without oil since sanctions against other kinds of dictatorship are likely to cause popular suffering without bringing down the dictatorship.

Before using sanctions against personalist dictators without oil, however, we need a careful, evidence-based assessment of what kind of government is likely to replace such a dictatorship brought down by foreign intervention. In the post–Cold War period, democracy is a little more likely than new autocracy to follow the overthrow of personalist dictatorships (Geddes, Wright, and Frantz 2014). Nevertheless, the likelihood of a new dictatorship is quite high, and the likelihood of civil war or disintegration into chaos, though low, is not insignificant. The four dictatorships in which the United States has intervened militarily since 2001 – Afghanistan, Iraq, Libya, and Syria – ranged from somewhat to extremely personalized before the interventions.[3] These military actions ended the dictatorships in Afghanistan, Iraq, and Libya, but none of the countries has democratized. Instead, they are among the places most likely to be home to terrorist organizations that target Western interests. At the time of writing, insurgents continue to control portions of each of these countries, and further disintegration seems possible.

Observation of events suggests that the more arbitrary, violent, and paranoid the personalist dictator is, the more likely an overthrow will result in another autocracy, civil war, or failed state. This is so because more paranoid dictators destroy more of the human talent and institutional competence in their countries, leaving them harder to govern in the future and more vulnerable to the breakdown of basic state services and the disintegration of order. In other words, the more the dictator "deserves" to be ousted, the more likely his ouster is to make conditions even worse for citizens in his country.

Quite a few personalist dictatorships rely on narrow ethnic, clan, or religious groups for support, as the Taliban, Saddam, and Qaddafi did, while Assad still does. We believe such dictatorships are especially likely to experience bloody transitions and violent, unstable futures. A dictatorship based on a narrow ascriptive category is more likely to continue fighting to survive despite low odds of winning, as we have seen in Syria in recent years. When some members of the ruling minority have grown fat at the expense of the rest of the population, popular hostility toward the dictatorship tends to spill over onto their nonelite co-ethnics. All members of the minority may then fear sharing the post-dictatorship fate of the elite, so they become willing to defend the dictatorship even at great cost.

If the dictatorship is eventually ousted, the government that follows it may have difficulty leading a return to normalcy because minority groups that lose power along with the dictator have reasons, and often the

---

[3] We have not included the countries in which military involvement was limited to drone strikes or support for military interventions led by allies, but most of them also fit the pattern described.

resources needed (because of the benefits and favoritism they experienced during the dictatorship), to organize warfare against the government that replaces them. This adds to the dangers faced by political leaders and citizens after transition.

The survival strategies typically used by personalist dictators also imply some further post-ouster consequences that well-intentioned foreigners considering intervention should ponder. During his years in power, the dictator with great power concentrated in his hands makes every effort to eliminate the most competent and politically gifted of his fellow citizens, whom he views as potential rivals. Some are killed and others jailed for years. At best, they will have spent long years in exile by the time the dictator falls. They will thus lack the networks of allies and mutual assistance that politics depends on, especially in places where rules are not enforced and institutions have been hollowed out. The dictator's effort to rid himself of rivals will limit the pool from which new leaders can come after his ouster and reduce the political resources they have to draw on. Consequently, the first post-personalist political leaders may lack the skills and political networks needed for a transition to competent, nonviolent government.

The destruction of both political and civil society institutions under personalist rule also leaves nations that have endured it with little human infrastructure with which subsequent political leaders can build stable government. Personalist dictators control appointments and promotions in all important areas of government and the security forces as well, and they promote on the basis of loyalty rather than competence or expertise. Over time, such appointment strategies not only reduce the talent of the government led by the dictator but can also strip the country of its ablest and best-educated citizens, many of whom flee rather than face the dangers, uncertainty, and limited opportunities available in the dictatorship. The decimation of institutions under personalist rule often includes the military and ordinary police, leaving them subsequently incapable of maintaining order or defending the new government from violent attacks.

In the frightening dog-eat-dog environment fostered by personalist dictatorship, interpersonal distrust aids survival. Only family or clan members can be counted on for help, which reinforces people's sense of responsibility toward extended family members. This intensified familism tends to persist after the fall of the personalist dictator and to undermine the neutrality and competence of government agencies, including the police and military. It affects hiring, promotions, and the delivery of government services, including safe streets.

For all of these reasons, the governments that follow personalist rule often lack competent, unbiased personnel. The dearth of capable personnel makes it difficult for an occupying army to deliver ordinary government services such as electricity, water, and garbage collection. The politicization of the police and security services under the dictatorship may mean that they have not been trained for the neutral maintenance of order and safe streets. Citizens may hate and distrust them. Foreign occupiers may undertake training new police and military forces, but they will have difficulty overcoming the distrust and intensified in-group loyalties developed during the dictatorship.

Corruption is usually high in personalist dictatorships. When corruption has become expected, it does not disappear just because political leadership has changed. No one knows whether the new government will be more honest than the last or whether it will survive. So, the get-it-while-you-can logic tends to persist.

The intervener is likely to be blamed for the political violence and disorder that follow intervention. In these circumstances, citizens who welcomed foreign intervention as a means of getting rid of a hated tyrant may very quickly come to revile the foreigners and the government allied with them for failing to keep them safe and foster the return of normal life. These attitudes undermine the occupier's efforts to promote the country's development into a stable ally willing to protect the intervener's economic and security interests. Governments contemplating intervention to rid other countries of personalist dictators should contemplate these likely outcomes.

These are probabilistic statements. We do not claim that foreign interventions against terrible dictators never improve things. We think the Vietnamese intervention to remove Pol Pot in Cambodia definitely improved life for Cambodians.

But we do urge policy makers not to assume that nothing can be worse than the current dictatorship or to make decisions under the illusion that democracy is somehow the "natural" consequence of freeing people from a tyrant.

References

Abbott, Elizabeth. 1988. *Haiti: The Duvaliers and Their Legacy*. New York: McGraw-Hill.

Acemoglu, Daron, and James Robinson. 2005. *Economic Origins of Dictatorship and Democracy*. New York: Cambridge University Press.

2001. "A Theory of Political Transitions." *American Economic Review* 91(4): 938–63.

Acemoglu, Daron, Simon Johnson, and James A. Robinson. 2005. "Institutions as a Fundamental Cause of Long-Run Growth." In *Handbook of Economic Growth*, eds. Philippe Aghion and Steven N. Durlauf. Amsterdam: Elsevier B.V, 385–472.

Adibe, Clement. 1995. "Managing Arms in Peace Processes: Somalia." United Nations Institute for Disarmament Research, Disarmament and Conflict Resolution Project. Geneva. www.unidir.org/files/publications/pdfs/disarmament-and-conflict-resolution-project-managing-arms-in-peace-processes-somalia-142.pdf.

Aksoy, Deniz, David B. Carter, and Joseph Wright. 2015. "Terrorism and the Fate of Dictators." *World Politics* 67(3): 423–68.

Albertus, Michael, and Victor Menaldo. 2014. "Dealing with Dictators: Negotiated Democratization and the Fate of Outgoing Autocrats." *International Studies Quarterly* 28(3): 550–65.

Allen, Chris. 1988. "Benin." In *Benin, The Congo, Burkina Faso: Economics, Politics and Society*, eds. Chris Allen, Michael S. Radu, Keith Somerville, and Joan Baxter. London: Pinter, 1–144.

Alt, James E., and David Dreyer Lassen. 2006. "Transparency, Political Polarization, and Political Budget Cycles in OECD Countries." *American Journal of Political Science* 50(3): 530–50.

Amnesty International. 1980. *Amnesty International Report 1980*. London: Amnesty International Publications.

"Analysis: Uzbek Eminence Falls from Grace." 2005. RFE/RL (Feb. 22). www.rferl.org/a/1057594.html.

Ardito-Barletta, Nicolás. 1997. "The Political and Economic Transition of Panama, 1978–1991." University of California, San Diego. Unpublished manuscript.

Arriagada Herrera, Genaro. 1988. *Pinochet: The Politics of Power.* Boston: Unwin Hymen.

Ashton, Nigel. 2008. *King Hussein of Jordan: A Political Life.* New Haven, CT: Yale University Press.

"Azerbaijan: Vulnerable Stability." 2010. International Crisis Group. Europe Report No. 207.

"Background Note: Jordan." 2011. US Department of State. https://2009-2017.state .gov/outofdate/bgn/jordan/192420.htm.

Bahry, Donna. 1993. "Society Transformed? Rethinking the Social Roots of Perestroika." *Slavic Review* 52(3): 512–54.

Baker, R. H. 1982. "Clientelism in the Post-Revolutionary State: The Soviet Union." In *Private Patronage and Public Power: Political Clientelism in the Modern State,* ed. Christopher Clapham. New York: St. Martin's Press.

Barany, Zoltan. 2011. "Comparing the Arab Revolts: The Role of the Military." *Journal of Democracy* 22(4): 28–39.

   2012. *The Soldier and the Changing State: Building Democratic Armies in Africa, Asia, Europe, and the Americas.* Princeton, NJ: Princeton University Press.

Baron, David and John Ferejohn. 1989. "Bargaining in Legislatures." *American Political Science Review* 83(4): 1181–206.

Barros, Robert. 2001. "Personalization and Institutional Constraints: Pinochet, the Military Junta and the 1980 Constitution." *Latin American Politics and Society* 43(1): 5–28.

Barzel, Yoram. 2002. *A Theory of the State: Economic Rights, Legal Rights, and the Scope of the State.* New York: Cambridge University Press.

Baturo, Alexander. 2014. *Democracy, Dictatorship, and Term Limits.* Ann Arbor: University of Michigan Press.

Beaulieu, Emily. 2014. *Electoral Protest and Democracy in the Developing World.* New York: Cambridge University Press.

Bebler, Anton. 1973. *Military Rule in Africa: Dahomey, Ghana, Sierra Leone, and Mali.* New York: Praeger.

Beck, Nathaniel, and Jonathan N. Katz. 1995. "What to Do (and Not to Do) with Time-Series Cross-Section Data." *American Political Science Review* 89(3): 634–47.

Be'eri, Eliezer. 1970. *Army Officers in Arab Politics and Society.* New York: Praeger.

Bermeo, Sarah Blodgett. 2016. "Aid Is Not Oil: Donor Utility, Heterogeneous Aid, and the Aid–Democratization Relationship." *International Organization* 70(1): 1–32.

   2011. "Foreign Aid and Regime Change: A Role for Donor Intent." *World Development* 39(11): 2021–31.

Bermeo, Sarah Blodgett, and David Leblang. 2015. "Migration and Foreign Aid." *International Organization* 69(3): 627–57.

Black, Jan Knippers, and Edmundo Flores. 1987. "Historical Setting." In *Panama: A Country Study,* eds. Sandra W. Meditz and Dennis M. Hanratty. Washington, DC: GPO for the Library of Congress.

Blair, David. 2002. *Degrees in Violence: Robert Mugabe and the Struggle for Power in Zimbabwe.* London: Continuum Books.

Blaydes, Lisa. 2011. *Elections and Distributive Politics in Mubarak's Egypt.* New York: Cambridge University Press.

Block, Steven A., Karen E. Ferree, and Smita Singh. 2003. "Multiparty Competition, Founding Elections and Political Business Cycles in Africa." *Journal of African Economies* 12(3): 444–68.

Blundy, David, and Andrew Lycett. 1987. *Qaddafi and the Libyan Revolution.* London: Weidenfeld and Nicholson.

Böhmelt, Tobias, and Ulrich Pilster. 2015. "The Impact of Institutional Coup-Proofing on Coup Attempts and Coup Outcomes." *International Interactions* 41(1): 158–82.

Boix, Carles, and Milan W. Svolik. 2013. "The Foundations of Limited Authoritarian Government: Institutions, Commitment, and Power-Sharing in Dictatorships." *The Journal of Politics* 75(2): 300–316.

Bolt, Jutta, and Jan Luiten van Zanden. 2014. "The Maddison Project: Collaborative Research on Historical National Accounts." *The Economic History Review* 67(3): 627–51.

Bove, Vincenzo, and Jennifer Brauner. 2014. "The Demand for Military Expenditure in Authoritarian Regimes." *Defence and Peace Economics*: 1–17.

Bras, Marisabal. 1993. "Historical Setting." In *Nicaragua: A Country Study*, ed. Tim Merrill. Washington, DC: Library of Congress Federal Research Division.

Bratton, Michael, and Nicolas van de Walle. 1997. *Democratic Experiments in Africa: Regime Transitions in Comparative Perspective.* Cambridge: Cambridge University Press.

Brender, Adi, and Allan Drazen. 2004. "Political Budget Cycles in New versus Established Democracies." The National Bureau of Economic Research. Working Paper.

Brinton, Crane. 1938. *The Anatomy of Revolution.* New York: Random House.

Brooker, Paul. 1997. *Defiant Dictatorships: Communist and Middle Eastern Dictatorships in a Democratic Age.* Basingstoke: Macmillan.

  1995. *Twentieth-Century Dictatorships: The Ideological One-Party States.* New York: New York University Press.

Brownlee, Jason. 2007. "Hereditary Succession in Modern Autocracies." *World Politics* 59(4): 595–628.

Bueno de Mesquita, Bruce, Alastair Smith, Randolph Siverson, and James Morrow. 2003. *The Logic of Political Survival.* Cambridge, MA: MIT Press.

Bullard, Monte R. 1985. *China's Political-Military Evolution: The Party and the Military in the PRC, 1960–1984.* Boulder, CO: Westview.

Bunce, Valerie, and S. L. Wolchik. 2010. "Defeating Dictators: Electoral Change and Stability in Competitive Authoritarian Regimes." *World Politics* 62(1): 43–86.

Burggraaff, William J. 1972. *The Venezuelan Armed Forces in Politics, 1935–1959.* Columbia: University of Missouri Press.

Burrowes, Robert D. 1987. *The Yemen Arab Republic: The Politics of Development, 1962–1986.* Boulder, CO: Westview Press.

Buzo, Adrian. 1999. *The Guerilla Dynasty: Politics and Leadership in North Korea.* London: I. B. Tauris.

Callaghy, Thomas. 1984. *The State–Society Struggle: Zaire in Comparative Perspective.* New York: Columbia University Press.

Carlisle, Donald S. 1995. "Islam Karimov and Uzbekistan: Back to the Future?" In *Patterns in Post-Soviet Leadership*, ed. Timothy J. Colton and Robert C. Tucker. Boulder, CO: Westview.

Carter, David B., and Curtis S. Signorino. 2010. "Back to the Future: Modeling Time Dependence in Binary Data." *Political Analysis* 18(3): 271–92.

Cederman, Lars-Erik, Andreas Wimmer, and Brian Min. 2009. "Ethnic Politics and Armed Conflict. A Configurational Analysis of a New Global Dataset." *American Sociological Review* 74(2): 316–37. Data downloaded from http://thedata.harvard .edu/dvn/dv/epr on 12/8/14, Version 1.1.

Chang, Eric C. C., and Miriam Golden. 2010. "Sources of Corruption in Authoritarian Regimes." *Social Science Quarterly* 91: 1–21.

Cheibub, José Antonio. 2006. *Presidentialism, Parliamentarism, and Democracy.* New York: Cambridge University Press.

Cheibub, José Antonio, Jennifer Gandhi, and James Raymond Vreeland. 2010. "Democracy and Dictatorship Revisited." *Public Choice* 143(1–2): 67–101.

Chenoweth, Erica, and Orion A. Lewis. 2013. "Unpacking Nonviolent Campaigns: Introducing the NAVCO 2.0 Dataset." *Journal of Peace Research* 50(3): 415–23.

Chirambo, Reuben. 2004. "'Operation Bwezani': The Army, Political Change, and Dr. Banda's Hegemony in Malawi." *Nordic Journal of African Studies* 13(2): 146–63.

Clapham, Christopher. 1988. "Epilogue: Political Succession in the Third World." *Third World Quarterly* 10(1): 281–88.

  1985. *Third World Politics: An Introduction.* Madison: University of Wisconsin Press.

Clark, Victoria. 2010. *Yemen: Dancing on the Heads of Snakes.* New Haven, CT: Yale University Press.

Clements, Benedict J., Sanjeev Gupta, and Masahiro Nozaki. 2011. *What Happens to Social Spending in IMF-Supported Programs?* No. 11/15. International Monetary Fund.

Codron, Jeremie. 2007. "Putting Factions 'Back in' the Civil-Military Relations Equation: Genesis, Maturation, and Distortion in the Bangladeshi Army." *South Asia Multidisciplinary Academic Journal.* http://samaj.revues.org/230.

Collins, Kathleen. 2006. *Clan Politics and Regime Transition in Central Asia.* Cambridge: Cambridge University Press.

Corbett, Charles D. 1972. "Military Institutional Development and Sociopolitical Change: The Bolivian Case." *Journal of Inter-American Studies and World Affairs* 14(4): 399–435.

Crassweller, Robert D. 1971. "Darkness in Haiti." *Foreign Affairs* 49(2): 315–29.

Crouch, Harold. 1978. *The Army and Politics in Indonesia.* Ithaca, NY: Cornell University Press.

Crystal, Jill. 1993. "Kuwait." In *Kuwait: A Country Study*, ed. Helen Chapin Metz. Washington, DC: Federal Research Division, Library of Congress.

Dann, Uriel. 1969. *Iraq under Qassem: A Political History, 1958–1963.* New York: Praeger.

De Boef, Suzanna, and Luke Keele. 2008. "Taking Time Seriously." *American Journal of Political Science* 52(1): 184.

De Waal, Alex. 2015. *The Real Politics of the Horn of Africa: Money, War and the Business of Power.* Cambridge: Polity Press.

Debs, Alexandre. 2016. "Living by the Sword and Dying by the Sword? Leadership Transitions in and out of Dictatorships." *International Studies Quarterly* 60(1): 73–84.

Debs, Alexandre, and Hein Goemans. 2010. "Regime Type, the Fate of Leaders and War." *American Political Science Review* 104(3): 430–46.

Decalo, Samuel. 1980. "Chad: The Roots of Centre-Periphery Strife." *African Affairs* 79(317): 490–509.

1990. *Coups and Army Rule in Africa: Motivations and Constraints.* New Haven, CT: Yale University Press.

1976. *Coups and Army Rule in Africa: Studies in Military Style.* New Haven, CT: Yale University Press.

1979. "Ideological Rhetoric and Scientific Socialism in Benin and Congo/Brazzaville." In *Socialism in Sub-Saharan Africa: A New Assessment,* eds. Carl G. Rosberg and Thomas M. Callaghy. Berkeley: Institute of International Studies, University of California.

1986. "The Morphology of Military Rule in Africa." In *Military Marxist Regimes in Africa,* eds. John Markakis and Michael Waller. London: Frank Cass.

1998. *The Stable Minority: Civilian Rule in Africa, 1960–1990.* Gainesville: Florida Academic Press.

DeNardo, James. 1985. *Power in Numbers.* Princeton, NJ: Princeton University Press.

Dietrich, Simone, and Joseph Wright. 2015. "Foreign Aid Allocation Tactics and Democratic Change in Africa." *The Journal of Politics* 77(1): 216–34.

Dodd, Thomas J. 2005. *Tiburcio Carías: Portrait of a Honduran Political Leader.* Baton Rouge: Louisiana State University Press.

Dominguez, Jorge. 1998. "The Batista Regime in Cuba." In *Sultanistic Regimes,* eds. H. E. Chehabi and Juan J. Linz. Baltimore, MD: Johns Hopkins University Press.

Doner, Richard, and Ansil Ramsay. 1997. "Competitive Clientelism and Economic Governance: The Case of Thailand." In *Business and the State in Developing Countries,* eds. Sylvia Maxfield and Ben Ross Schneider. Ithaca, NY: Cornell University Press.

Draper, Theodore. 1965. *Castroism: Theory and Practice.* New York: Praeger.

Dragu, Tiberiu, and Yonatan Lupu. Forthcoming. "Collective Action and Constraints on Repression at the Endgame." *Comparative Political Studies.* DOI: 10.1177/0010414017730077.

Dragu, Tiberiu, and Adam Przeworski. 2017. "Preventive Repression: Two Types of Moral Hazard." Paper presented at the American Political Science Association meeting, San Francisco, CA.

Dreher, Axel. 2006. "IMF and Economic Growth: The Effects of Programs, Loans, and Compliance with Conditionality." *World Development* 34(5): 769–88.

Dunning, Thad. 2004. "Conditioning the Effects of Aid: Cold War Politics, Donor Credibility, and Democracy in Africa." *International Organization* 58(2): 409–23.

2008. *Crude Democracy: Natural Resource Wealth and Political Regimes.* New York: Cambridge University Press.

Eck, Kristine, and Lisa Hultman. 2007. "One-Sided Violence against Civilians in War: Insights from New Fatality Data." *Journal of Peace Research* 44(2): 233–46.

Englebert, Pierre. 1998. *Burkina Faso: Unsteady Statehood in West Africa.* New York: Routledge.

2003. "Cote d'Ivoire: Recent History." In *Africa South of the Sahara 2004.* London: Europa Publications, 328–32.

Erlich, Haggai. 1983. "The Ethiopian Army and the 1974 Revolution." *Armed Forces and Society* 9(3): 455–81.

Escribà-Folch, Abel. 2013. "Accountable for What? Regime Types, Performance, and the Fate of Outgoing Dictators, 1946–2004." *Democratization* 20(1): 160–85.

Escribà-Folch, Abel, and Joseph Wright. 2015. *Foreign Pressure and the Politics of Autocratic Survival*. Oxford: Oxford University Press.

"The Execution of Power." 2013. *Economist* (Dec. 21). www.economist.com/news/asia/21591906-greed-mortal-sin-so-disloyalty-kims-execution-power (accessed Nov. 20, 2015).

Ezrow, Natasha, and Erica Frantz. 2011. *Dictators and Dictatorships: Understanding Authoritarian Regimes and Their Leaders*. London: Bloomsbury Publishing.

Fahmy, Ninette S. 2002. *The Politics of Egypt: State–Society Relationship*. London: RoutledgeCurzon, Taylor & Francis Group.

Fainsod, Merle. 1967. *How Russia Is Ruled*, rev. ed. Cambridge, MA: Harvard University Press.

Farouk-Sluglett, Marion, and Peter Sluglett. 1987. *Iraq since 1958: From Revolution to Dictatorship*. London: Kegan Paul International.

Fathi, Nazila. 2013. "The Leader." *The Cairo Review of Global Affairs* 10(Summer).

Fearon, James D. 2007. "Iraq's Civil War." *Foreign Affairs* 86(2): 2–15.

Fernández, Damian J. 1989. "Historical Background: Achievements, Failures, and Prospects." In *The Cuban Military under Castro*, ed. Jaime Suchlicki. Miami, FL: University of Miami, North-South Center Publications for the Research Institute for Cuban Studies.

Finer, Samuel. E. 1976. *The Man on Horseback: The Role of the Military in Politics*. New York: Praeger.

First, Ruth. 1974. *Libya: The Elusive Revolution*. New York: Africana Publishing, Holmes & Meier.

Fitch, John Samuel. 1977. *The Military Coup D'état as a Political Process: Ecuador, 1948–1966*. Baltimore, MD: Johns Hopkins University Press.

Fitzpatrick, Sheila. 2015. *On Stalin's Team: The Years of Living Dangerously in Soviet Politics*. Princeton, NJ: Princeton University Press.

Fontana, Andrés. 1987. "Political Decision-Making by a Military Corporation: Argentina, 1976–83." Ph.D. dissertation, University of Texas.

Forrest, Joshua B. 1987. "Guinea-Bissau since Independence: A Decade of Domestic Power Struggles." *Journal of Modern African Studies* 25(1): 95–116.

Frantz, Erica, and Natasha Ezrow. 2011. *The Politics of Dictatorship: Institutions and Outcomes in Authoritarian Regimes*. Boulder, CO: Lynne Rienner.

Frantz, Erica, and Andrea Kendall-Taylor. 2014. "A Dictator's Toolkit: Understanding How Co-optation Affects Repression in Autocracies." *Journal of Peace Research* 51(3): 332–46.

Frantz, Erica, and Elizabeth Stein. 2017. "Countering Coups: Leadership Succession Rules in Dictatorships." *Comparative Political Studies* 50(7): 935–62.

Freedom House. 2016. Freedom on the Net. https://freedomhouse.org/sites/default/files/FOTN_2016_Full_Report.pdf.

Galíndez, Jesús de. 1973. *The Era of Trujillo: Dominican Dictator*, ed. Russell H. Fitzgibbon. Tucson: University of Arizona Press.

Gallab, Abdullahi A. 2008. *The First Islamic Republic: Development and Disintegration of Islamism in the Sudan*. Aldershot: Ashgate.

Gandhi, Jennifer. 2008. *Political Institutions under Dictatorship*. New York: Cambridge University Press.

Gandhi, Jennifer, and Ellen Lust-Okar. 2009. "Elections under Authoritarianism." *Annual Review of Political Science* 12 (1): 403–22.

Gandhi, Jennifer, and Adam Przeworski. 2007. "Authoritarian Institutions and the Survival of Autocrats." *Comparative Political Studies* 40(11): 1279–301.

2006. "Cooperation, Cooptation, and Rebellion under Dictatorship." *Economics and Politics* 18(1): 1–26.

Garrido de Sierra, Sebastián. 2011. "Eroded Unity and Clientele Migration: An Alternative Explanation of Mexico's Democratic Transition." Paper presented at the Annual Meeting of the Midwest Political Science Association, Chicago, IL.

Geddes, Barbara. 2003. *Paradigms and Sand Castles: Theory Building and Research Design in Comparative Politics*. Ann Arbor: University of Michigan Press.

1999. "What Do We Know about Democratization after Twenty Years?" *Annual Review of Political Science* 2(1): 115–44.

2005. "Why Parties and Elections in Authoritarian Regimes?" Paper delivered at the American Political Science Association annual meeting, Washington, DC.

Geddes, Barbara, Erica Frantz, and Joseph Wright. 2014. "Military Rule." *Annual Review of Political Science* 17(1): 147–62.

Geddes, Barbara, Joseph Wright, and Erica Frantz. 2014. "Autocratic Breakdown and Regime Transitions: A New Data Set." *Perspectives on Politics* 12(2): 313–31.

2017. "A Measure of Personalism." Unpublished manuscript.

Gleditsch, Kristian Skrede. 2002. "Expanded Trade and GDP Data." *The Journal of Conflict Resolution* 46(5): 712–24.

Gleditsch, Nils Petter, Peter Wallensteen, Mikael Eriksson, Margareta Sollenberg, and Håvard Strand. 2002. "Armed Conflict 1946–2001: A New Dataset." *Journal of Peace Research* 39(5): 615–637. Data downloaded from www.pcr.uu.se/research/ ucdp/datasets/ucdp prio armed conflict dataset/ on 12/8/14. version: 4-2014a.

Goemans, Hein, Kristian Skrede Gleditsch, and Giacomo Chiozza. 2009. "Introducing Archigos: A Dataset of Political Leaders." *Journal of Peace Research* 46(2): 269–83.

González, Edward. 1974. *Cuba under Castro: The Limits of Charisma*. Boston: Houghton Mifflin.

González, María de los Ángeles. 2002. "Do Changes in Democracy Affect the Political Budget Cycle? Evidence from Mexico." *Review of Development Economics* 6(2): 204–24.

Gorman, Stephen. 1981. "Power and Consolidation in the Nicaraguan Revolution." *Journal of Latin American Studies* 13(1): 133–49.

Greitens, Sheena Chestnut. 2016. *Dictators and Their Secret Police: Coercive Institutions and State Violence*. Cambridge: Cambridge University Press.

Grieder, Peter. 1999. *The East German Leadership 1946–1973: Conflict and Crisis*. Manchester: Manchester University Press.

2012. *The German Democratic Republic*. New York: Palgrave Macmillan.

Haber, Steven. 2006. "Authoritarian Government." In *The Oxford Handbook of Political Economy*, eds. Donald Wittman and Barry Weingast. New York: Oxford University Press.

Haber, Steven, and Victor Menaldo. 2011. "Do Natural Resources Fuel Authoritarianism? A Reappraisal of the Resource Curse." *American Political Science Review* 105(1): 1–26.

Haddad, George. 1973. *Military Rule in the Middle East: The Arab States, Part II: Egypt, the Sudan, Yemen and Libya.* Vol. 3. New York: Robert Speller and Sons.
  1971. *Revolutions and Military Rule in the Middle East: The Arab States, Part I: Iraq, Syria, Lebanon and Jordan.* New York: Robert Speller & Sons.

Hadenius, Axel, and Jan Teorell. 2007. "Pathways from Authoritarianism." *Journal of Democracy* 18(1): 143–56.

Haile-Selassie, Teferra. 1997. *The Ethiopian Revolution 1974–1991: From a Monarchical Autocracy to a Military Oligarchy.* London: Kegan Paul International.

Harkness, Kristen A. 2014. "The Ethnic Army and the State: Explaining Coup Traps and the Difficulties of Democratization in Africa." *Journal of Conflict Resolution* 60(4): 587–616.

Hartlyn, Jonathan. 1998. "The Trujillo Regime in the Dominican Republic." In *Sultanistic Regimes*, eds. H. E. Chehabi and Juan Linz. Baltimore, MD: Johns Hopkins University Press.

Heath, Jonathan. 1999. *Mexico and the Sexenio Curse.* Washington, DC: Center for Strategic and International Studies.

Heitzman, James, and Robert Worden, eds. 1989. *Bangladesh: A Country Study.* Washington, DC: GPO for the Library of Congress.

Henze, Paul B. 2007. *Ethiopia in Mengistu's Final Years: The Derg in Decline.* Vol. I. Addis Ababa: Shama Books.

Herb, Michael. 1999. *All in the Family: Absolutism, Revolution, and Democracy in the Middle Eastern Monarchies.* Albany: State University of New York Press.

Higgott, Richard, and Finn Fuglestad. 1975. "The 1974 Coup d'Etat in Niger: Towards an Explanation." *Journal of Modern African Studies* 13(3): 383–98.

Hinnebusch, Raymond. 2011. "The Ba'th Party in Post-Ba'thist Syria: President, Party and the Struggle for 'Reform.'" *Middle East Critique* 20(2): 109–25.

Hoefte, Rosemarijn. 2013. *Suriname in the Long Twentieth Century.* New York: Palgrave Macmillan.

Horowitz, Donald. 1985. *Ethnic Groups in Conflict.* Berkeley: University of California Press.

Horowitz, Michael C., and Allan C. Stam. 2014. "How Prior Military Experience Influences the Future Militarized Behavior of Leaders." *International Organization* 68(3): 527.

Hyde, Susan D., and Nikolay Marinov. 2012. "Which Elections Can Be Lost?" *Political Analysis* 20(2): 1.

Hyde, Susan D., and Angela O'Mahoney. 2010. "International Scrutiny and Pre-Electoral Fiscal Manipulation in Developing Countries." *Journal of Politics* 72(3): 690–704.

Iazhborovskaia, Inessa. 1997. "The Gomulka Alternative: The Untraveled Road." Trans. Anna M. Cienciala. In *The Establishment of Communist Regimes in Eastern Europe, 1944–1949*, eds. Norman Naimark and Leonid Gibianskii. Boulder, CO: Westview, 123–38.

Ilkhamov, Alisher. 2007. "Neopatrimonialism, Interest Groups and Patronage Networks: The Impasses of the Governance System in Uzbekistan." *Central Asian Survey* 26(1): 65–84.

Janowitz, Morris. 1977. *Military Institutions and Coercion in the Developing Nations.* Chicago, IL: University of Chicago Press.

Johnson, Chalmers. 1962. *Peasant Nationalism and Communist Power.* Stanford, CA: Stanford University Press.

Jones, Benjamin F. and Benjamin A. Olken. 2005. "Do Leaders Matter? National Leadership and Growth since World War II." *Quarterly Journal of Economics* 120(3): 835–64.

Jones, Donald W. 1991. "How Urbanization Affects Energy-Use in Developing Countries." *Energy Policy* 19(7): 621–30.

Jowitt, Kenneth. 1975. "Inclusion and Mobilization in European Leninist Regimes." *World Politics* 28(1): 69–96.

Jua, Nantang. 2001. "Democracy and the Construction of Allogeny/Autochthony in Postcolonial Cameroon." *African Issues* 29(1–2): 37–42.

Kalt, Joseph P., and Mark A. Zupan. 1984. "Capture and Ideology in the Economic Theory of Politics." *American Economic Review* 74(3): 279–300.

Kalu, Kalu N. 2009. *State Power, Autarchy, and Political Conquest in Nigerian Federalism.* Washington, DC: Rowman and Littlefield.

Kapuściński, Ryszard. [1983] 1989. *The Emperor: Downfall of an Autocrat.* San Diego, CA: Harcourt Brace Jovanovich.

Kayser, Mark Andreas. 2005. "Who Surfs, Who Manipulates? The Determinants of Opportunistic Election Timing and Electorally Motivated Economic Intervention." *American Political Science Review* 99(1): 17–27.

Kendall-Taylor, Andrea, and Erica Frantz. 2014. "How Autocracies Fall." *The Washington Quarterly* 37(1): 35–47.

2016. "When Dictators Die." *Journal of Democracy* 27(4): 159–71.

Kiernan, Ben. 1982. "Pol Pot and the Kampuchean Communist Movement." In *Peasants and Politics in Kampuchea, 1942–1981,* eds. Ben Kiernan and Chantou Boua. London: Zed Press.

Kim, Nam Kyu, and Alex M. Kroeger. 2018. "Regime and Leader Instability under Two Forms of Military Rule." *Comparative Political Studies* 51(1): 3–37.

Knutsen, Carl Henrik, Håvard Mokleiv Nygård, and Tore Wig. 2017. "Autocratic Elections: Stabilizing Tool or Force for Change?" *World Politics* 69(1): 98–143.

Koehler, John O. 1999. *Stasi: The Untold Story of the East German Secret Police.* Boulder, CO: Westview.

Kokkonen, Andrej, and Anders Sundell. 2014. "Delivering Stability: Primogeniture and Autocratic Survival in European Monarchies 1000–1800." *American Political Science Review* 108(2): 438–53.

Kovrig, Bennett. 1979. *Communism in Hungary: From Kun to Kádár.* Stanford, CA: Hoover Institution Press.

1984. "Hungary." In *Communism in Eastern Europe,* ed. Teresa Rakowska-Harmstone. Bloomington: Indiana University Press, 86–114.

Kuntz, Philipp, and Mark R. Thompson. 2009. "More Than Just the Final Straw: Stolen Elections as Revolutionary Triggers." *Comparative Politics* 41(3): 253–72.

Kuran, Timur. 1991. "Now Out of Never: The Element of Surprise in the East European Revolution of 1989." *World Politics* 44(1): 7–48.

1989. "Sparks and Prairie Fires: A Theory of Unanticipated Political Revolution." *Public Choice* 61(1): 41–74.

"Kuwait." 2012. In *Political Handbook of the World 2012,* ed. Tom Lansdorf. Washington, DC: CQ Press, 793–98.

Lankov, Andrei. 2013. *The Real North Korea: Life and Politics in the Failed Stalinist Utopia*. Oxford: Oxford University Press.

Lee, Joyce. 2015. "China's Most Powerful Man: Xi Jinping." *Time Magazine* (Sep. 25).

Levi, Margaret. 1997. *Consent, Dissent, and Patriotism*. New York: Cambridge University Press.

Levitsky, Steven, and Lucan Way. 2010. *Competitive Authoritarianism: Hybrid Regimes after the Cold War*. Cambridge: Cambridge University Press.

    2013. "The Durability of Revolutionary Regimes." *Journal of Democracy* 24(3): 5–17.

Lewis, Mark. 1989. "Historical Setting." In *Jordan: A Country Study*, ed. Helen Chapin Metz. Washington, DC: Federal Research Division, Library of Congress.

Lewis, Paul H. 1980. *Paraguay under Stroessner*. Chapel Hill: University of North Carolina Press.

    1978. "Salazar's Ministerial Elite, 1932–1968." *Journal of Politics* 40(3): 622–47.

Little, Andrew T., Joshua A. Tucker, and Tom LaGatta. 2015. "Elections, Protest, and Alternation of Power." *Political Science Research and Methods* 7(3): 1142–56.

Lohmann, Suzanne. 1994. "The Dynamics of Informational Cascades: The Monday Demonstrations in Leipzig, East Germany, 1989–91." *World Politics* 47(1): 42–101.

Londregan, John, and Keith Poole. 1990. "Poverty, the Coup Trap, and the Seizure of Executive Power." *World Politics* 42(2): 151–83.

Lorentzen, Peter. 2014. "China's Strategic Censorship." *American Journal of Political Science* 58(2): 402–14.

Luckham, Robin. 1971. *The Nigerian Military: A Sociological Analysis of Authority and Revolt 1960–67*. Cambridge: Cambridge University Press.

Lust-Okar, Ellen. 2006. "Elections under Authoritarianism: Preliminary Lessons from Jordan," *Democratization* 13 (3): 455–70.

    2005. *Structuring Conflict in the Arab World: Incumbents, Opponents and Institutions*. Cambridge: Cambridge University Press.

MacIntyre, Andrew. 1994. "Power, Prosperity and Patrimonialism: Business and Government in Indonesia." In *Business and Government in Industrializing Asia*, ed. Andrew MacIntyre. Ithaca, NY: Cornell University Press.

Magaloni, Beatriz. 2008. "Credible Power-Sharing and the Longevity of Authoritarian Rule." *Comparative Political Studies* 41(4–5): 715–41.

    2006. *Voting for Autocracy*. New York: Cambridge University Press.

Magee, Christopher S. P., and John A. Doces. 2014. "Reconsidering Regime Type and Growth: Lies, Dictatorships, and Statistics." *International Studies Quarterly* 59(2): 223–37.

Malesky, Edmund, and Paul Schuler. 2010. "Nodding or Needling: Analyzing Delegate Responsiveness in an Authoritarian Parliament." *American Political Science Review* 104(3): 482–502.

Malesky, Edmund, Regina Abrami, and Yu Zheng. 2011. "Institutions and Inequality in Single-Party Regimes: A Comparative Analysis of Vietnam and China." *Comparative Politics* 43(4): 401–21.

Mampilly, Zachariah. 2011. *Rebel Rulers: Insurgent Governance and Civilian Life during War*. Ithaca, NY: Cornell University Press.

Manning, Kimberley Ens, and Felix Wemheuer. 2011. *Eating Bitterness: New Perspectives on China's Great Leap Forward and Famine.* Vancouver: University of British Columbia Press.

Marinov, Nikolay, and Hein Goemans. 2014. "Coups and Democracy." *British Journal of Political Science* 44(4): 799–825.

Marshall, Monty G., and Donna Ramsey Marshall. 2014. "Coup D'État Events, 1946–2013 Codebook." Center for Systemic Peace.

Martin, Michel. 1986. "The Rise and 'Thermidorianization' of Radical Praetorianism in Benin." In *Military Marxist Regimes in Africa*, eds. John Markakis and Michael Waller. London: Frank Cass.

Martz, John. 1962. *Colombia: A Contemporary Political Survey.* Chapel Hill: University of North Carolina Press.

McCubbins, Matthew D., and Thomas Schwartz. 1984. "Congressional Oversight Overlooked: Police Patrols versus Fire Alarms." *American Journal of Political Science* 28(1): 165–79.

McFaul, Michael. 2005. "Transitions from Postcommunism." *Journal of Democracy* 16(3): 5–19.

McLaughlin, James L., and David Owusu-Ansah. 1994. "Historical Setting." In *Ghana: A Country Study*, ed. La Verle Berry. Washington, DC: Federal Research Division, Library of Congress.

Micgiel, John. 1994. *"Frenzy and Ferocity": The Stalinist Judicial System in Poland, 1944–47, and the Search for Redress.* Pittsburgh, PA: Center for Russian and East European Studies, University of Pittsburgh.

Miller, Michael. 2015. "Elections, Information, and Policy Responsiveness in Autocratic Regimes." *Comparative Political Studies* 48(12): 1526–62.

Miranda, Roger, and William Ratliff. 1993. *The Civil War in Nicaragua: Inside the Sandinistas.* New Brunswick, NJ: Transaction.

Mohamedi, Fareed. 1994. "Oman." In *Persian Gulf States: Country Studies*, ed. Helen Chapin Metz. Washington, DC: Federal Research Division, Library of Congress.

Molteno, Robert. 1974. "Cleavage and Conflict in Zambian Politics: A Study in Sectionalism." In *Politics in Zambia*, ed. William Tordoff. Berkeley: University of California Press.

Morency-Laflamme, Julien. 2017. "A Question of Trust: Military Defection during Regime Crises in Benin and Togo." *Democratization* (published online): 1–17.

Morganbesser, Lee. 2016. *Behind the Façade: Elections under Authoritarianism in Southeast Asia.* Albany: State University of New York Press.

Nepstad, Sharon Erickson. 2013. "Mutiny and Nonviolence in the Arab Spring: Exploring Military Defections and Loyalty in Egypt, Bahrain, and Syria." *Journal of Peace Research* 50(3): 337–49.

2015. *Nonviolent Struggle: Theories, Strategies, and Dynamics.* New York: Oxford University Press.

Nguyen Van Canh. 1983. *Vietnam under Communism, 1975–1982.* Stanford, CA: Hoover Institution Press.

Nichol, Jim. 2006. "Democracy in Russia: Trends and Implications for U.S. Interests." Congressional Research Services Report for Congress, Library of Congress.

Noland, Marcus, and Stephan Haggard. 2011. *Witness to Transformation: Refugee Insights into North Korea*. Washington, DC: Peterson Institute for International Economics.

Nordhaus, William D. 1975. "The Political Business Cycle." *The Review of Economic Studies* 42(2): 169–90.

Nordlinger, Eric. 1977. *Soldiers in Politics: Military Coups and Governments*. Englewood Cliffs, NJ: Prentice-Hall.

North, Douglass. 1990. *Institutions, Institutional Change and Economic Performance*. Cambridge: Cambridge University Press.

North, Lisa. 1983. "Ideological Orientation of Peru's Military Rulers." In *The Peruvian Experiment Reconsidered*, eds. Cynthia McClintock and Abraham Lowenthal. Princeton, NJ: Princeton University Press.

"North Korean Leader Kim Jong-il Dies 'of Heart Attack.'" 2011. BBC News (Dec. 19). www.bbc.co.uk/news/world-asia-16239693 (accessed Nov. 20, 2015).

O'Donnell, Guillermo A. 1973. *Modernization and Bureaucratic-Authoritarianism: Studies in South American Politics*. Berkeley: Institute of International Studies, University of California.

　1978. "State and Alliances in Argentina, 1956–1976." *Journal of Development Studies* 15(1): 3–33.

O'Donnell, Guillermo, and Philippe C. Schmitter. 1986. *Transitions from Authoritarian Rule*, vol. IV: *Tentative Conclusions about Uncertain Democracies*. Baltimore, MD: Johns Hopkins University Press.

Otayek, Rene. 1986. "The Revolutionary Process in Burkina Faso: Breaks and Continuities." In *Military Marxist Regimes in Africa*, eds. John Markakis and Michael Waller. London: Frank Cass.

Owusu-Ansah, David. 2014. *Historical Dictionary of Ghana*. Lanham, MD: Rowman & Littlefield.

Paik, Woo Yeal. 2009. "Political Participation, Clientelism, and State–Society Relations in Contemporary China." Ph.D. dissertation, University of California, Los Angeles.

Panier, Bruce. 2016. "Who Could Replace Uzbekistan's Ailing President?" RFE/RL (Aug. 29). www.rferl.org/a/who-would-replace-uzbekistan-Karimov-president/27952766.html.

Payne, Anthony, and Paul K. Sutton. 1993. *Modern Caribbean Politics*. Baltimore, MD: Johns Hopkins University Press.

Payne, Stanley. 1961. *Falange: A History of Spanish Fascism*. Stanford, CA: Stanford University Press.

Payne, Stanley. 1987. *The Franco Regime, 1936–1975*. Madison: University of Wisconsin Press.

Pazzanita, Anthony G. 2008. *Historical Dictionary of Mauritania*. Plymouth, UK: Scarecrow Press.

Pearson, Neale J. 1982. "Honduras." *Latin America and Caribbean Contemporary Record I*: 439–54.

Pepinsky, Thomas. 2007. "Autocracy, Elections, and Fiscal Policy: Evidence from Malaysia." *Studies in Comparative International Development* 42(1): 136–63.

　2014. "The Institutional Turn in Comparative Authoritarianism." *British Journal of Political Science* 44(3): 631–53.

Perlmutter, Amos. 1974. *Egypt: The Praetorian State*. New Brunswick, NJ: Transaction Books.

Peterson, Edward N. 2002. *The Secret Police and the Revolution: The Fall of the German Democratic Republic*. Westport, CT: Praeger.

Pinkney, Robert. 1972. *Ghana under Military Rule, 1966–1969*. London: Methuen.

Pion-Berlin, David, and Harold Trinkunas. 2010. "Civilian Praetorianism and Military Shirking during Constitutional Crises in Latin America." *Comparative Politics* 42(4): 395–411.

Plate, Thomas Gordon, and Andrea Darvi. 1981. *Secret Police: The Inside Story of a Network of Terror*. New York: Doubleday Books.

Plekhanov, Sergey. 2004. *A Reformer on the Throne: Sultan Qaboos Bin Said Al Said*. London: Trident Press.

Policzer, Pablo. 2009. *The Rise and Fall of Repression in Chile*. Notre Dame, IN: University of Notre Dame Press.

Popkin, Samuel L. 1979. *The Rational Peasant: The Political Economy of Rural Society in Vietnam*. Berkeley: University of California Press.

Porter, Gareth. 1993. *Vietnam: The Politics of Bureaucratic Socialism*. Ithaca, NY: Cornell University Press.

Potash, Robert A. 1969. *The Army and Politics in Argentina*. Stanford, CA: Stanford University Press.

 1980. *The Army and Politics in Argentina, 1945–1962: Perón to Frondizi*. Stanford, CA: Stanford University Press.

 1996. *The Army and Politics in Argentina, 1962–73: From Frondizi's Fall to the Peronist Restoration*. Stanford, CA: Stanford University Press.

Powell, Jonathan M., and Clayton L. Thyne. 2011. "Global Instances of Coups from 1950–2010: A New Dataset." *Journal of Peace Research* 48(2): 249–59.

Press, Robert M. 1991. "Togo's Reforms Stymied by Army." *Christian Science Monitor* (Dec. 3).

Priestley, George. 1986. *Military Government and Popular Participation: The Torrijos Regime, 1968–1975*. Boulder, CO: Westview Special Studies on Latin America and the Caribbean.

Przeworski, Adam. 1986. "Some Problems in the Study of the Transition to Democracy." In *Transitions from Authoritarian Rule: Comparative Perspectives*, vol. III, eds. Guillermo O'Donnell, Philippe C. Schmitter, and Laurence Whitehead. Baltimore, MD: Johns Hopkins University Press.

Przeworski, Adam, Michael E. Alvarez, José Antonio Cheibub, and Fernando Limongi. 2000. *Democracy and Development: Political Institutions and Well-Being in the World, 1950–1990*. Cambridge: Cambridge University Press.

Quinlivan, James T. 1999. "Coup-Proofing: Its Practice and Consequences in the Middle East." *International Security* 24(2): 131–65.

Remmer, Karen. 1991. *Military Rule in Latin America*. Boulder, CO: Westview.

Rizvi, Gowher. 1985. "Riding the Tiger: Institutionalizing the Military Regimes in Pakistan and Bangladesh." In *The Political Dilemmas of Military Regimes*, eds. Christopher Clapham and George Philip. London: CroomHelm, 201–36.

Roessler, Philip. 2011. "The Enemy Within: Personal Rule, Coups, and Civil War in Africa." *World Politics* 63(2): 300–346.

 2016. *Ethnic Politics and State Power in Africa: The Logic of the Coup–Civil War Trap*. Cambridge: Cambridge University Press.

Ropp, Stephen C. 1982. *From Guarded Nation to National Guard*. Stanford, CA: Hoover Institution Press.

Ross, Michael. 2012. *The Oil Curse: How Petroleum Wealth Shapes the Development of Nations*. Princeton, NJ: Princeton University Press.

Rousseau, Jean Jacques. [1762] 2010. *The Social Contract*. Trans. G. D. H. Cole. Seattle, WA: Pacific Publishing Studio.

Rozenas, Arturas. 2012. "Elections, Information, and Political Survival in Autocracies." Ph.D. dissertation, Duke University.

Rubinstein, Ariel. 1982. "Perfect Equilibrium in a Bargaining Model," *Econometrica* 50 (1): 97–110.

Saidazimova, Gulnoza. 2005. "Uzbekistan: Can New Governments Bring Any Change?" RFE/RL (Feb. 8). www.rferl.org/a/1057340.html.

Schatzberg, Michael. 1997. "Beyond Mobutu: Kabila and the Congo." *Journal of Democracy* 8(4): 70–84.

Schirmer, Jennifer. 1998. *The Guatemalan Military Project: A Violence Called Democracy*. Philadelphia: University of Pennsylvania Press.

Schneider, Ben Ross. 2004. *Business Politics and the State in Twentieth-Century Latin America*. New York: Cambridge University Press.

Schooley, Helen. 1987. *Conflict in Central America*. Harlow: Longman.

Schwarz, Adam. 2000. *A Nation in Waiting: Indonesia's Search for Stability*. Boulder, CO: Westview.

Selznick, Philip. 1952. *The Organizational Weapon: A Study of Bolshevik Strategy and Tactics*. Santa Monica, CA: Rand Corporation.

Shi, Min, and Jakob Svensson. 2006. "Political Budget Cycles: Do They Differ across Countries and Why?" *Journal of Public Economics* 90(8): 1367–89.

Sieczkowski, Cavan. 2011. "Kim Jong Un: Who Is Son of Dead North Korean Leader, Kim Jong Il?" *International Business Times* (Dec. 19). www.ibtimes.com/kim-jong-un-who-son-dead-north-korean-leader-kim-jong-il-385134 (accessed Nov. 20, 2015).

Singh, Naunihal. 2014. *Seizing Power: The Strategic Logic of Military Coups*. Baltimore, MD: Johns Hopkins University Press.

Skidmore, Thomas. 1988. *The Politics of Military Rule in Brazil, 1964–85*. Oxford: Oxford University Press.

Slater, Dan. 2010. *Ordering Power: Contentious Politics and Authoritarian Leviathans in Southeast Asia*. New York: Cambridge University Press.

Smyth, William. 1994. "Historical Setting." In *Persian Gulf States: Country Studies*, ed. Helen Chapin Metz. Washington, DC: Federal Research Division, Library of Congress.

Snyder, Richard. 1998. "Paths out of Sultanistic Regimes: Combining Structuralist and Voluntarist Perspectives." In *Sultanistic Regimes*, ed. H. E. Chehabi and Juan J. Linz. Baltimore, MD: Johns Hopkins University Press.

Soper, Karl Wheeler. 1989. "National Security." In *Romania: A Country Study*, ed. Ronald D. Bachman. Washington, DC: Federal Research Division, Library of Congress.

Spalding, Rose J. 1994. *Capitalists and Revolution in Nicaragua: Opposition and Accommodation 1979–1993*. Chapel Hill: University of North Carolina Press.

Spooner, Mary Helen. 1999. *Soldiers in a Narrow Land: The Pinochet Regime in Chile*. Berkeley: University of California Press.

Stepan, Alfred C. 1971. *The Military in Politics: Changing Patterns in Brazil*. Princeton, NJ: Princeton University Press.

Stokes, Susan Carol. 2001. *Mandates and Democracy: Neoliberalism by Surprise in Latin America*. Cambridge: Cambridge University Press.

Svolik, Milan. 2008. "Authoritarian Reversals and Democratic Consolidation." *American Political Science Review* 102(2): 153–68.

2012. *The Politics of Authoritarian Rule*. New York: Cambridge University Press.

Szulc, Tad. 1959. *Twilight of the Tyrants*. Charlottesville: University of Virginia Press.

Themner, Lotta, and Peter Wallensteen. 2014. "Armed Conflict, 1946–2013." *Journal of Peace Research* 51(4): 541–54.

Thomson, John H. 1988. "The Liberian Coup d'état: Its Impact on Economic and Security Assistance." US Army War College Individual Study Project.

Tismaneanu, Vladimir. 2002. "Gheorghiu-Dej and the Romanian Workers' Party: From De-Sovietization to the Emergence of National Communism." Washington, DC: Woodrow Wilson International Center for Scholars Working Paper No. 37.

2003. *Stalinism for All Seasons: A Political History of Romanian Communism*. Berkeley: University of California Press.

Tordoff, William, and Robert Molteno. 1974. "Introduction." In *Politics in Zambia*, ed. William Tordoff. Berkeley: University of California Press.

Tripp, Charles. 2007. *A History of Iraq*. Cambridge: Cambridge University Press.

Truex, Rory. 2016. *Making Autocracy Work: Representation and Responsiveness in Modern China*. New York: Cambridge University Press.

Tucker, Joshua A. 2007. "Enough! Electoral Fraud, Collective Action Problems, and Post-Communist Colored Revolutions." *Perspectives on Politics* 5(3): 535–51.

Tullock, Gordon. 1987. *Autocracy*. Boston: Kluwer Academic Publishers.

Ulfelder, Jay, and Benjamin Valentino. 2008. "Assessing Risks of State-Sponsored Mass Killing." Political Instability Task Force.

"Uzbekistan: Islam Karimov vs. the Clans." 2005. RFE/RL (Apr. 22). www.rferl.org/a/1058611.html.

"Uzbekistan: Karimov Appears to Have Political Clans Firmly in Hand." 2006. RFE/RL (Aug. 31). www.rferl.org/a/1070977.html.

Vickery, Michael. 1984. *Cambodia 1975–1982*. Boston: South End Press.

Vu Tuong. 2014. "Persistence amid Decay: The Communist Party of Vietnam at 83." In *Politics in Contemporary Vietnam: Party, State, and Authority Relations*, ed. Jonathan D. London. New York: Palgrave Macmillan.

Wagner, María Luíse. 1989. "Historical Setting." In *Bolivia: A Country Study*, eds. Rex A. Hudson and Dennis M. Hanratty. Washington, DC: Federal Research Division, Library of Congress.

Webre, Stephen. 1979. *José Napoleón Duarte and the Christian Democratic Party in Salvadoran Politics, 1960–1972*. Baton Rouge: Louisiana State University Press.

Weeks, Jessica L. P. 2014. *Dictators at War and Peace*. Ithaca, NY: Cornell University Press.

2012. "Strongmen and Straw Men: Authoritarian Regimes and the Initiation of International Conflict." *American Political Science Review* 106(2): 326–47.

Wheatley, Jonathan. 2005. *Georgia from National Awakening to Rose Revolution: Delayed Transition in the Former Soviet Union*. Aldershot: Ashgate Publishing.

Whitson, William W. 1973. *The Chinese High Command: A History of Communist Military Politics, 1927–71*. London: Palgrave Macmillan

Wiarda, Howard. 1975. "Dictatorship, Development, and Disintegration: Politics and Social Change in the Dominican Republic." Ph.D. dissertation, University of Massachusetts.

Wig, Tore, and Espen Geelmuyden Rød. 2016. "Cues to Coup Plotters: Elections as Coup Triggers in Dictatorships." *Journal of Conflict Resolution* 60(5): 787–812.

"Will Kabila Go?" 2015. *Economist* (Dec. 12): 50.

Wilson, Andrew. 2011. *Belarus: The Last European Dictatorship*. New Haven, CT: Yale University Press.

Wilson, Mary C. 1990. *King Abdullah, Britain and the Making of Jordan*. New York: Cambridge University Press.

Wimmer, Andreas, Lars-Erik Cederman, and Brian Min. 2009. "Ethnic Politics and Armed Conflict: A Configurational Analysis of a New Global Data Set." *American Sociological Review* 74(2): 316–37. Data downloaded from http://thedata.harvard.edu/dvn/dv/epr on 12/8/14, Version 1.1.

Wintrobe, Ronald. 1998. *The Political Economy of Dictatorship*. Cambridge: Cambridge University Press.

Wiseman, John A. 1996. "Military Rule in the Gambia: An Interim Assessment." *Third World Quarterly* 17(5): 917–40.

Woodward, Peter. 1990. *Sudan 1898–1989: The Unstable State*. Boulder, CO: Lynne Rienner.

World Development Indicators (WDI) 2015. http://data.worldbank.org/data-catalog/world-development-indicators, downloaded on 12/8/14. Version: November 6, 2014.

Wright, Joseph. 2009. "How Foreign Aid Can Foster Democratization in Authoritarian Regimes." *American Journal of Political Science* 53(3): 552–71.

2018. "The Latent Characteristics That Structure Autocratic Rule." Unpublished manuscript.

Zisser, Eyal. 2000. *Asad's Legacy: Syria in Transition*. London: Hurst & Co.

Zolberg, Aristide. 1966. *Creating Political Order: The Party-States of West Africa*. Chicago, IL: Rand McNally.

1964. *One-Party Government in the Ivory Coast*. Princeton, NJ: Princeton University Press.

1968. "The Structure of Political Conflict in the New States of Tropical Africa." *American Political Science Review* 62: 70–87.

Index

Afghanistan, 14, 30, 32, 138, 233
Ahidjo, Ahmadou, 7
Al Said family, 9
Al Saud dynasty, 5
Algeria, 29
Allende, Salvador, 25
Amin, Idi, 11
Aref, 'Abd al-Salam, 183
Argentina, 3, 31, 46, 161, 208
army. *See* military
Assad family, 28, 84, 166
Authoritarian Regimes Data Set, 13, 21
authoritarianization, 4, 27, 31–2, 41, 220, 224
    Peru, 29, 31
    Turkey, 220
    Venezuela, 4, 29
    Zambia, 9
autogolpe. *See* authoritarianization

Ba'th party (Iraq), 32, 78, 218, 227
Ba'th party (Syria), 32
Balaguer, Joaquin, 202
Banda, Hastings, 70, 165
Bangladesh, 69, 102
Barre, Siad, 105
Belarus, 143
Ben Ali, Zine El-Abidine, 158
Benin, 39, 69, 95–6, 173
Bignone, Reynaldo, 208
Biya, Paul, 7, 142
Boix, Carles, 12
Bratton, Michael, 209

Brazil, 31, 106, 161
Burkina Faso, 7, 31
Burundi, 14

Cambodia, 14, 40, 50, 130, 235
Cameroon, 7, 142
Cárdenas, Cuauhtémoc, 183
Ceauşescu, Nicolae, 157
Cerezo, Vinicio, 29
Chad, 29, 157
Chávez, Hugo, 4, 12, 29, 186, 224
child mortality, 148–50
Chile, 25, 28, 69, 161
China, 3, 5, 35, 82–4, 130, 141, 169, 188, 221
Chinese Communist Party, 82
civil war, 1, 17, 159, 219, 233
civilian-led dictatorship
    coups in, 49
    democratization and, 214, 217
    initiation of, 42
    leadership succession in, 216
    personalism in, 200
    personalization of, 231
Colombia, 106, 208
Colorado Party (Paraguay), 84, 102–3
Communist Party (Uzbekistan), 61
Cote d'Ivoire, 29, 137, 140
counterbalancing, *see also* coup-proofing
coup, 14, 27, 178
    Afghanistan, 32
    Argentina, 3, 31, 46
    Bangladesh, 69

coup (cont.)
  Benin, 69, 95–6
  bloodless, 103
  Brazil, 31
  Burkina Faso, 31
  causes of, 44–57
  Chile, 25, 28, 69, 161
  definition of, 6, 20
  democratic breakdown and, 52–4
  Egypt, 44, 46, 70, 158, 177–8, 221
  end of dictatorship, 179
  Guatemala, 32
  Honduras, 220
  Indonesia, 84
  inequality and, 54–6
  initiation of dictatorship, 28, 31, 89, 221
  Iraq, 10, 32, 37, 46, 78, 183
  leadership shuffle, 7, 46, 55, 72, 122,
    204
  Liberia, 224
  Libya, 31, 46, 224
  Mali, 220
  Mauritania, 10, 46
  Niger, 32
  paramilitary forces and, 164
  party creation and, 95–125
  plotting, 31, 33, 36, 38, 44, 69, 99, 102, 120,
    163, 167, 220
  regime change, 6, 46, 49–52, 55, 72, 122,
    180, 229
  Sudan, 10
  Syria, 28, 32
  Tunisia, 204
  Turkey, 8
coup attempt, 33, 101, 159, 164, 173,
    229
  Benin, 96
  Paraguay, 103
  semi-competitive elections and, 180–1
  Somalia, 105
  Soviet Union, 62
  Turkey, 221
coup failure. *See* coup attempt
coup-proofing, 50, 114, 120, 163–5,
    167–8
Coups for Various Purposes, 46

De Waal, Alex, 63, 97
Déby, Idriss, 29
Decalo, Samuel, 102
democracy
  definition, 5

Democratic Republic of Congo, 26, 81, 161,
    165, 204, 208
democratization
  costs of losing power and, 206–11
  personalism in military-led regimes and,
    213
  personalization and, 211
Deng Xiaoping, 83
dictatorial legislatures, 136
dictatorship
  beginning of, 5, 18, 27
  coding rules, 5, 18
  definition of, 1
  end of, 6, 19, 72, 179
Diori, Hamani, 136
Doe, Samuel, 36, 90, 99, 224
Dominican Republic, 116, 201
Duvalier family, 29, 158, 163

East Germany, 130, 156
economic crisis, 187–90
Ecuador, 161
Egypt, 14, 44, 46, 70, 98, 138, 142–3, 158,
    177–8, 207, 221
El Salvador, 143
Erdogan, Recep Tayyip, 221
Escribà Folch, Abel, 232
Evren, Kenan, 8
Eyadéma, Gnassingbé, 208

failed state, 17, 219, 233
foreign aid, 150
  elections and, 138
  leadership selection and, 138
foreign imposition of dictatorship, 26–8, 219
foreign invasion, 52, 219, 233
  end of dictatorship, 180
Franco, Francisco, 134, 136
Fujimori, Alberto, 29, 89, 224

Galtieri, Leopoldo, 208
Gandhi, Jennifer, 12
Gbagbo, Laurent, 29
Georgia, 140, 158
Ghana, 6, 36, 80, 207
Gorbachev, Mikhail, 61
government spending, 144–7
Greitens, Sheena, 157
Grieder, Peter, 130
Guatemala, 29, 32, 102
Guéï, Robert, 29
Guinea Bissau, 136

Haber, Steven, 3
Habré, Hissène, 29
Haddad, George, 28, 44, 70, 177
Hadenius, Axel, 12
Haiti, 29, 158, 163
Hashemite dynasty, 10
health spending, 147–50
Ho Chi Minh, 83
Honduras, 220
Hungary, 80, 103, 169
Hussein, Saddam, 17, 80, 82, 157, 166,
    218–19, 224

indirect military rule, 5, 19–20, 29
    Guatemala, 29
Indonesia, 5, 84, 199
inequality and coups, 54
insurgency, 27, 29, 33, 35, 40, 159
    Algeria, 29
    Cambodia, 40
    Chad, 29
    China, 35
    Democratic Republic of Congo, 26
    end of dictatorship, 180
    Mexico, 40
    Mozambique, 29
    Nicaragua, 29
    Vietnam, 29, 35
internal security agencies, 160–2
    coup-proofing, 168
    loyalty of, 168–73
international war, 1, 188
Iran, 26, 140, 218–19
Iraq, 10, 14, 17, 32, 37, 46, 78, 82, 138, 157,
    166, 183, 218–19, 224, 233

Jordan, 10, 137
Jurabekov, Ismail, 63–4

Kabila, Laurent, 26
Karimov, Islam, 61–5, 69, 71, 77–8, 85
Karzai, Hamid, 30
Kaunda, Kenneth, 9
Kendall-Taylor, Andrea, 139
Kérékou, Mathieu, 39, 69, 96–7
Khmer Rouge (Cambodia), 40, 50
Khomeini, Ruhollah, 26
Kim Il-sung, 81, 83, 194
Kim Jong Il, 132
Kim Jong Un, 132
Korean Workers' Party, 81
Kountché, Seyni, 102

Kuomintang (Taiwan), 140
Kuwait, 224

Lê Duẩn, 83
leadership selection, 68–74, 98
    foreign aid and, 138
    party-based dictatorship, 192
    Togo, 208
legislatures, 136–7
Levitsky, Steven, 12, 82, 195, 213
Lewis, Paul, 102
Liberia, 36, 90, 99, 224
Libya, 14, 17, 31, 38, 46, 90, 165, 207, 219,
    224, 233
Lukashenka, Aliaksandr, 143
Lust-Okar, Ellen, 136

Madagascar, 39
Maduro, Nicolás, 186
Magaloni, Beatriz, 115
Malawi, 70, 165
Mali, 220
Mao Zedong, 83–4, 169, 194
Mauritania, 10, 46
Mexico, 40, 116, 182
military, 162–3
    leadership control over, 166–7
    leadership interference, 167
military dictatorship, 51, 226
    Argentina, 39, 208
    Benin, 95
    Burkina Faso, 7
    Chile, 161
    civilianization of, 102
    Colombia, 106, 208
    compared with personalist dictatorship, 12
    costs of losing power in, 207
    definition of, 194
    democratization and, 208
    dispersal of arms, 192
    Egypt, 102
    Ghana, 207
    internal security agencies in, 157, 159
    leadership rotation in, 108
    leadership shuffle coups and, 55
    military marginalization in, 109
    Niger, 102
    party creation and, 107
    personalization in, 208, 213, 231
    regime breakdown and, 192, 197,
        199
    transition to indirect military rule, 20

Milošević, Slobodan, 30, 140
Mobutu, Joseph, 26, 81, 104, 116–17, 161, 208
monarchic dictatorship
  costs of losing power in, 210
  Egypt, 44, 177
  initiation of, 7, 9, 28
  Iraq, 30
  Jordan, 10
  Oman, 9
  Saudi Arabia, 188
Montenegro, 30
Mozambique, 29
Mubarak, Hosni, 142–3, 177

Nasser, Gamel Abdel, 44, 70, 102, 177
National Democratic Party of Uzbekistan, 62
National Union party (Egypt), 102
Nepal, 210
Ngo Dinh Diem, 163
Nicaragua, 29, 78, 161
Niger, 32, 102, 136
Nordlinger, Eric, 14, 45
North Korea, 81, 83–4, 132, 157, 213

O'Donnell, Guillermo, 190
Oman, 9

Paraguay, 84, 102–3, 143
Partido Revolucionario Institucional (Mexico),
  116, 182–3
parties, 131
party-based dictatorship, 137
  China, 188
  costs of losing power, 209
  definition of, 193
  democratization and, 209
  initiation of, 28, 159
  internal security agencies, 159
  patron–client networks in, 187
  personalization of, 201, 209
  regime breakdown and, 192, 199
  Zambia, 9
party creation, 95–125
  Bangladesh, 102
  causes of, 113
  coup type and, 122
  coups and, 119, 121
  Egypt, 102
  elections and, 110
  leadership characteristics and, 112
  leadership rotation and, 108
  military marginalization and, 110

Niger, 102
Paraguay, 102–3
  regime survival and, 118
  Somalia, 105
  trends over time, 114
People's Revolutionary Party (Benin), 96
personalism, *see also* personalist dictatorship;
    personalization
  causes of, 65–94
  costs of losing power and, 206
  factionalism and, 89–92
  intitial regime leaders and, 86–8
  measurement, 79
  patterns, 85
  regime consolidation and, 88–9
personalist dictatorship, 17
  compared with military dictatorship, 11
  consequences of, 224, 232
  costs of losing power in, 191, 210, 213
  definition of, 11, 70
  democratization and, 219
  Iraq, 17, 219
  leadership succession in, 230
  Libya, 17, 219
  Malawi, 70
  regime breakdown and, 191, 202
  Uganda, 12
  Uzbekistan, 61
  Venezuela, 12
  Yemen, 71
personalization, 12–13, 65–94, 115, 124,
    161–2, 224
  democratization and, 211
  internal security agencies and, 160
  leadership death and, 204
  leadership succession and, 203
  regime breakdown and, 190–201
  Uzbekistan, 61–5
Peru, 29, 31, 161, 224
Philippines, 154
Pinochet, Agosto, 25, 69, 161
Pol Pot, 130, 235
Poland, 157
Popkin, Samuel, 35
popular uprising, 27, 29, 33, 41, 52, 90, 178,
    229
  Colombia, 208
  Cote d'Ivoire, 29
  end of dictatorship, 179
  Haiti, 29
  Iran, 26
  Nepal, 210

Qaddafi, Moammar, 17, 31–2, 38, 90, 165, 182, 219, 224, 233
Qassem, 'Abd al-Karim, 183

Rákosi, Mátyás, 80
Ratsiraka, Didier, 39
Rawlings, Jerry, 6, 36, 207
regime
  definition of, 5
  revolutionary, 82, 195
regime breakdown
  economic crisis and, 187–90
  leadership change and, 201–6
  leadership death and, 205
  personalization and, 190–201
Rivera, Julio, 143
Roessler, Philip, 48
Rojas Pinilla, Gustavo, 106, 208
Romania, 157, 210

Saleh, Ali Abdullah, 71
Sandinistas, 29
Sankara, Thomas, xv, 7
Saudi Arabia, 3, 5, 10, 188
Schmitter, Philippe C., 190
seizure group, 4, 10
  beginning of dictatorship, 30
  costs of losing power (military), 207
  costs of losing power (party-based), 209
  costs of losing power (ruling family), 210
  definition of, 3
  dispersal of arms, 99–101, 118, 124, 192, 200–1, 215, 224
  factionalism, 11, 97–101, 107, 124, 160, 222–3
  initiation of dictatorship, 25–43
  military, 4, 7, 34, 39–40, 70, 79, 89, 105, 194, 200, 224
  party-based, 4, 8, 32, 37, 159
  personalization of dictatorship, 65–94
  preexisting traits of, 3, 5, 11–13, 193, 207
  regime breakdown and, 190–201
  ruling family, 9
self-coup. *See* authoritarianization
semi-competitive elections, 137–50, 180, 187, 211, 227–8
  child mortality and, 144–50
  definition, 138

  foreign aid and, 138
  government spending and, 144–50
  health spending and, 144–50
Serbia, 30, 140
Shah of Iran, 26
Shevardnadze, Eduard, 140, 158
Somali Revolutionary Socialist Party, 105–6
Somalia, 105
Somoza family, 29, 78, 161
South Korea, 154
Soviet Union, 114, 157, 221
Spain, 134
Stroessner, Alfredo, 84, 102–3, 143
Sudan, 10
Suharto, 5, 84, 136
Svolik, Milan, 12, 45, 54, 57, 68, 89, 160
Syria, 28, 32, 84, 166, 213, 233

Taiwan, 140, 154
Teorell, Jan, 12
Third Force Movement (Colombia), 106
Togo, 173, 208
Trujillo, Rafael, 117, 201–2
Tunisia, 158, 204
Turkey, 8, 221

Uganda, 11
United National Independence Party (Zambia), 9
Uruguay, 161
Uzbekistan, 61–4, 71, 76

van de Walle, Nicolas, 209
Venezuela, 4, 12, 29, 140, 186, 224
Vietnam, 29, 35, 50, 83, 235
Vietnam (South), 163

Way, Lucan, 12, 82, 195, 213
Weeks, Jessica, 198

Xi Jinping, 83

Yemen, 14, 71
Yugoslavia, 30

Zambia, 9
Zerbo, Saye, 7
Zia, Mohammad, 69, 102
Zolberg, Aristide, 140

CPSIA information can be obtained
at www.ICGtesting.com
Printed in the USA
FSHW011300191219
65278FS

9 781107 535954